SOYINKA

COLLECTED PLAYS

1

Wole Soyinka was educated at the Universities of Ibadan and Leeds. He has been actively involved in the theatre both as an actor and producer, and formed his own company, the *1960 Masks*. He has also held several teaching posts. In 1986 he won the Nobel Prize for literature. As well as plays he has written two novels, two volumes of poetry, and *The Man Died*, notes of his prison experience. His latest book is *The Open Sore of a Continent* (OUP 1996).

Also available from Oxford Paperbacks

Collected Plays 2: *The Lion and the Jewel*
Kongi's Harvest
The Trials of Brother Jero
Jero's Metamorphosis
Madmen and Specialists

WOLE SOYINKA

COLLECTED PLAYS

1

Oxford New York

OXFORD UNIVERSITY PRESS

Oxford University Press, Great Clarendon Street, Oxford OX2 6DP

Oxford New York
Athens Auckland Bangkok Bogota Bombay
Buenos Aires Calcutta Cape Town Dar es Salaam
Delhi Florence Hong Kong Istanbul Karachi
Kuala Lumpur Madras Madrid Melbourne
Mexico City Nairobi Paris Singapore
Taipei Tokyo Toronto Warsaw

and associated companies in
Berlin Ibadan

Oxford is a registered trade mark of Oxford University Press

A Dance of the Forests first published by Oxford University Press 1963
The Swamp Dwellers, The Strong Breed first published by
Oxford University Press 1964
The Road first published by Oxford University Press 1965
The Bacchae of Euripides first published by Oxford University Press 1973
These five plays first published together as an
Oxford University Press paperback 1973

British Library Cataloguing in Publication Data
Data available

Library of Congress Cataloging in Publication Data
Data available
ISBN 0-19-281136-3

17 19 20 18 16

Printed in Great Britain by
Cox & Wyman Ltd,
Reading, Berkshire

CONTENTS

A DANCE
OF THE
FORESTS

A DANCE OF THE FORESTS was first performed as part of the Nigerian Independence Celebrations, October 1960.

Production was by the 1960 Masks, with the following cast:

DEAD WOMAN *Elizabeth Osisioma*

DEAD MAN *Taiye Ayorinde*

ADENEBI (and HISTORIAN)
   Ralph Opara

DEMOKE (and COURT POET)
   Yemi Lijadu

ROLA (and MADAME TORTOISE)
   Olga Adeniyi-Jones

AGBOREKO *Funmilayo Asekun*

OLD MAN
PHYSICIAN } *Patrick Ozieh*

DIRGE-MAN, SLAVE-
DEALER and CRIER } *Femi Euba*

COUNCILLOR *Wole Siyanbola*

MATA KHARIBU *Sola Rhodes*

POET'S NOVICE
HALF-CHILD } *Tokunbo Odunjo*

ARONI *Adisa Ajetunmobi*

MURETE *Segun Sofowote*

OGUN *Afolabi Ajayi*

FOREST HEAD
(OBANEJI) } *Elow Gabonal*

ESHUORO *Remi Adeleye*

Dancers *The Ezeagu District Dancing Union*

Other parts *The Company*

Characters

The Guests of Honour
DEAD WOMAN

DEAD MAN

The Town Dwellers
ADENEBI Council Orator

OBANEJI

DEMOKE A Carver

ROLA A Courtesan

AGBOREKO Elder of Sealed Lips

OLD MAN A Council Elder
(father of Demoke)

A DIRGE-MAN

HIS ACOLYTE

COUNCILLORS

BEATERS

DRUMMERS

The Forest Dwellers
ARONI the Lame One

MURETE tree-imp

ESHUORO a wayward cult-spirit

OGUN patron god of carvers

FOREST HEAD masquerading as
Obaneji

FOREST CRIER

THE QUESTIONER

THE INTERPRETER

JESTER to Eshuoro

THE TRIPLETS

THE HALF-CHILD

THE ANTS

SPIRITS of the PALM, DARKNESS,
RIVERS, etc.

The Court of MATA KHARIBU
MADAME TORTOISE (Rola)

COURT POET (Demoke)

HIS NOVICE

MATA KHARIBU

A CAPTAIN (the Dead Man)

HIS WIFE (the Dead Woman)

PHYSICIAN

HISTORIAN (Adenebi)

SLAVE-DEALER

SOOTHSAYER (Agboreko)

A PAGE, GUARDS, ATTENDANTS, etc.

'From ARONI, the Lame One, this testimony . . .

'I know who the Dead Ones are. They are the guests of the Human Community who are neighbours to us of the Forest. It is their Feast, the Gathering of the Tribes. Their councillors met and said, Our forefathers must be present at this Feast. They asked us for ancestors, for illustrious ancestors, and I said to FOREST HEAD, let me answer their request. And I sent two spirits of the restless dead . . .

'THE DEAD MAN, who in his former life was a captain in the army of Mata Kharibu, and the other, . . . THE DEAD WOMAN, in former life, the captain's wife. Their choice was no accident. In previous life they were linked in violence and blood with four of the living generation. The most notorious of them is ROLA, now, as before, a whore. And inevitably she has regained the name by which they knew her centuries before—MADAME TORTOISE. Another link of the two dead with the present is ADENEBI, the Court Orator, oblivious to the real presence of the dead. In previous life he was COURT HISTORIAN. And I must not forget DEMOKE, the Carver. In the other life, he was a POET in the court of Mata Kharibu. AGBOREKO, the Elder of Sealed Lips performed the rites and made sacrifices to Forest Head. His trade was the same in the court of Mata Kharibu. When the guests had broken the surface of earth, I sat and watched what the living would do.

'They drove them out. So I took them under my wing. They became my guests and the Forests consented to dance for them. Forest Head, the one who we call OBANEJI, invited Demoke, Adenebi, and Rola to be present at the dance. They followed him, unwillingly, but they had no choice.

'It was not as dignified a Dance as it should be. ESHUORO had come howling for vengeance and full of machinations. His professed wrongs are part of the story.

'Eshuoro is the wayward flesh of ORO—Oro whose agency serves much of the bestial human, whom they invoke for terror. OGUN, they deify, for his playground is the battle field, but he loves the anvil and protects all carvers, smiths, and all workers in iron.

'For this Feast of the Human Community their Council also resolved that a symbol of the great re-union be carved. Demoke, son of the Old

Man, was elected to carve it. Undoubtedly Ogun possessed him for Demoke chose, unwisely, to carve Oro's sacred tree, *araba*. Even this might have passed unnoticed by Oro if Demoke had left araba's height undiminished. But Demoke is a victim of giddiness and cannot gain araba's heights. He would shorten the tree, but apprentice to him is one OREMOLE, a follower of Oro who fought against this sacrilege to his god. And Oremole won support with his mockery of the carver who was tied to earth. The apprentice began to work above his master's head; Demoke reached a hand and plucked him down . . . the final link was complete—the Dance could proceed.'

PART ONE

An empty clearing in the forest. Suddenly the soil appears to be breaking and the head of the Dead Woman pushes its way up. Some distance from her, another head begins to appear, that of a man. They both come up slowly. The man is fat and bloated, wears a dated warrior's outfit, now mouldy. The woman is pregnant. They come up, appear to listen. They do not seem to see each other. Shortly after, Adenebi enters. He passes close to the Dead Man.

DEAD MAN: Will you take my case, sir?
   [*Adenebi starts, stares, and runs off.*]
DEAD MAN [*shaking his head.*]: I thought we were expected.
   [*They both seem to attempt to sense their surroundings.*]
DEAD WOMAN: This is the place.
DEAD MAN: ... Unless of course I came up too soon. It is such a
   long time and such a long way.
DEAD WOMAN: No one to meet me. I know this is the place.
   [*Obaneji enters, passes close by the woman.*]
DEAD WOMAN: Will you take my case?
   [*Obaneji stops and looks thoughtfully at them. The Dead Man,
   listening hard, goes quickly towards him. Obaneji withdraws, looking
   back at the pair.*]
DEAD WOMAN: I thought he might. He considered it long enough.
   [*Demoke enters. He is tearing along.*]
DEAD WOMAN: Will you take my case?
DEMOKE [*stops.*]: Can't you see? I am in a hurry.
DEAD WOMAN: But you stopped. Will you not take my case?
DEMOKE: When you see a man hurrying, he has got a load on his
   back. Do you think I live emptily that I will take another's
   cause for pay or mercy?
DEAD WOMAN: And yet we'll meet there.
DEMOKE: You say you know. I am merely on my business.
   [*Going.*]
DEAD WOMAN: Stop. I lived here once.
DEMOKE: That was before my time. [*Going, stops again.*] Perhaps we
   will meet. But the reveller doesn't buy a cap before he's invited.

[*Goes. The Dead Woman shakes her head sadly. Rola enters, swinging her hips.*]

DEAD MAN: Madam please, will you take my case?

ROLA: Even before you ask it.

DEAD MAN [*gladly.*]: Will you?

ROLA [*who has gone nearer him.*]: Oh! [*She backs away.*] What is the matter with you!

DEAD MAN: Don't ask.

ROLA [*stamps her foot angrily.*]: What is the matter with you?

DEAD MAN [*writhing.*]: Do I have to answer?

ROLA: You look disgusting. I suppose you are not even a man at all. [*The Dead Man turns away. His head falls forward on his chest.*]

ROLA: What a nerve you have. Do you think because you are out of town you, in your condition, can stop me and talk to me? Next time I'll get people to flog you. [*She goes off.*]

DEAD MAN [*swaying unhappily.*]: O O O I am so ashamed. To be found out like that, so soon, so soon. I am so ashamed.

DEAD WOMAN: Could it be I am not qualified after all? After a hundred generations, it is rather difficult to know.

DEAD MAN: I am so ashamed, so ashamed . . .

DEAD WOMAN: I know they told me to come. I know I was summoned. What is it to them from whom I descended— if that is why they shun me now? The world is big but the dead are bigger. We've been dying since the beginning; the living try but the gap always widens. What is it to them from whom I descended!

DEAD MAN: It was a mistake from the beginning. It is a long way to travel the understreams to be present where the living make merry. What is it to me? I want nothing more. Nothing at all.

DEAD WOMAN: I have been made a fool. It is a hard thing to carry this child for a hundred generations. And I thought . . . when I was asked, I thought . . . here was a chance to return the living to the living that I may sleep lighter. [*Sound of bells, shouts, gunshots from afar. The Dead Man listens.*]

DEAD MAN: That is hardly the sound of welcome.

DEAD WOMAN: They would never have tempted me another way. It is a hard thing to lie with the living in your grave.

DEAD MAN [*still listening.*]: Anyway, I have forgotten the procedure. I will only betray myself a stranger. [*Goes.*]

DEAD WOMAN [*hears the noise.*]: Not the procession of welcome. [*Going.*] I've been made a fool. Again. [*Goes off, same direction.*] [*The noise, very much like that of beaters, comes quite near the clearing. Gunshots are let off, bells rung, etc. It builds to a crescendo and then dies off in the distance. Enter the four who passed by the Dead Pair—Rola, Adenebi, Obaneji, Demoke.*]

ROLA: . . . So I told her to get out. Get out and pack your things. Think of it. Think of it yourself. What did she think I was? I can't take anyone who happens to wander in, just because she claims to be my auntie. My auntie!

ADENEBI: It is rather difficult. I suppose one has to be firm. You start your own family, expect to look after your wife and children, lead—you know—a proper family life. Privacy . . . very important . . . some measure of privacy. But how do you manage that when a lot of brats are delivered at your door because their great grandparents happen to have been neighbours of your great grand-uncles.

ROLA: This whole family business sickens me. Let everybody lead their own lives. [*Throws away her cigarette and takes another.*]

OBANEJI: It never used to be a problem.

ROLA: It is now.

OBANEJI: People like you made it so.

ROLA: Hm. I see we've got another of the good old days.

OBANEJI: On the contrary . . .

ROLA: Never mind. You'd only waste your breath anyway. [*By now they've seated themselves on tree trunks, stones, etc.*]

ROLA: The whole sentimentality cloys in my face. That is why I fled. The whole town reeks of it . . . The gathering of the tribes! Do you know how many old and forgotten relations came to celebrate?

OBANEJI: Now we've got it. They pushed you out of house.

ROLA: I've a mind to go back and set fire to it. If I haven't got a house, they can't stay with me.

DEMOKE: It's a good thing in a way. I mean, as long as they don't do it too often. I am sure none of them had even been down here before.

ROLA: O . . . oh. The silent one has broken his vow. I suppose you wouldn't like to come and live with a pack of dirty, yelling grandmas and fleabitten children?

[*Demoke remains silent.*]

ROLA: I thought not.

DEMOKE: Don't jump to conclusions. I suddenly realized that I was foolish to talk. When the cockerel decides it's fire burning on his head, the only thing to do is pour water on it.

[*Obaneji smiles; Rola splutters and crushes her cigarette.*]

OBANEJI: You are the carver, aren't you?

DEMOKE: How did you know?

OBANEJI [*laughs.*]: Look at your hands.

[*Demoke has been shaping a piece of wood with a stone.*]

DEMOKE: As the saying goes, if the red monkey only tumbled in his parlour, no one would know he had any sons.

ADENEBI: Are you *the* carver?

DEMOKE: I am.

ADENEBI: So you are the man. Why aren't you in town? Today is your day of triumph, sir. Every neck is creaking with looking up at the totem.

ROLA [*wide-eyed.*]: Oh. So you did that?

OBANEJI: Unfortunately I have seen so much and I am rarely impressed by anything. But that . . . it was the work of ten generations. I think your hands are very old. You have the fingers of the dead.

ROLA [*with unexpected solemnity.*]: And you did not even cut it down. Climbing the king of trees and carving it as it stood—I think that was very brave.

OBANEJI: It is the kind of action that redeems mankind, don't you think so?

ROLA: But how did you work on it? Did you use ladders and nets or did you straddle it like a palm wine tapper?

DEMOKE [*with sudden irritation.*]: The knife doesn't carve its own handle you know. There were others who lopped off the branches and skinned the trunk. In fact it took quite a few of us to do it. And one man fell to his death.

ROLA: Oh. Did you see it?

DEMOKE: I was beneath him at the time. He fell right past me. I could have touched him if I wished.

ADENEBI: You must have been glad it wasn't you. But I don't see why you are sitting here. You should be in town drinking in the admiration.

DEMOKE: For one thing, I did not know what it was all about.
The council met and decided that they wanted it done. In secret.
The tree was in a grove of Oro, so it was possible to keep it
hidden. Later I learnt it was meant for the gathering of the
tribes. When I finished it, the grove was cleared of all the
other trees, the bush was razed and a motor road built right up
to it. It looked different. It was no longer my work. I fled from it.

OBANEJI: I merely fled from the noise. I suppose we all did.

ADENEBI: Speak for yourself.

OBANEJI: I am sorry. Why are you here?

ADENEBI: You say you fled. I don't believe it. Especially you, a
carver. Have you no sense of history?

ROLA: What history? Or doesn't it matter?

ADENEBI: The accumulated heritage—that is what we are
celebrating. Mali. Chaka. Songhai. Glory. Empires. But you
cannot feel it, can you?

OBANEJI: But what made you leave it and come to this quiet?

ROLA: He got lost in the maze of purple and gold.

ADENEBI: I have a weak heart. Too much emotion upsets me. This
is the era of greatness. Unfortunately it is to those who cannot
bear too much of it to whom the understanding is given . . .
Wait. Listen. [*Distant noise of bells, shouts, etc.*] *They* know what
it is all about. I belong with them. And so do you, if you'd
only drop your superior airs and admit it.
[*Re-enter the Dead Man and Dead Woman.*]

ROLA [*takes Demoke by the arm.*]: Those obscenities again. Let us
wander off by ourselves. The others can deal with them.

DEMOKE [*rises. Goes towards them.*]: I must question them.

ROLA [*pulling him back.*]: What can you want with them? Come
with me. What on earth is the matter with you?

ADENEBI [*leaving quickly.*]: I came here to get away from the
excitement.

OBANEJI: Anyway, one begins to hear the revellers even from here.
Come on carver, we'll go deeper into the forest.
[*He takes Demoke by the hand and leads him firmly away, Rola
in tow. The two creatures stop. They want to go after, but the noise
which they have just heard is increasing. They turn and go out the
way they came.*]

*

[*A tree trunk to one side of the scene. Murete, a tree-demon, is about to come out of it when he hears some noise. Ducks back. Enter Aroni, the one-legged. He looks as if he is going to hop right past the tree when he stops suddenly and gives it a stout wallop. The tree-demon yelps.*]

ARONI: So you are not afraid.

[*Murete's head emerges warily.*]

MURETE: No. When the leaves tremble it is no concern of the roots.

ARONI: You become more and more human every day. I suppose you took that saying from your friend, Agboreko.

MURETE: *He* at least is amusing. And his language is full of colour.

ARONI: Yes, I can see where the colour has run and left ugly patches on you. Be quiet! You are unreliable Murete. You too meant to leave today. Don't lie.

MURETE: I never denied it.

ARONI: Today, when Forest Head needed you all. You meant to desert him.

MURETE: Today there happens to be much more fun among the living.

ARONI: Among the living? Fool, are you dead then?

MURETE: No, but it is dead enough here. Even my home looks dead. You see how the leaves have served someone for a feast?

ARONI: So I noticed. I thought you did it yourself.

MURETE: What for?

ARONI: So I would think you have moved house.

MURETE: Well, frankly, that is why I stayed on. But I didn't do it myself. Eshuoro came here and bit off the top. Said someone else—some woodcutter or something—had cut off his own, so he came to take it out on me.

ARONI: Hm. So that's it. He is sulking somewhere. I was wondering why we hadn't seen him for a while.

MURETE: I'll do him a mischief one of these days.

ARONI: Don't boast uselessly. Murete, I want you at the feast.

MURETE: The welcoming of the dead? No, I am going to drink millet wine at the feast of the living.

ARONI: Doesn't Agboreko bring you enough?

MURETE: Only when he remembers. And then he brings too much and the ants get the rest. I can take my own measure at their feasting.

ARONI: Villain!

MURETE: These rites of the dead, I don't know why you take them on.

ARONI: Do not question. You have not done your share.

MURETE: You wanted witnesses. I guided four human beings towards you.

ARONI: [*lifting up a mighty fist.*]: You did what?

MURETE: Well, they passed by me and didn't miss their way. So you might almost say I provided them.

ARONI: Come out. Come out at once.

[*Murete gingerly pops up his head. Comes out, sheepish-impudent.*]

ARONI [*eyes him sternly.*]: I could force you to stay, you know that. [*Murete maintains a stubborn silence.*]

ARONI: You say you saw four human beings. Did you notice anyone else?

MURETE: Which others?

ARONI: The two dead. The ones they asked for, and no longer want.

MURETE: I did not see them. Do you think I never go to sleep?

ARONI: One more impertinence out of you and I'll tie you backwards and leave you with your tongue licking the earthworm's discharge at every fall of a leaf.

MURETE: It won't be the first time.

ARONI: Take care how you tempt me. I have some more questions. If you answer them sanely, you may save your skin. Now which of the townspeople did you talk to?

MURETE: The one who summoned me, naturally.

ARONI [*bellows.*]: And who was that?

MURETE [*instinctively raises his arms for protection.*]: Agboreko. Their Elder of Sealed Lips.

ARONI: No one else?

MURETE: No one.

ARONI: Not even the Old Man, their Councillor?

MURETE: He never comes himself. Always he sends Agboreko.

ARONI: What did he complain of?

MURETE: How you tricked them. He said they asked Forest Father for illustrious ancestors and you sent them accusers. He wanted to know what lay in your mind.

ARONI: . . . And did he?

MURETE: How could he? I don't know myself do I?

ARONI: You are a bad liar. And you also take bribes.

MURETE: I told him to ask you.

ARONI: You said four human beings passed by you. That means you were drunk.

MURETE: Why?

ARONI: Or else you had no eyes in your head. You should have recognized the fourth.

MURETE: Maybe I was sleepy.

ARONI: Be quiet. When last did you see Ogun?

MURETE: Not for a long time.

ARONI: If he comes to you, let me know at once. One of the three witnesses is his servant. I don't want interference from him.

MURETE: What does that mean?

ARONI: Don't leave your house for the moment. I'll send word when you may go on your debauchery.

[*Exit Aroni. Murete makes a rude sign, re-enters the tree. Enter Agboreko, Elder of the Sealed Lips. He wears a white agbada and a white wrapper. Carries a clay pot full of millet wine. A bulky, unhurried man.*]

AGBOREKO [*sprinkles some of the wine at the foot of the tree and leaves the pot beside it.*]: It is I, Agboreko. Murete, it is Agboreko that calls you. Ear that never shuts, eye that never closes. Murete, Agboreko brings you the unhappiness of his children.

MURETE: Come back later. I have told you, the forest is big and I pay no heed to the footsteps of the dead.

AGBOREKO: Murete, if the hunter loses his quarry, he looks up to see where the vultures are circling. Proverb to bones and silence.

MURETE: All right, all right. Come back later. I may have learnt something then.

[*Agboreko sighs, goes. Murete pops up, looks after him.*]

MURETE: [*mimicking.*] Proverb to bones and silence. Somehow I couldn't bear him today. That is Aroni's influence. He spoils everything.

[*Reaches for the pot and takes a deep draught. Enter Ogun who holds the pot against his mouth and forces him to drink the lot at once. Ogun then takes him and turns him quickly round and round. Murete staggers about, quite drunk and unbalanced.*]

OGUN: Drunk again, Murete?

MURETE [*hiccups. Tries to speak but waffles.*]

OGUN: The four humans—which way did they go?

MURETE [*points.*]

OGUN: How recently?

MURETE: How . . . how?

OGUN: Was it a long time?

[*Murete picks up a leaf. Lets it fall. Takes a twig and breaks it off piece by piece, giggling all the while. Ogun impatiently slaps his hand.*]

OGUN: You know Demoke, servant of Ogun. Demoke the worker of iron and of wood. Was he among the four?

MURETE [*drunkenly.*]: You.

OGUN: Aroni bade me ask you. He says, was the carver among them? Demoke, the servant of Ogun.

MURETE: You . . . Ogun . . . you . . . Ogun.

OGUN: No you drunkard. Ogun is nowhere here. Aroni sent me. He spoke to you . . . recently.

MURETE: Yes, yes, Aroni.

OGUN: And Eshuoro, did he speak to you?

MURETE [*wildly flailing.*]: Eshuoro, you bit off my shelter. I'll bite your head off. I'll bite your head off . . .

OGUN: Gently . . . gently . . . of course you'll bite my head off. Don't forget, you are no friend to Eshuoro, are you . . . ?

MURETE [*baring his teeth.*]: I'll bite off yours . . . come here . . . just you come here . . . is it my affair if the woodcutter lopped off your big top. You take up too much room anyway . . . who do you think you are?

[*Aims a wild blow at Ogun. He ducks. Murete passes out.*]

OGUN [*examining him.*]: Mm. Mm. [*Props him up against the tree.*] He should bear no love for Eshuoro. It is not much but it is something. Let Eshuoro strip a few more dwellings naked and he won't have a friend at the welcome. Demoke the carver, my friend and servant, it was my axe you drove into araba, pride among the trees of Eshuoro. It was my iron that cicatrized his naked skin—I'll not forget you Demoke. I shall not forget.

[*Re-enter Obaneji, Demoke, Adenebi and Rola.*]

DEMOKE: They are gone.

OBANEJI: We will follow them if you like.

ROLA: No. Demoke, stay here.

OBANEJI: You really think they are the people your father spoke of?

DEMOKE: I do. Anyway, what does it matter? I still don't know what brought me here.

ADENEBI: Well, don't be over-anxious to find out. At least not from those ...

DEMOKE: I know we are bound to meet somewhere.

ADENEBI: For heaven's sake let's change the subject.

ROLA: For once I agree with you.

DEMOKE: The man who fell to his death—from the tree—I wonder if he was the other one ...

ROLA: Dressed like that? For God's sake ...

ADENEBI: I'm going back if you don't stop this.

OBANEJI: But you said you thought they were the ones Agboreko invoked—at your father's request.

DEMOKE: They say Aroni has taken control. That is when the guilty become afraid.

ROLA: Can't we talk of something else? You ... you haven't told us why you came. What are you hiding?

OBANEJI: No crime, if that's what you mean. Like your carver here, I was thrown out by the nose. I know too much ... about people ... far too much. When I saw them all, actually rejoicing—that much is true at least—most of them did experience joy ... but you see ... when they laughed, I was looking down their throats.

ROLA: And what did you see?

OBANEJI: Only what I know already.

ROLA: Hm. If it isn't the sage himself.

OBANEJI: Don't misunderstand me. It is just that I work as a filing clerk for the Courts. Senior clerk, mind you. I know about people even before I've met them. Know their whole history sometimes. And against my will, I find that all the time, I am guessing which name belongs to who. You don't know how unnerving that can be, especially when one is so often right.

ROLA: A sort of keeper of the nation's secrets, eh? What a chance! But I suppose you don't much enjoy it. You only pry against your will.

ADENEBI [*hurriedly*.]: Look, somehow we all seem to be keeping together. So why don't we forget all about unpleasantness?

ROLA [*coyly at Demoke.*]: Do *you* think I was being unpleasant? Anyway, I think people ought to be more honest about their work. I know I would enjoy that sort of thing.

OBANEJI: To be quite honest, I do enjoy some of it. I would never deny that it had its enjoyable side. You know, the lighter side. As I said, we collect records of the most peculiar things. You'd never guess how varied is our collection.

ROLA: I know what *I* would collect mostly.

OBANEJI: Wealthy men?

ROLA: You are turning nasty.

OBANEJI: On the contrary, you suggested we should be more honest towards each other. And I intend to try it out. Now, I for instance. My favourite is motor lorries. You know, passenger lorries. I have a passion for them.

ROLA: What a choice!

OBANEJI: Take one lorry I was examining only yesterday—the records that is—now wait a minute ... what was the name of it again? I never can remember the number ... oh yes ... The Chimney of Ereko.

ADENEBI: That is not its real name.

OBANEJI: Oh, you know it too?

ADENEBI: Of course I do. All the passenger lorries pass through our hands in the council. We perform all the formalities. The name of this one is 'God My Saviour'.

OBANEJI: Yes, that is the name painted on it. But we prefer to call our collection, human or vehicular, by the names by which they are generally known. This one, the Chimney of Ereko. What a lorry! What a record it has. You put it off the road very recently, didn't you?

ADENEBI: We had to. It was smoking like a perpetual volcano.

OBANEJI: Pity. I was very fond of it. Chimney of Ereko. It had survived eight serious crashes, apart from falling in a pit two or three times. Yes, it was something of an old warrior. I grew a real affection for it.

ADENEBI: If you like that sort of thing.

OBANEJI: Oh yes I do. Now take another casebook which we closed only yesterday. Another passenger lorry. They call it the Incinerator.

ADENEBI: Never heard the name.

OBANEJI: You couldn't have. It got that name only yesterday—
after what happened.

ROLA: What?

OBANEJI: Before I tell you, I must let you know the history of
the lorry. When it was built, someone looked at it, and
decided that it would only take forty men. But the owner took
it to the council . . . now, my friend, this is something for you
to investigate. One of your office workers took a bribe. A real
substantial bribe. And he changed the capacity to seventy.

DEMOKE: Seventy!

OBANEJI: Yes. Seventy. From forty.

ROLA: That's nearly twice.

OBANEJI: You said it—nearly twice. Now what do you think
would happen if such a trap suddenly caught fire?

DEMOKE: When?

ROLA [shuts her eyes tightly.]: No, no, no, no . . .

OBANEJI: Yesterday. That is why they have called it the
Incinerator since yesterday. Of the seventy people in it, five
escaped. It overturned you see, and the body was built of
wood. . . . Dry and brittle in the Harmattan season too. They
were all on their way here—to the gathering of the tribes.
[There is a short silence.]

ADENEBI: Seventy did you say?

OBANEJI: Excepting five. Only five escaped.

ADENEBI: Seventy. It couldn't have been one of ours.

OBANEJI: Mr. Adenebi. What office do you hold in the
council?

ADENEBI [angrily.]: What do you imply?

OBANEJI: You misunderstand me. I only meant, are you in a
position to find out something for me?

ADENEBI [warily.]: That depends. I am only the official Orator to
the Council, but . . .

OBANEJI: You do wield some authority.

ADENEBI: Yes, Certainly.

OBANEJI: You see, I want to close my files on this particular
lorry—the Incinerator. And my records won't be complete
unless I have the name of the man who did it—you know,
the one who took the bribe. Do you think you can help me
there?

ADENEBI: Since you are so clever and so knowledgeable, why don't you find that out yourself?

OBANEJI: Please . . . it is only for the sake of records . . .

ADENEBI: Then to hell with your records. Have you no feeling for those who died? Are you just an insensitive, inhuman block?

OBANEJI: I didn't kill them. And anyway, we have our different views. The world must go on. After all, what are a mere sixty-five souls burnt to death? Nothing. Your bribe-taker was only a small-time murderer; he wasn't even cold-blooded. He doesn't really interest me very much. I shall be writing his name in small print.

ROLA: He deserves to be hanged.

OBANEJI: Now that's a bloodthirsty woman. No, you cannot really punish the man. After all, how was he to foresee the consequences of his actions? How was he to know that in two months from the deed, the lorry would hit another, overturn completely, and be set on fire?

ROLA [fiercely.]: You seem to relish talking about it.

OBANEJI: Oh, no. I have seen so much. It simply doesn't impress me, that's all.

[There is a short silence.]

DEMOKE: I work with fire. Carving and smelting. Sometimes I merely trace patterns on wood. With fire. I live by the forge and often hold the cinders in my hands. So you see I am not afraid of fire. But I wish to be saved from death by burning. Living, I would rather not watch my body dissolve like alloy. There must be happier deaths.

ROLA: Like what?

OBANEJI: Yes, go on. Tell us. What kind of death would you prefer?

DEMOKE: A fall from a great height.

OBANEJI [sharply.]: Why?

DEMOKE: Why?

OBANEJI: Yes, why? Why should you prefer to fall?

DEMOKE: Because I know what it is. I have seen it happen. Didn't I tell you about my apprentice . . .

OBANEJI: Yes, your apprentice. But what has that to do with you?

DEMOKE: I watched it. I took part in it. There is nothing ignoble in a fall from that height. The wind cleaned him as he fell.

And it goes further. I mean, for me, it goes further.

Perhaps it is because I am a slave to heights. You see, I can go so far so high, but one step further than that and I am seized with dizziness. Where my hands are burning to work, where my hands are trembling to mould, my body will not take me. Is that not a lack of fulfilment? If I can pull my body up, further than it will go, I would willingly fall to my death after.

ROLA: That doesn't make sense.

DEMOKE: Oh yes it does. For me it does.

OBANEJI: Hm. And our friend the Orator to the Council ... what sort of death shall we pray that you meet with?

ADENEBI [*furiously.*]: No, you tell us. How would you like to be killed?

OBANEJI: Oh. I shall have to think a minute or two over that ... Let me see ...

ROLA: Why don't you confess it? You are the type who would rather die in your bed. You look it.

OBANEJI: You say that as if one should be ashamed of it.

ROLA [*contemptuously.*]: No. I suppose there are things which do crawl into a hole to die.

OBANEJI [*laughs softly.*]: And you? Since the Orator won't tell us his death-wish, perhaps you will.

ROLA [*throws her head back and laughs.*]: So you'd like to know. Are you quite sure that you would like to know?

OBANEJI: I asked you, didn't I?

[*Rola swings round suddenly, embraces him and tries to kiss him.*]

OBANEJI [*struggling.*]: Please ... please ... let me go.

ROLA: Oh no. If you think I am just pretending, go ahead and kill me right now. You'll see I don't mind at all. Of course, if I was really going to die, I would go further than that.

[*Obaneji eventually succeeds in throwing her off; Rola loses her balance and falls. Adenebi runs to assist her to get up.*]

ROLA: Pig! Pig!

ADENEBI: That was quite unnecessary. What sort of a man do you call yourself anyway?

ROLA [*struggling with Adenebi.*]: Let me get at him. I've scratched out duller eyes than yours.

OBANEJI: I am sorry. Believe me, I didn't mean to hurt you.

ROLA: Of course you didn't. You are just naturally uncouth. Pig!

OBANEJI: Again I apologize. But please keep your distance in future. I have a particular aversion to being mauled by women.

ROLA [*furiously*.]: I suppose you weren't born by one. Filth! You should be back among your moths and dust you nosy conceited prig. Who do you think you are anyway, looking perpetually smug and pushing people around?

ADENEBI: I hope you like what you've started. After all you asked the question. You should not complain if you get an unexpected answer.

OBANEJI: You are wrong there. It was not unexpected. It was only the method of reply for which I wasn't prepared.

ROLA [*looks at him with withering contempt*.]: No wonder you were not prepared. I don't suppose you have ever in your life dared to hold a woman in your arms . . .

OBANEJI: Please . . . please . . . let us change the subject.

ROLA: You started it. And anyway who are you to think that we will only talk of whatever happens to please you? I am getting sick of the way you step back when it seems you are about to get splashed, especially as you swing your feet about as much as you do . . .

OBANEJI: Once again, I am sorry. But please don't . . .

ROLA [*teasing, quite bitchily, makes a sudden dart and pulls at his beard*.]: He'll die in his bed but he'll die alone
He'll sleep in his bed but he'll sleep alone
He'll wake in the morning and he'll eat alone.
So good up in heaven he sang praises alone.

OBANEJI: I beg you not to impress yourself on me so hard. I have told you, recognition is the curse I carry with me. I don't want to know any more. I thought I was safe with you. I thought that you all wanted to be quiet.

DEMOKE: Let me tell you a story. Once upon a time . . .

ROLA: Shut up. It is he who ought to tell us a story. Let him tell us of his life. How came it he was born not fully formed?

ADENEBI: Really, this is too much. A lady shouldn't . . .

OBANEJI: I know you already. But do you have to betray yourself to these people?

ROLA: Don't you dare suggest you know me. Whatever it is you keep in your filthy records, I am not in them. I am not a criminal. I don't work in the council and I never drove your Incinerator. I have never been to court in all my life.

OBANEJI: Let me beg you to be quiet then.

ROLA: There is the graveyard. Find yourself a graveyard if you want some silence.

OBANEJI: I don't think that would be any better than here. Isn't the graveyard filled with your lovers?

ROLA: What!

[*There is silence.*]

ADENEBI: Now, really . . .

OBANEJI: Well, look at her. Doesn't she look the type who would drive men to madness and self-destruction!

ROLA: What do you mean? Say it outright. What do you mean?

OBANEJI: Nothing. I merely hoped that would keep you silent.

ROLA: You have a filthy mind. Coward! Why don't you say what is in your mind?

OBANEJI: I beg you to let us change this subject.

ROLA: Out with it! I have nothing to be ashamed of. Because your ears are stuck to gossip, you throw out perpetual feelers for muck. Do you think I do not know what you meant?

DEMOKE : Why? Why? Why? The man said nothing. Only a feeble effort to be cruel. Why do you take it to heart?

ROLA: Shut up or I'll get those who will tear the skin off your back. You and your complacent friend.

DEMOKE [*suddenly.*]: Madame Tortoise! Blind. Blind. [*Hitting himself on the forehead.*] Madame Tortoise, that is who you are! [*Rola stands stock-still, her face drained of expression.*]

OBANEJI [*quietly.*]: You've been begging for a stone to hit you on the head. Couldn't you be quiet?

ROLA [*breaking down.*]: What have I done to you? What have I ever done to you?

[*She falls on her knees, still sobbing.*]

ADENEBI: Do you know what you have just said? You had better be sure it is true.

OBANEJI: He seems to know her. I thought she was tougher.

DEMOKE: Madame Tortoise. Just think . . . I have been with her all day . . .

ROLA [*raises her head suddenly.*]: Isn't that enough? Have you all suddenly earned the right to stare at me as if I was leprous?

You want me to wallow in self-disgust. Well, I won't.
I wasn't made the way you think women are.

ADENEBI: What! No shame. No shame at all.

DEMOKE: Please, don't upset yourself—not over *him*.

ROLA: Ho. You are very kind, are you not? You think you have
enough for yourself that you can spare me some pity.
Well keep it. Keep it. Just what is it you all accuse me of?

OBANEJI [*placatingly*.]: Nothing. Nothing.

ADENEBI: Nothing? Do you call that nothing? Two lovers in
the graveyard. And the sordidness of it. The whole horrible
scandal. How did I ever get in your company?

ROLA: Go. It is people like you . . . Psh! Since when did I ever
begin to waste a glance on fools. You know that, I hope.
You are a fool. A foolish man. The word has meaning when
I look at you. I wouldn't be sorry to see you under the ground,
except that it wouldn't be because you were my lover.

ADENEBI: Her brazenness. Do you see? She is utterly unrepentant!

ROLA: People like you beg to be shaven clean on the skull.
Except that I couldn't bear to touch you.

DEMOKE: I carved something to you. Of course I didn't know
you then, I mean, I had never met you. But from what I heard,
you were so . . .

ADENEBI: Bestial. Yes, just the sort of thing you would carve, isn't
it? Like your totem. Bestial it was. Utterly bestial.

DEMOKE: Actually, that is what I mean. Madame Tortoise is the
totem—most of it anyway. In fact, you might almost say she
dominated my thoughts—she, and something else. About
equally.

ADENEBI: Something equally revolting I am sure.

DEMOKE [*simply*.]: Oh no. Equally . . . Anyway, it had to do with me.
[*Adenebi sniggers*.]

OBANEJI: One moment. I thought I heard you say, earlier on,
that this work was quite remarkable.

ADENEBI: That didn't mean I thought it even worth the trouble.
And anyway, we had only met. I wanted to see if he was at
all fooled by his own monstrosity.

ROLA: You see. Men like that, who can pity them? Do they not
beg that their lives be wrung out of them? That their heads
be turned inside out?

ADENEBI: Are you making excuses?

ROLA: Not to you. Not to anyone. I owe all that happened to my
nature. I regret nothing. They were fools, fools to think they
were something better than . . . the other men. My other men.

ADENEBI: Men! Some of them were hardly grown up. We heard
you liked them young, really young.

ROLA: I regret nothing. You men are conceited fools. Nothing
was ever done on my account. Nothing. What you do is boost
yourselves all the time. By every action. When that one killed
the other, was it on my account? When he killed himself,
could he claim that he did it for me? He was only big with
himself, so leave me out of it.

ADENEBI: I suppose you didn't really run merely because you
were beset by your relations. They simply didn't leave you
room to entertain your lovers. And this could have been a
profitable season. A generous season.

ROLA: Draw your filthy conclusions. I only know I am master
of my fate. I have turned my training to good account. I
am wealthy, and I know where my wealth came from.

ADENEBI: Oh yes, you ruined countless. Young and old. Old,
peaceful ones who had never even set eyes on you; who simply
did not know what their son was up to; didn't know he was
draining the home away—for you.

ROLA: Don't go on or you'll make me cry. Fool! What is it to me?
When your business men ruin the lesser ones, do you go crying
to them? I also have no pity for the one who invested foolishly.
Investors, that is all they ever were—to me.

OBANEJI [nodding, with a faint faraway smile.]: Madame Tortoise . . .
Madame Tortoise . . . Do you realize, I even knew your
ancestors. I knew . . .

ROLA: And you, I suppose you have no ancestors. You are merely
the dust that came off a moth's wing.

[Obaneji appears to be shut up by this. There is an uncomfortable
silence.]

DEMOKE: You don't look one bit similar to your other face—you
know, the one that rises from legends. That was the one I
thought of. I thought of you together, but . . . you are not the
same. Anyway, you can have a look at my totem and tell me.
I needed some continuity and you provided it—You do see

why, don't you? I take it you do know of the legendary
Madame Tortoise.

ROLA [*subdued.*]: No. What was she?

DEMOKE [*shrugs.*]: A woman.

ADENEBI [*rises.*]: I think I must leave your company. He talks like
a lost lunatic and you are worse than the devil. I don't want
to be involved in your types.

[*Goes off. Rushes back immediately and goes off the opposite way.
The Dead Pair enter.*]

OBANEJI: Perhaps we ought to go too.

[*Demoke rises sharply. Goes to the Dead Man.*]

DEMOKE: Are you the one who fell from the tree?

ROLA: Use your eyes. He cannot be. Come away for heaven's
sake.

DEMOKE: Did you meet? Does he accuse me?

DEAD MAN: I always did want to come here. This is my home. I
have always yearned to come back. Over there, nothing held
me. I owned nothing, had no desire to. But the dark trees and
the thick earth drew me. When I died, I fell into the
understreams, and the great summons found me ready.
I travelled the understreams beneath the great ocean; I travelled
the understreams beneath the great seas. I flowed through the
hardened crust of this oldest of the original vomits of Forest
Father . . .

DEMOKE: And did you meet Oremole the bonded carver? Does
he accuse me?

OBANEJI: Must you be in such haste? Everything will come to you
sooner or later.

DEAD MAN [*jerks up suddenly.*]: Like palsy. How suddenly you shake
with violence!

DEAD WOMAN: What is this? The one who was to take my case—
has he sent another down? Into the pit?

DEAD MAN: What have they thought that it fills the air so suddenly
with stench?

DEAD WOMAN: A hundred generations has made no difference.
I was a fool to come.

DEAD MAN: It is death you reek of. Now I know what the smell is.

DEMOKE: I did . . . I asked you, did he accuse me?

DEAD WOMAN: I said the living would save me. What fingers are

those whom I begged to let down my child gently? What
have you thought to push me further down the pit? [*Goes.*]

DEAD MAN: May you be cursed again. May you be cursed again.
[*Goes.*]

DEMOKE: I pushed him. I pushed him down.

ROLA: Who?

DEMOKE: He climbed higher and I pushed him down. The one
who did not fall from the tree. Apprentice to my craft, till I
plunged him into hell.

OBANEJI: Save it. Save it for later.

ROLA: Leave him alone. What is it all to you?

OBANEJI: He needn't speak. Why does he? Why do you all? I want
nothing, asked nothing.

DEMOKE: Now, now, and from his nest, I will again
Pluck him, Oremole servant of Oro and fling him
Screaming downwards into hell.

OBANEJI: Hatred. Pride. Blindness. Envy. Was it envy?

DEMOKE: Envy, but not from prowess of his adze.
The world knew of Demoke, son and son to carvers;
Master of wood, shaper of iron, servant of Ogun,
Slave, alas, to height, and the tapered end
Of the silk-cotton tree. Oremole
My bonded man, whetted the blades,
Lit the fires to forge Demoke's tools.
Strong he was; he whirled the crooked wheel
When Oro puffed himself, Oro who was born
With a pebble in his throat, and frightens children
Begging for their tiny hands to pull it out.
Oremole was the cat by night. The cloth that hangs
Above tall branches, Oremole left it there.
Nimble like a snake, he had no foot to trip him.
And now he sat above my head, carving at the head
While I crouched below him, nibbling hairs
Off the chest of araba, king among the trees.
So far could I climb, one reach higher
And the world was beaten like an egg and I
Clasped the tree-hulk like a lover.
Thrice I said I'll cut it down, thread it,
Stride it prostrate, mould and master araba

Below the knee, shave and scrape him clean
On the head. But thrice Oremole, slave,
Server to Eshuoro laughed! 'Let me anoint
The head, and do you, my master, trim the bulge
Of his great bottom.' The squirrel who dances on
A broken branch, must watch whose jaws are open
Down below. Thrice I said I would behead it
Where my feet would go no further. Thrice
Oremole, slave, fawner on Eshuoro laughed.
'No one reduces Oro's height, while I serve
The wind. Watch Oremole ride on Aja's head,
And when I sift the dust, master, gather it
Below.' The water-pot, swept up suddenly.
Boasted, Aja is my horse. Has it got wings
Or is it not made of clay? I plucked him down!
Demoke's head is no woman's cloth, spread
To receive wood shavings from a carpenter.
Down, down I plucked him, screaming on Oro.
Before he made hard obeisance to his earth,
My axe was executioner at Oro's neck. Alone,
Alone I cut the strands that mocked me, till head
And boastful slave lay side by side, and I
Demoke, sat in the shoulders of the tree,
My spirit set free and singing, my hands,
My father's hands possessed by demons of blood
And I carved three days and nights till tools
Were blunted, and these hands, my father's hands
Swelled big as the tree-trunk. Down I came
But Ogun touched me at the forge, and I slept
Weary at his feet.

MAN'S VOICE [*quite near.*]: Demoke!

OBANEJI: Who was that?

VOICE: Demoke!

OBANEJI: Do you know that voice?

DEMOKE: My father's.

OBANEJI: Quickly then. This way. It came from here.
[*He leads them in the wrong direction.*
Enter Ogun. Rapidly.]

OGUN: Once again, he foiled me. Forest Father,

Deeper still you lead my ward into your
Domain, where I cannot follow. To stay him,
I assumed his father's voice, who follows now
Hard upon my heels. I'll not desert him.
The crime, if crime it was, lies on my head.
My instrument he was, plucking out Oremole
Worshipper of Oro, slayer of my disciples.
I set his hand to the act. I killed
The proud one, who would not bow araba's head
When the gifted hands of Demoke, son and son
To carvers would pass his spirit into wood,
Would master wood with iron, fibre with fire!
Forest Father, masquerading as a human,
Bringing them to judgement, I'll not desert
My servant. I am no less son to you than others
And if my voice is not heard, my hand must
Be felt.
[*The beaters' noise comes over, increasing during Ogun's speech.
He goes off as the Old Man, followed by two of the councillors,
enters, surrounded by the whole chaos of beaters.*]

OLD MAN: You are sure it wasn't my son Demoke?

COUNCILLOR: Very sure. I am absolutely certain.

OLD MAN: Anyway, you say the person was heading for home.

COUNCILLOR: It was Adenebi, the Court Orator. I couldn't
mistake him.

OLD MAN: Never mind. I'm only worried because he went into
hiding. But I don't think he would wander into the forest.
I begged him not to.
[*Adenebi enters.*]

COUNCILLOR: That's the man himself. I thought I saw you
returning home.

ADENEBI: So I was. And then I heard all the commotion. And I
met one of your men who said you were hunting some shady
characters.

OLD MAN: And so we are.

ADENEBI: What are they like?

OLD MAN: I don't know. I haven't seen them.

ADENEBI: But in that case . . .

OLD MAN: Look here, we haven't got nets or cages, so you can

sce we are not really trying to capture them. If we can drive
them away from here, it will be sufficient. [*To the Councillor.*]
Tell the men to scatter. They are not covering sufficient
ground. They must move wider. I can't hear them. I cannot
hear them. They must make a lot more noise.

ADENEBI: Won't they get away before you . . .

OLD MAN: My friend, we want them to go; to go before we get
there, wherever there is. And if the guest won't go quietly,
we must shout out the price of food.

ADENEBI: What guest?

OLD MAN: What guest? Oh, go, go!

ADENEBI: I'm sorry, but if you will talk in riddles . . . Talking
about guests, what about the half dozen or so special guests
whom we were supposed to expect.

OLD MAN [*very restlessly.*]: They are the very people we are trying
to drive off.

ADENEBI: What! What kind of welcome is that?

OLD MAN: Look. Go on, look. Do I seem mad?

ADENEBI: No.

OLD MAN: Well, believe me when I tell you that everything has
misfired. These people who have come to claim our hospitality
do not wish us well. We were sent the wrong people. We
asked for statesmen and we were sent executioners.
[*One of the crowd enters.*]

ADENEBI: I don't understand. I thought we left it all to you.

OLD MAN: Ah, petrol. You, get me one of the councillors.
[*The man goes.*] I have just remembered. They cannot stand
the smell of petrol.
[*Councillor enters.*]
Get some petrol. Pour it all over the forest. They cannot
stand the smell.

COUNCILLOR: Baba, don't you think that . . .

OLD MAN: Now what am I thinking of? I must be getting tired.
No sensible man burns the house to cook a little yam. I
know what I want. Remember the old decrepit wagon we
put off the road?

COUNCILLOR: Oh. The Chimney of Ereko?

OLD MAN: That's the one. Tell the owner it is back on the road—
in the forest, that is. Get him to drive it right through here

and he can let it smoke as much as he likes. Fill up his tank
and charge it to the council.

COUNCILLOR: Baba, no vehicle could move a foot in this bush.

OLD MAN: The Chimney can. He's survived at least half a dozen
head-on crashes; not to mention the number of houses he's
knocked down for being too near the street. Don't worry,
it will tame this jungle.

[*The Councillor goes.*]

ADENEBI: Sir, will you kindly explain what is happening?

OLD MAN [*not listening.*]: Yes, yes, the Chimney ought to do it.
When that monster travels at anything over two miles per
hour you can't see the world for smoke or smell a latrine for
petrol fumes. If any ghost can survive it, then there is no power
that can help me.

ADENEBI: Sir, I am still waiting for some sort of explanation. I
know I am not dreaming.

OLD MAN: What is the matter with you? [*Looks up as if he is seeing
him for the first time.*]

ADENEBI: Nothing I hope. But such a lot seems to be happening.
Just tell me one thing. Did I or did I not hear aright when
you said that all this was to drive off the very people we had
invited to be our guests?

OLD MAN: Yes.

ADENEBI: I beg your pardon sir. Did you say 'Yes'?

OLD MAN: Yes, yes, yes!

ADENEBI: But ... but ... this is madness.

OLD MAN: Why? Was it or was it not you who spoke in favour
of my idea in the council? Did you not threaten to finance
the whole programme yourself if the council turned it down?

ADENEBI: Certainly I did. It fell to me as official Orator.

OLD MAN: Well then, are you backing out now?

ADENEBI [*completely flabbergasted.*]: But ... I don't see how ...
wait a minute. Let me understand where I am. I remember
what I said, what we promised to do. An occasion such as the
gathering of the tribes—a great thing ... it would happen only
once in several lifetimes ... only once in centuries of history.
It is a whole historical epoch in itself. We resolved to carve
a totem, a totem that would reach to the sky.

OLD MAN: Yes. My son carved it.

ADENEBI: Your son? Was that your son?

OLD MAN: Yes, don't look so surprised. We come from a long line of carvers.

ADENEBI: Oh. Well, in addition I said; . . . no, you said, and I took it up, that we must bring home the descendants of our great forebears. Find them. Find the scattered sons of our proud ancestors. The builders of empires. The descendants of our great nobility. Find them. Bring them here. If they are half-way across the world, trace them. If they are in hell, ransom them. Let them symbolize all that is noble in our nation. Let them be our historical link for the season of rejoicing. Warriors. Sages. Conquerors. Builders. Philosophers. Mystics. Let us assemble them round the totem of the nation and we will drink from their resurrected glory.

OLD MAN: Yes. It was a fine speech. But control, at some point was lost to our enemies. The guests we were sent are slaves and lackeys. They have only come to undermine our strength. To preach to us how ignoble we are. They are disgruntled creatures who have come to accuse their tormentors as if this were a court of law. We have courts for the oppressed. Let them go somewhere else.

ADENEBI: I see. I had thought how splendid it would all be. Purple robes. White horses dressed in gold. Processions through the town with communion and service around our symbol . . . by the way, I really ought to tell you how disappointed I was with your son's handiwork. Don't you think it was rather pagan? I should have thought that something more in keeping with our progress would be more appropriate.

OLD MAN: You should have told him.

ADENEBI: I never saw it till it was finished. In fact I saw the carver himself—your son—only today. But I didn't have time to tell him . . .

OLD MAN: Did you say you saw him? When?

ADENEBI: Not very long ago. There were two other people at the time. Strange people.

OLD MAN [thoughtfully.]: I fear for him. I greatly fear for him.

ADENEBI: Why? Is he unwell? He seemed quite healthy when we . . .

OLD MAN: No, no. It is nothing. Forget I spoke.

[Enter the Councillor.]

OLD MAN: Will he do it?

COUNCILLOR: Yes. He's on his way.

OLD MAN: I hope he kills them all over again. [*Angrily.*] Slaves! Can't they forget they once had lives of their own? How dare they pester the living with the petty miseries of their lives!

ADENEBI: Mali. Songhai. Perhaps a descendant of the great Lisabi. Zimbabwe. Maybe the legendary Prester John himself. . . . I was thinking of heroes like they.

OLD MAN: Isn't it time Agboreko was back? If he has learnt nothing by now then the whole Forest is against us.

COUNCILLOR: He went to consult Murete of the Trees.

OLD MAN: Hm. It shows how helpless we are. Murete, the most unreliable of the tree demons, but he is the only one who will even respond when he is called. It serves me right. The cricket didn't know he was well off until he asked the sparrow to admire his hole.

ADENEBI: Mali. Songhai. Lisabi. Chaka . . . but who did we get?

OLD MAN: Nonentities without a doubt. It is only the cockroach who shouts vanity when the chicken struts.

AGBOREKO [*entering*.]: Proverb to bones and silence.

OLD MAN: Agboreko. At last.

AGBOREKO: I heard them again.

OLD MAN: Was there some change?

AGBOREKO: They notice nothing. They are so full of themselves and their grievances. The worst possible type to deal with.

OLD MAN: They won't go among the people will they?

AGBOREKO: It won't be necessary. Aroni has taken them under his wing. And anyway, they have met one of their old adversaries. Madame Tortoise.

COUNCILLOR: The one who still bears that name?

AGBOREKO: The same. And that is one descendant we overlooked. Illustrious too beyond a doubt. And they are strongly linked to her. Through what crime, I do not know.

OLD MAN: And where does Aroni mean to hold court? If we knew that . . .

AGBOREKO: If the flea had a home of his own, he wouldn't be out on a dog's back. Proverb to bones and silence.

OLD MAN: And Murete . . . wouldn't tell?

AGBOREKO: Nine times I asked Murete of the trees. And nine times he said to me, Aroni will tell you. Ask him.

OLD MAN: Well, ask him.

AGBOREKO [*shakes his head.*]: Aroni is Wisdom itself. When he means to expose the weaknesses of human lives, there is nothing can stop him. And he knows how to choose his time.

OLD MAN [*drawing him aside.*]: Oremole ... the one who ... fell from the tree. Is he among the dead?

AGBOREKO: Not yet. Perhaps not at all.

OLD MAN: And would the others accuse on his behalf?

AGBOREKO: The lips of the dead did not open thus far. I cannot tell.

OLD MAN: Does the Old Man of the Forest himself pass judgement or is it his wayward court?

AGBOREKO: Would that affect the scales of Aroni? The chameleon dances, his father claps and you exclaim, 'How modestly the young one keeps silence.' Proverb to bones and silence.

COUNCILLOR: There is still hope. We have heard nothing of Forest Father. Perhaps Aroni merely acts on his own.

AGBOREKO [*shakes his head.*]: Oro cried last night and Bashiru vanished from his bed. Do you still wonder what became of your friend? Proverb to bones and silence.

COUNCILLOR: I am sorry.

ADENEBI: But where does your Forest Father come in? Who is he anyway?

[*There is total silence while they all stare at him.*]

AGBOREKO [*sighs.*]: Perhaps I should go and summon Murete once more. He might have eaten by now.

OLD MAN [*quickly.*]: Agboreko, pay no attention to ...

AGBOREKO: Did you think I took notice? Because it rained the day the egg was hatched the foolish chicken swore he was a fish. Proverb to bones and silence. [*Goes.*]

OLD MAN [*shouts after him.*]: Offer Murete millet wine for a whole year.

ADENEBI: I don't think my place is here. Perhaps this is some sort of play for the gathering, but I am too busy to worry my head a moment longer about all this mystery. I can see now that the carver is your son ... such peculiar behaviour.

OLD MAN: You should go. And if you see my son again tell him not to forget what I told him.

ADENEBI: You'll probably run into him yourself. He is still somewhere around here.

OLD MAN: Here? In the bush? [*Adenebi is going.*] Wait! Did you say you saw my son here?

ADENEBI: I told you. I was with him.

OLD MAN: But here? In the forest? [*Angrily.*] Why didn't you tell me that before?

ADENEBI: You didn't ask.

OLD MAN: Forgive me. Were there others?

ADENEBI: Yes. One man, and another, a woman. I was fourth.

OLD MAN: Was it near here?

ADENEBI [*looks around.*]: Yes. In fact I think we rested in this clearing for some time.

OLD MAN: Did you hear or notice anything?

ADENEBI: Like what?

OLD MAN: Anything! Did you meet other people for instance?

ADENEBI: There was nobody else ... oh no ... there were two mad creatures ... you know, those mad people you find everywhere. They were very unpleasant looking. In fact, it was the reason why I decided to go back. They seemed to follow us all over the place. They made me feel like vomiting. Oh yes, and I found that the woman who was with us was that notorious lady they call Madame Tortoise. That was really why I left. Think, if I, a councillor, was discovered with her!

OLD MAN [*agitatedly.*]: Madame Tortoise! And my son was with you?

ADENEBI: He was.

OLD MAN: Who was the fourth?

ADENEBI: I don't know. An impertinent old man. Said he was a Chief Clerk or something.

OLD MAN: I feared it. Eshuoro was the fourth. Eshuoro must have been the fourth, leading you all to your destruction. How did you escape him?

ADENEBI: I ... I don't know ... What is this?

OLD MAN: A servant of Oro was killed. Nothing will rest until we are all bathed in blood. ... [*Raises his voice suddenly.*] Agboreko! Agboreko—o!
[*Agboreko hurries in almost at once.*]

AGBOREKO: They passed here. They stayed at this very spot and spoke with four people.

OLD MAN: I shouted to tell you the same. Something Adenebi said awoke all the suspicions in me. And my son was among the four. With Madame Tortoise. Did you not know that?

AGBOREKO: Murete consented at last to unseal his lips. Two of the dead spoke to four people; they wanted human advocates.

OLD MAN: At whose prompting?

AGBOREKO: No doubt it is another cunning thought of Aroni. To let the living condemn themselves.

OLD MAN: [pointing to Adenebi.] He was with them. Why? What has he ever done?

ADENEBI: Don't class me with Madame Tortoise. I am no murderer . . .

AGBOREKO: He is still in the forest isn't he? It will all come out.

ADENEBI [frightened.]: Don't speak of me at all. Leave me out of your thoughts altogether.

AGBOREKO: Anyway, the man is a fool. Is that not enough crime for Aroni?

OLD MAN: The fourth. Who was the fourth then? There were four of them.

AGBOREKO: Until the last gourd has been broken, let us not talk of drought. Proverbs to bones and silence. [Beaters' noises audible again.]

OLD MAN: Then you too have thought the same. Eshuoro it must have been.

AGBOREKO: A hundred and twenty-one of the sons and servants of Forest Father it could have been. Even the Father of Forests himself. Let us be busy. I have sent for my man.

OLD MAN: Yes, yes. They passed here. He says they passed here and stayed a while. If we drive off the witnesses Aroni has no power. Where is your man? Isn't he here yet?

AGBOREKO: He is on his way.

[Definite rhythm of drums above beaters' noises.]

OLD MAN: He'll come too late.

AGBOREKO: No. Patience, Baba. Patience.

ADENEBI: Who is this man? Shall we send somebody for him? I will go if you like.

AGBOREKO: If the wind can get lost in the rainstorm it is useless to send him an umbrella. Proverb to bones and silence.

OLD MAN: Yes, yes, we'll be patient.

AGBOREKO: The eye that looks downwards will certainly see the nose. The hand that dips to the bottom of the pot will eat the biggest snail. The sky grows no grass but if the earth called her barren, it will drink no more milk. The foot of the snake is not split in two like a man's or in hundreds like the centipede's, but if Agere could dance patiently like the snake, he will uncoil the chain that leads into the dead . . .

[*Enter the beaters, shouting. The flogger immediately breaks through them and sets out to clear a space with his long whip, which he freely exercises. The dancer follows almost at once, followed by his acolyte (a very intense young girl). She sprinkles the cleared space after the flogger. The dirge-man begins to recite within a few minutes of their entry. An assistant hands Agboreko the divination board, the bowl and kernels.*]

DIRGE-MAN: Move on eyah! Move apart
I felt the wind breathe—no more
Keep away now. Leave the dead
Some room to dance.

If you see the banana leaf
Freshly fibrous like a woman's breasts
If you see the banana leaf
Shred itself, thread on thread
Hang wet as the crêpe of grief
Don't say it's the wind. Leave the dead
Some room to dance.

[*Agboreko has already tossed the kernels. The Old Man goes up inquiringly to him. Agboreko draws lines and pronounces.*]

AGBOREKO: The loft is not out of reach when the dust means to settle. Oracle to the living and silence.

[*The Old Man turns away, disappointed. The dancer does not, of course, ever stop, although the drumming is lowered for Agboreko, and for the dirge-man.*]

DIRGE-MAN [*goes to the drummer and gives him the two-fisted greeting. The acolyte, who has finished her sprinkling, begins to dance softly, growing rapidly more intense.*]:

Ah, your hands are vanished and if it thunders
We know where the hands are gone.
But we name no names, let no god think
We spy his envy. Leave the dead
Some room to dance.

[*The process is repeated between Agboreko and the Old Man.*]

AGBOREKO: Have you seen a woman throw away her pestle when she really means to pound yam? When Iredade took her case to Orunmila, he said, If the worm doesn't jig near the roost, the fowl may still want to peck, but at least it can't say the worm was throwing dust in his face. Go home therefore, go home. Iredade turned sadly away so Orunmila called her back. He said, They say the forest is more cunning any time of the year, but who ever lay back in his house and watched the creepers grow over him? Oracle to the living and silence.

[*The dirge-man has been circling the acolyte.*]

DIRGE-MAN: Daughter, your feet were shod
In eeled shuttles of Yemoja's loom
But twice your smock went up
And I swear your feet were pounding
Dust at the time. Girl, I know
The game of my ancestors. Leave the dead
Some room to dance.

A touch, at that rounded moment of the night
And the dead return to life
Dum-belly woman, plantain-breasted
Mother! What human husband folds
His arms, and blesses randy ghosts?
Keep away now, leave, leave the dead
Some room to dance.

[*The dirge-man joins one or two others in a casual dance in the background. Agboreko again consults his board and kernels.*]

AGBOREKO: When they heard the thunder, Osumare said, That was only me laughing at mice. If they are the dead and we are the living, then we are their children. They shan't curse us.

When the busy-body neighbour said to the child, you haven't
been home-trained, the mother went and tore her wrapper.
She said it is not my child you cursed, it is I.

OLD MAN [*very disgruntled.*]: Ho, They say when the rock hit the
tortoise, he shrugged his shoulder and said, I've always been
cracked. When his wife met him, she asked, When did you
begin to clatter?

AGBOREKO [*putting away his bowl.*]: Proverb to bones and ...
That was thunder!
[*He hastily retrieves his paraphernalia.*]

OLD MAN: No sign of rain. I can't see a cloud, can you?

AGBOREKO [*casting nuts.*]: It was thunder. Thunder. I must cast
afresh!
[*The rumble which they all heard continues to increase. It soon
reveals itself as the roar of a high-powered lorry, bearing down on
them, headlights full on.*]

ADENEBI: Look! It is not thunder at all. There is a drunkard at
the wheel.

OLD MAN: I sent for it. For fumigation. It is the Chimney of Ereko.

AGBOREKO: The Chimney of Ereko! A-a-ah, Baba, Will you
never believe that you cannot get rid of ancestors with the
little toys of children ...

A BEATER: The Chimney of Ereko! The Chimney of Ereko!
[*The cry is taken up. Within seconds they have all panicked.
They scatter in every direction. Adenebi is knocked down. As he
attempts to rise he is knocked down again and trampled by flying
feet. Agboreko and the Old Man stand their ground for a while,
but Agboreko eventually yields, shouting what is probably a fitting
proverb to the Old Man before making a not very dignified exit, but
nothing is heard for the roar of the lorry and the panic of the crowd.
Before Agboreko is out of sight, the Old Man takes another look
at the headlamps and disappears. Adenebi rises slowly. The noise
of the engine is quite deafening. He looks round, half-dazed but
becomes suddenly active on discovering that he is alone. Runs
around shouting names, then turns to run into the headlamps,
stops suddenly and stands with raised arms, screaming. There is a
crash, the noise stops suddenly, and the lights go out. Adenebi's
scream being heard above it and after, stopping suddenly as he
hears his own terror in the silence.*]

ADENEBI [*sags slowly to his knees and gropes around.*]: . . . Demoke, Demoke. Where is that carver! And where is that woman who drains the life from men, slowly or in violence. Madame Tortoise. Madame Tortoise! My friends. My friends . . .

[*A slow rumble of scattered voices, and the forest creatures pass through, from the direction of the lorry, coming straight down and turning right and left. They all hold leaves to their noses, and grumble all the way. Some sniff in disgust, others spit, all stop their noses, disapproving strongly of the petrol fumes. Adenebi tries to make himself as inconspicuous as possible. Some fan their faces, and one has encased his head completely in a clay pot. They are all assortments of forest spirits, from olobiribiti, who rolls himself like a ball, to the two-headed puruboro, whose four horns belch continuous smoke.*]

ADENEBI [*emerging when all is again quiet. Looks around him.*]: I have always lived in mortal terror of being lost.

[*Obaneji, Rola and Demoke enter. They walk across and out on the other side without seeing Adenebi. Obaneji returns at once.*]

OBANEJI: Did you find out?

ADENEBI [*quickly on the defensive.*]: What? What ought I to have found out?

OBANEJI: You promised me. You said you would use your influence. For my records. Who did it? Who burnt out sixty-five souls?

ADENEBI: I . . . do not wish . . . to know you. I want to be left alone.

[*Obaneji turns to go with a shrug.*]

ADENEBI: Wait. I want to find my way out. I am lost here.

OBANEJI [*pointing to the direction they were taking.*]: Not this way. This leads deeper into the forest.

ADENEBI: Where are you taking them?

OBANEJI: To the welcoming of the dead. Your people refuse to acknowledge them. And yet they sacrificed until my dwelling reeked of nothing but sheep's blood and I granted their request. Now they drive them out like thieves. [*Goes.*]

[*Adenebi faces the opposite direction. Takes a step forward, peers into the darkness. Turns and runs after Obaneji.*]

PART TWO

Scene as Murete's dwelling. Murete is about to leave home for the human festivities. Stops to clean his nails against the bark of the tree.

MURETE [*grumbling.*]: Fine time to tell me he no longer needs me. What will I find at this hour but the dregs of emptied pots? If it wasn't considered obscene I would compensate my loss from the palm tree. Can't understand why not. Human beings drink their mother's milk. Drink the milk of mothers other than their own. Drink goat's milk. Cow's milk. Pig's blood. So just because I am Murete of the trees is no reason why I shouldn't climb the palm tree and help myself. I'll do it too. One of these days when I am drunk enough. [*Stops.*] Hm, there doesn't seem to be any sense in that. If I'm drunk, then I am not thirsty, so what would I be doing up the palm? [*Examines his nails with satisfaction. Straightens up his finery.*] But I'll do it just the same. If Aroni likes, he can ostracize me. [*Eshuoro enters from behind, grasps him by the throat.*]

ESHUORO: Swear, not a word.

MURETE [*choking.*]: I swear.

ESHUORO: Not a word to anyone that you saw me.

MURETE: I swear.

ESHUORO: Swear again. And don't forget that Eshuoro does not forgive the sacrilegious. [*Forces a leaf between his teeth and tears it off.*] Swear!

MURETE: I swear.

[*Eshuoro lets him go, Murete stumbles angrily spitting out the piece of leaf in his mouth.*]

MURETE [*with impotent fury.*]: Have you had your fill of eating others' roofs that you now think you can spare Murete a leaf or two of my own house!

ESHUORO [*looks at the trees.*]: That was nothing. And don't make me prove to you it was nothing. Answer quickly. Today is the day, isn't it?

MURETE: So you say. But what day is it, forest sage?

ESHUORO: Be careful . . . I asked you whether or not today was
the day for Aroni's harmless little ceremony. His welcome of
the dead. Another mild lesson for those fleas he calls humans.
Is it or isn't it?

MURETE: How do I know?

ESHUORO: Don't lie to me. Today is their gathering of the tribes.
I know they asked for conquerors and Aroni has sent them
accusers, knowing they would never welcome them. So he
holds his little feast. A few human witnesses who are returning
to their holes, supposedly wiser.

MURETE: Go and complain to Forest Father.

ESHUORO: I was not even invited. Another convenient forgetfulness
of Aroni's, isn't it?

MURETE: Don't bring me into your squabbles. They don't interest
me.

ESHUORO: Answer quickly. On whose side are you?

MURETE: I hadn't been told we were taking sides.

ESHUORO: Fool. How you survived till now I do not know. Have
you seen how they celebrate the gathering of the tribes? In our
own destruction. Today they even dared to chase out the
forest spirits by poisoning the air with petrol fumes. Have you
seen how much of the forest has been torn down for their
petty decorations?

MURETE: I know it wasn't the humans who ate my roofing.

[Eshuoro presses his arm so hard Murete yelps with pain.]

ESHUORO: Don't talk back, tree gleaner. I'm telling you today must
be a day of reprisals. While they are glutted and full of
themselves that is the time. Aroni's little ceremony must be
made into a bloody sentence. My patience is at an end. Where
the humans preserve a little bush behind their homes, it is only
because they want somewhere for their garbage. Dead dogs and
human excrement are all you'll find in it. The whole forest
stinks. Stinks of human obscenities. And who holds us back?
Forest Father and his lame minion, Aroni. They and their little
ceremonies of gentle rebuke.

MURETE: You feel strongly about it. That is commendable. Isn't
Forest Father the one who can help you? Go and talk to him.
Or if you are afraid to go, tell me and I'll make you an
appointment.

ESHUORO: You had better not go to him if that is in your mind. I'll have you bitten for seven years by ants.

MURETE: Oh. Oh. So you can count on them can you? You have been poisoning the mind of the ants.

ESHUORO: They were not difficult to win over. And they'll be present at the welcoming. Four hundred million of their dead will crush the humans in a load of guilt. Four hundred million callously smoked to death. Since when was the forest so weak that humans could smoke out the owners and sleep after?

MURETE: No one has complained much. We have claimed our own victims—for every tree that is felled or for every beast that is slaughtered, there is recompense, given or forced.

ESHUORO [*twists his arm.*]: Be sure then to take yourself off today. Every one of you that won't come clearly on my side must take himself off. Go into the town if you love them so much and join the gathering of the tribes.

MURETE: What will you do?

ESHUORO: My jester will accompany me. Aroni means to let the humans judge themselves. Good. My jester will teach them how Aroni means to let them go, afterwards. Means to let them live. Are they not guilty people?

MURETE: Let who go?

ESHUORO: Are you still pretending. The human witnesses he has abducted. He means to let them go afterwards.

MURETE: Eshuoro, you won't dare.

ESHUORO: Not by my hand. But if the humans, as always, wreak havoc on their own heads, who are we to stop them? Don't they always decide their own lives?

MURETE: I am not much concerned. But it seems to me that, limb for limb, the forest has always proved victor.

ESHUORO: This great assemblage of theirs is an affront. And I have suffered the biggest insult any son of Forest Head has ever experienced from the hand of a human insect.

MURETE: Ask for justice from Forest Head.

ESHUORO: Am I his son or am I not? I have told him. I have asked that he pass judgement for my limbs that were hacked off piece by piece. For my eyes that were gouged and my roots disrespectfully made naked to the world. For the desecration of my forest body.

MURETE: What are you talking about? Is it still about the
woodcutter who chopped off your top?

ESHUORO: Have you not been to the town centre? Have you not
seen this new thing he made for me? The beacon for the
gathering of the tribes. Have you not seen the centrepiece of
their vulgarity?

MURETE: What?

ESHUORO: The totem, blind fool, drunk fool, insensitive fool.
The totem, my final insult. The final taunt from the human
pigs. The tree that is marked down for Oro, the tree from which
my follower fell to his death, foully or by accident, I have still
to discover when we meet at the next wailing. But my body
was stripped by the impious hands of Demoke, Ogun's favoured
slave of the forge. My head was hacked off by his axe.
Trampled, sweated on, bled on, my body's shame pointed at
the sky by the adze of Demoke, will I let this day pass without
vengeance claimed blood for sap?

MURETE: Why . . . you . . . mucus off a crab's carbuncle. You
stream of fig pus from the duct of a stumbling bat. That is an
offering which would have gladdened the heart of Forest Father
himself. He would have called it adulation. Did he not himself
teach them the arts, and must they be confined to little rotted
chips which fall off when Eshuoro peels like a snake of the
previous year. Offal of the hyena tribe, all you want is an
excuse to feed on carrion! Dare you call yourself of the Forest
blood? You are only the greasy recesses of a rodent's nest . . .
[Eshuoro breaks a branch off the tree, whirls and whirls it round him
in an effort to smash Murete once for all. Murete runs off. Eshuoro
drops the stick and rages. Does a frenetic jig as he flings his
grievance to the world.]

ESHUORO: Demoke, son and son to carvers, who taught you
How you impale me, abuse me! Scratching my shame
To the dwellers of hell, where
The womb-snake shudders and the world is set on fire.
Demoke, did you know? Mine is the tallest tree that grows
On land. Mine is the head that cows
The Messengers of heaven. Did you not know?
Demoke, did you not know? Only the tree may eat itself
Oro alone is the worm that strips himself

Denudes the forest in a night. Only I
May eat the leaves of the silk-cotton tree
And let men cower and women run to hole.
My voice is thin, my voice is shrill, my voice
Is no child's lullaby to human ears.
Place mariwo[1] between your gates and let my knives
Seek the curious eye of the unbidden stranger.
Demoke, watch for the sudden fall of slighted trees
The tallest tree alone is mine, and mine alone.
Skin of my loins, see where it holds the branches.
Where the wind goes, a shred of Oro
Marks the trail, and when it drips, it is not
From camwood dye. Red, red is the colour of the wind
Oro is the nothing that the eye beholds
Spirits of the dead eat and drink of me
Long since the beginning. Spirits of the dead
Have feasted on Oro but do I grow less?
Do I grow thin? Do I cry when the night-bird pecks?
Oro is the nothing that the eye beholds
The child that vanishes and the silent lips of men.
Bathe children of my dead in ram's blood
That I may know them, and spare them
But do not forget the following year, or the year
That comes after; aye, Oro also can forget
And women cry when Oro rubs off yesterdays
Covers with sand the smear of blood proclaiming
That the father rested on the horns of rams.
Demoke, son and son again to pious carvers,
Have you lost fear? Demoke, renegade, beware
The slanted eye of night. Beware
The anger of the silent wind that rustles
Not a leaf. I'll be revenged. Eshuoro, I,
I'll be revenged, I'll be revenged . . . [*Rushes out.*]

*

[*Another part of the forest.*
Approaching sound of a gong. Enter the Forest Crier with a scroll.
Strikes his gong. A few Forest Spirits emerge from hiding places.

1. Palm fronds.

*Mostly, only their faces can be seen. The Crier walks with a kind
of mechanical to and fro movement.*]

CRIER: To all such as dwell in these Forests; Rock devils,
Earth imps, Tree demons, ghommids, dewilds, genie
Incubi, succubi, windhorls, bits and halves and such
Sons and subjects of Forest Father, and all
That dwell in his domain, take note, this night
Is the welcome of the dead. When spells are cast
And the dead invoked by the living, only such
May resume their body corporeal as are summoned
When the understreams that whirl them endlessly
Complete a circle. Only such may regain
Voice auditorial as are summoned when their link
With the living has fully repeated its nature, has
Re-impressed fully on the tapestry of Igbehinadun
In approximate duplicate of actions, be they
Of good, or of evil, of violence or carelessness;
In approximate duplicate of motives, be they
Illusory, tangible, commendable or damnable.
Take note, this selection, is by the living.
We hold these rites, at human insistence.
By proclamation, let the mists of generations
Be now dispersed. Forest Father, unveil, unveil
The phantasmagoria of protagonists from the dead.
[*Exit the crier. Forest Father enters, accompanied by Aroni.
They remain to one side.*]

FOREST HEAD: Oh, they made amusing companions. It was really
their latent violence which frightened me. I did not know
what I would do if it involved me.

ARONI: They appear tame enough now.

FOREST HEAD: So tame in fact, I could send them home. But they
forget too easily.

ARONI: They had no suspicion of you?

FOREST HEAD: Only uncertainty. I threw dark hints to preserve
my mystery and force them into an acceptance of my aloofness.
It held them all except the woman.

ARONI: Madame Tortoise.

FOREST HEAD: The same. You have done very well to choose her
Aroni. I am very pleased. Ah—Eshuoro?

ARONI: He will find us. I have laid a trail that will bring him to us.

FOREST HEAD: We will make use of him. If the child needs a fright, then the mother must summon the witch. Proverbs to ... How is it spoken by that busy man—Agboreko?

ARONI [*mimicking*.]: Proverb to bones and silence.

[*They laugh.*]

FOREST HEAD: Murete's blood brother is he not? Brother in fermented millet blood. Well, is everything prepared?

ARONI: We are ready.

FOREST HEAD: Remind me, how far back are we?

ARONI: About eight centuries. Possibly more. One of their great empires. I forget which.

FOREST HEAD: It matters nothing ...

[*Aroni waves his hand in a circle. The court of Mata Kharibu lights up gradually. Two thrones. One contains Mata Kharibu, the other, his queen, Madame Tortoise, both surrounded by splendour. A page plucks an African guitar. Mata Kharibu is angry; his eyes roll terribly; the court cowers. His queen, on the other hand, is very gay and cruel in her coquetry. She seems quite oblivious of the king's condition. The court poet (Demoke) stands a few feet from her. Behind him stands his scribe, a young boy, pen and scroll at the ready. Those not involved in the action at any time, freeze in one position.*]

MADAME TORTOISE [*gaily*.]: I am sad.

COURT POET: It is a mantle, my lady, woven only for the gracious. Sadness is noble my lady, and you wear it like the night.

[*Aside.*] And I hope it smothers you like one.

MADAME TORTOISE: The sadness will not leave me. I have lost my canary.

COURT POET: Your canary, Madame? Would you say—and I do wish it Madame—that you had lost your head?

MADAME TORTOISE: Unriddle me.

COURT POET: My lady, I would not say, look up. It is not given to the eye to perceive its own beauty. Reflection is nothing, except in the eye of a sensitive soul. Mirror is dross.

MADAME TORTOISE [*gaily*.]: I am impatient.

COURT POET: Your hair is the feathers my lady, and the breast of the canary—your forehead my lady—is the inspiration of your servant. Madame, you must not say you have lost your canary—[*aside*] unless it also be your virtue, slut!

MADAME TORTOISE: And yet I would have it here, with me. Can you fly as high with your feet as you conjure so easily with words?

COURT POET: Madame, it is my turn to be unriddled.

MADAME TORTOISE: I know where my canary is, but will you fetch it for me. I want it here with me.

COURT POET: Command me, my lady!

MADAME TORTOISE: On the roof-top. Fetch it, poet.

COURT POET [leans out of a window. Whistles.]

MADAME TORTOISE: No fool. Do you want it to tire itself with flying?

COURT POET: My lady, you were born on satin, on brocades and red velvet. A canary, was born on wings.

MADAME TORTOISE: Go after it. The canary will like you better for it.

[The poet's novice quickly lays down his scroll.]

NOVICE: Indeed, a royal bird may not be tired. And my hands are soft. I will fetch the canary.

MADAME TORTOISE: If your tutor gives permission, certainly. What do you say, my poet?

COURT POET: Did not a soldier fall to his death from the roof two days ago my lady?

MADAME TORTOISE: That is so. I heard a disturbance, and I called the guard to find the cause. I thought it came from the roof and I directed him there. He was too eager and he fell.

COURT POET: From favour Madame?

MADAME TORTOISE [eyeing him coolly.]: From the roof.

[They look at each other.]

MADAME TORTOISE: Well?

COURT POET: I forbid him to go.

MADAME TORTOISE: I order him to go.

[The novice runs off.]

MADAME TORTOISE: And I order you to follow him. When he has retrieved my canary, bring it here to me, like a servant.

[The poet bows and leaves. Madame Tortoise and her attendants remain statuesque.]

[From the opposite side, a warrior is pushed in, feet chained together. Mata Kharibu leaps up at once. The warrior is the Dead Man. He is still in his warrior garb, only it is bright and new.]

MATA KHARIBU [*advancing slowly on him.*]: It was you, slave!
   You it was who dared to think.

WARRIOR: I plead guilty to the possession of thought. I did not
   know that it was in me to exercise it, until your Majesty's
   inhuman commands.
   [*Mata Kharibu slaps him across the face.*]

MATA KHARIBU: You have not even begun to repent of your
   madness.

WARRIOR: Madness your Majesty?

MATA KHARIBU: Madness! Treachery! Frothing insanity traitor!
   Do you dare to question my words?

WARRIOR: No, terrible one. Only your commands.
   [*Mata Kharibu whips out his sword. Raises it. The soldier bows his
   head.*]

PHYSICIAN: Your Majesty! [*He hurries forward. Whispers in
   Kharibu's ear. Kharibu subsides, goes back to his throne, and watches
   them, glowering.*] You know me. You know you can trust me.

WARRIOR: I know you are in the pay of Mata Kharibu.

PHYSICIAN: But you cannot accuse me of inhumanity. I saved you
   twice from being tortured. And just now I saved your life.
   Try and think of me only as a friend.
   [*The soldier remains silent.*]
   I am trying to help you. Not only you, but your men who
   regard you so much as their leader that they can refuse to fight
   when you order them not to.

WARRIOR: It is an unjust war. I cannot lead my men into battle
   merely to recover the trousseau of any woman.

PHYSICIAN: Ah. But do you not see? It goes further than that.
   It is no longer the war of the queen's wardrobe. The war is now
   an affair of honour.

WARRIOR: An affair of honour? Since when was it an honourable
   thing to steal the wife of a brother chieftain?

PHYSICIAN: Can you really judge the action of another?

WARRIOR: No. But the results, and when they affect me and men
   who place their trust in me. If the king steals another's wife,
   it is his affair. But let it remain so. Mata Kharibu thought,
   hoped that the dishonoured king would go to war on her
   account. There he was wrong. It seems her rightful husband
   does not consider that your new queen is worth a battle. But

Mata Kharibu is so bent on bloodshed that he sends him a new
message. Release the goods of this woman I took from you
if there will be peace between us. Is this the action of a ruler
who values the peace of his subjects?

PHYSICIAN: A man cannot take a wife without a dowry. Mata
Kharibu asks what is rightly his. The dowry of a woman he
takes to wife.

WARRIOR: I understand. I thank you for enlightening me,
Physician.

PHYSICIAN: And will you fight?

WARRIOR: You have done your work. You may tell the king that
I was mad before, but now I am fully returned to my senses.
[*The Physician looks at him doubtfully.*]
Go to him sir. Or perhaps I ought to say, go and make your
report to the woman who now rules all our lives—even Mata
Kharibu. Go to the woman who draws the frown on his face
and greases the thunder of his voice. Tell her I know her
ambitions. I will not fight her war.

PHYSICIAN: Fool. A soldier does not choose his wars.

WARRIOR: Is Mata Kharibu not a soldier?

PHYSICIAN: Was ever a man so bent on his own destruction!

WARRIOR: If that referred to the king, you have spoken your first
true word today.

PHYSICIAN: Future generations will label you traitor. Your son,
your children will all call you . . . a-ah I remember now.
You have a wife have you not? An expectant mother?

WARRIOR: I know what runs in your head. But it will not help
you. Summon the tears of my wife and her unborn child if
you so desire. But there is no leader who will not feel a
stronger tie of blood with soldiers than with a stranger he took
to wife. My duty is to my men.
[*The Physician shuffles, uncertain how to proceed.*]

PHYSICIAN: Unborn generations will . . .

WARRIOR: Unborn generations will be cannibals most worshipful
Physician. Unborn generations will, as we have done, eat up
one another. Perhaps you can devise a cure, you who know how
to cure so many ills. I took up soldiering to defend my
country, but those to whom I gave the power to command
my life abuse my trust in them.

PHYSICIAN: Liar! Is Mata Kharibu not your general!

WARRIOR: Mata Kharibu is leader, not merely of soldiers but of men. Let him turn the unnatural pattern of men always eating up one another. I am suddenly weary of this soldiering where men must find new squabbles for their cruelty. Must I tell the widowed that their men died for another's trousseau?

PHYSICIAN: You think your own life is yours to dispose of?

WARRIOR: I have the right to choose how I mean to die.

PHYSICIAN: Your own life. Are you sure that no one else may waste your life except you?

WARRIOR: Why do you continue this useless questioning? I have told you that I am ready to submit my neck to . . .

PHYSICIAN: But the others . . . the others . . . Have you a right to submit the neck of another?

WARRIOR: What do you mean?

PHYSICIAN: Your men. The soldiers who follow you. The men you have misled. They have become traitors like you or do you not know that?

WARRIOR: They made their choice themselves. They must do as they decide.

PHYSICIAN: You have told them what to think. You have ordered their feelings. These men are used to obeying you. If you are so determined to die, you must first release them of their allegiance to you.

WARRIOR [looks up. Breaks into a smile.]: I see. Now I understand what you want. You are afraid. Mata Kharibu is afraid.

PHYSICIAN [scared.]: Be quiet. For heaven's sake do not speak so loud.

WARRIOR: But I am right. Perhaps I have started a new disease that catches quickly.

[Enter the Historian (Adenebi) with scrolls.]

HISTORIAN: Don't flatter yourself. Every blade of grass that has allowed its own contamination can be burnt out. This thing cannot last. It is unheard of. In a thousand years it will be unheard of. Nations live by strength; nothing else has meaning. You only throw your life away uselessly.

MATA KHARIBU [apprehensive.]: Did you find anything?

HISTORIAN: There is no precedent, your Highness.

MATA KHARIBU: You have looked thoroughly?

HISTORIAN: It is unheard of. War is the only consistency that past
ages afford us. It is the legacy which new nations seek to
perpetuate. Patriots are grateful for wars. Soldiers have never
questioned bloodshed. The cause is always the accident your
Majesty, and war is the Destiny. This man is a traitor. He must
be in the enemy's pay.

MATA KHARIBU: He has taken sixty of my best soldiers with him.

HISTORIAN: Your Highness has been too lenient. Is the nation to
ignore the challenge of greatness because of the
petty-mindedness of a few cowards and traitors.

WARRIOR: I am no traitor!

HISTORIAN: Be quiet Soldier! I have here the whole history of Troy.
If you were not the swillage of pigs and could read the
writings of wiser men, I would show you the magnificence of
the destruction of a beautiful city. I would reveal to you the
attainments of men which lifted mankind to the ranks of gods
and demi-gods. And who was the inspiration of this divine
carnage? Helen of Troy, a woman whose honour became as
rare a conception as her beauty. Would Troy, if it were standing
today lay claim to preservation in the annals of history if a
thousand valiant Greeks had not been slaughtered before its
gates, and a hundred thousand Trojans within her walls? Do
you, a mere cog in the wheel of Destiny, cover your face and
whine like a thing that is unfit to lick a soldier's boots, you,
a Captain . . . Your Majesty, I am only the Court historian
and I crave your august indulgence for any excess of zeal.
But history has always revealed that the soldier who will not
fight has the blood of slaves in him. For the sake of
your humble subjects, this renegade must be treated as a
slave.

MATA KHARIBU: Not only he. Every one who thinks like him,
be he soldier or merchant. I will have no moral termites a
thousand miles within my domain. Mata Kharibu is not the
idle eye that watches contemptible insects eat away the strength
of his kindgom.

[The Soothsayer (Agboreko) enters.]

MATA KHARIBU: If you come to tell me of unfavourable stars,
soothsayer, turn round and go out again. We will fight this
war in spite of cowards or auguries.

SOOTHSAYER: I see much blood Mata Kharibu. On both sides of the plough.

MATA KHARIBU: I will be satisfied with that. Does it not mean a great battle? On Kharibu's side at least, there will be real soldiers fighting. Sell that man down the river. He and his men. Sell them all down the river.

PHYSICIAN: Think again your Highness. It is a whole company.

HISTORIAN: His Majesty has decided wisely. Those men can never again be trusted.

MATA KHARIBU: I want them taken away immediately. I do not want sight or smell of them after sunset. If no boat can be found drown them.

SLAVE-DEALER: Your Majesty!

MATA KHARIBU: I will hear no petitions today.

SLAVE-DEALER [throwing himself forward.]: I am no petitioner Mata Kharibu. I merely place my vessel at the disposal of your august Majesty.

MATA KHARIBU: Oh! you. Are you not the slave-dealer?

SLAVE-DEALER: Your humble servant is amply rewarded. Your Highness has deigned before to use me as an agent, and hearing that there was to be another war, I came to offer my services. However, if there are slaves even before the battle has begun ...

MATA KHARIBU: They are yours. If they are out of my Kingdom before an hour, I shall not forget you.

PHYSICIAN: Mata Kharibu, most humane of monarchs, the crime of your soldiers is a terrible one, but do not place men who once served you faithfully in the hands of that merchant.

MATA KHARIBU: Why? What is this?

PHYSICIAN: Sir, I know the man of old, and I know the slight coffin in which he stuffs his victims. He knows how to get them down alive; it is his trade. But until he nears the slave-market, the wretches have gone through the twenty torments of hell.

SLAVE-DEALER: I have a new vessel. A true palace worthy of renegade soldiers. You malign me Physician?

HISTORIAN: Mata Kharibu need not be troubled about their fate. Their lives are forfeit.

PHYSICIAN: Then execute them at once your Highness. Kill them all but do not deliver them into his hands.

SLAVE-DEALER: Come down to the shore and into my vessel, and

I will not ask you before you strip your body and lie contented
as . . .

PHYSICIAN: Don't try your oily words with me, liar!

SLAVE-DEALER: But I assure you Mr. Physician . . .

MATA KHARIBU: Silence! Have I now become the market overseer
that you squabble before me which stick drives the cattle to
the sale? Beware lest the blood that is let at the battle be
nothing compared to the heads that will roll if one more voice
forgets to lower itself in my hearing. Villains! Has the rot
that has beset my soldiers already spread into my court that
I cannot even think because a bazaar has been opened before
my throne!

[*He storms off. He is about to pass by the Soothsayer when he stops,
pulls him aside.*]

MATA KHARIBU: I saw it on your face. The stars were unfavourable?

SOOTHSAYER: Then why do you proceed?

MATA KHARIBU: It is too late to stop. I have been frightened.
I dare not stop. I cannot stop. That captain of my army has
put a curse on me.

SOOTHSAYER: A curse? Then that may explain . . .

MATA KHARIBU: No. Not like that. They have not cursed me as
you think. But this new thing . . . You are wise. Surely you can
understand. It is unheard of. I shall be shamed before generations
to come. What does it mean? Why should my slave, my subject,
my mere human property say, unless he is mad, I shall not
fight this war. Is he a freak?

SOOTHSAYER: No.

MATA KHARIBU: I could understand it if he aimed at my throne.
But he is not even man for that. What does it mean? What
do you see for me in the future? Will there be more like him,
born with this thought cancer in their heart?

SOOTHSAYER: Mata Kharibu, have you ever seen a smudge on the
face of the moon.?

MATA KHARIBU: What do you mean?

SOOTHSAYER: Have you?

MATA KHARIBU: No.

SOOTHSAYER: And yet it happens. Once in every million years,
one of the sheep that trail the moon in its wanderings does dare
to wipe its smutty nose on the moon. Once in a million years.

But the moon is there still. And who remembers the
envy-ridden sheep?

MATA KHARIBU: So the future holds nothing for men like him?

SOOTHSAYER: Nothing. Nothing at all.

MATA KHARIBU [going.]: At least, in the reign of Mata Kharibu,
I shall see that your words are true.

SOOTHSAYER [looking after him, musingly.]: No. It does not depend
on you, Mata Kharibu. It is in the nature of men to seek power
over the lives of others, and there is always something lower
than a servant. [Goes.]

[During the foregoing, the Slave-dealer and the Historian exchange
furtive whispers. As soon as Mata Kharibu leaves the court, the
Physician marches purposefully towards the Slave-dealer.]

PHYSICIAN: You shifty, miserable flesh merchant, how dare you
suggest that you have the space in that finger-bowl to transport
sixty full-grown men?

SLAVE-DEALER: Honourable Physician to the court of Mata
Kharibu, why this concern for the health of traitors condemned
to a fate worse than death?

PHYSICIAN: Mata Kharibu is not so devoid of humanity as
to . . .

SLAVE-DEALER: I have no wish to argue that point. Mr. Physician,
I assure you most sincerely that you are mistaken. My new
vessel is capable of transporting the whole of Kharibu's court
to hell—when that time does come. The Honourable Historian
here can testify to it. I took him aboard . . . [Behind his back,
he passes a bag of money to the Historian, who takes it, feels it
and pockets it.] . . . only this afternoon, and showed him every
plank and rope . . . ask him yourself.

HISTORIAN: That is a fact. Mata Kharibu and all his ancestors
would be proud to ride in such a boat.

PHYSICIAN: In that case . . . I . . .

SLAVE-DEALER: I take my leave of you. Be good enough to give
me your official clearance. I have only an hour, remember.
[Goes.]

HISTORIAN: Do come for some sherbert at my house . . . [places
his arm round the Physician.] . . . You are a learned man and I
would appreciate an opportunity to discuss the historical
implications of this . . . mutiny . . . if one can really call it

that ... We were so near to the greatness of Troy and
Greece ... I mean this is war as it should be fought ... over
nothing ... do you not agree?

[*They go off.*]

[*The Court Poet enters with a golden cage, containing a canary.*]

MADAME TORTOISE: You were late returning, poet.

COURT POET: Such is the generosity of my lady's smiles, the poet
is now indulged, and cannot abide storms. Madame, I waited
until sunshine was restored—[*aside*] hoping it would shrivel you.

MADAME TORTOISE: Is that my canary? I no longer desire it.

COURT POET: It is the privilege of Beauty to be capricious.

MADAME TORTOISE: You return alone. Where is your novice?

COURT POET: My pupil Madame? He was so eager to earn the good
graces of your Highness.

MADAME TORTOISE: And may no one deserve them but you?

COURT POET: No one, your Highness. No one else.

MADAME TORTOISE: You have not told me. Where is your
pupil?

COURT POET: Being a good pupil Madame, he has just learned a
new lesson.

MADAME TORTOISE: I am waiting to learn too, poet. What lesson
was this?

COURT POET: In short Madame, he was too eager, and he fell.

MADAME TORTOISE: How fell? What do you mean? Is he dead?

COURT POET: No Madame. Only a mild fall. He broke an arm.

[*They stare each other in the eye.*]

MADAME TORTOISE: So, so.

COURT POET: That roof is dangerous Madame. Did not a soldier
also fall from the same spot?

MADAME TORTOISE [*mocking.*]: He was too eager, and he fell.

[*Again, they look each other in the eye.*]

COURT POET: So, so, your Highness ...

MADAME TORTOISE: Leave me now poet. And take the bird with
you. And look out my poet; sometimes, you grow wearisome.
[*Court Poet bows, and departs. The queen looks around. Eyes the
kneeling soldier for a few moments, then claps her hands. The court
is instantly cleared, except for the soldier and his guard. She angrily
signals the guard off and he disappears.*]

MADAME TORTOISE: Come here soldier.

[*When there is still no response, she smiles, and rises voluptuously. Stands very close to the soldier.*]

MADAME TORTOISE [*jerks up his head suddenly, laughing.*]: You are the one that will not fight for me?

WARRIOR: Madame, I beg you to keep your distance. Restraint is a difficult exercise for a man condemned to dishonour.

MADAME TORTOISE: Restraint ha! That is a virtue lacked by your soldiers . . . or did you not know that?

WARRIOR: I did not mean that kind of restraint. Madame, I know what havoc you have wreaked among my men, and we now face the final destruction of a good band of loyal men. Somehow, I do not hate you. But I do know the power of blood on the brain. I beg you to keep beyond my hands.

MADAME TORTOISE [*thrusts herself quite close to him.*]: A man. You speak like a man. No wonder your men are all men, every one of them. They have been well taught by their leader. It is a marvellous thing. These men were stupid, but they come under a leader, a man, and suddenly they stand upright and demand more than what is theirs. I did not know until now that you spoke through them all.

WARRIOR: Madame, desist from this torture.

MADAME TORTOISE: Torture! I have cause to torture you. Did you know the one who fell from the roof? The one who leapt to his death, on my account?

WARRIOR: Madame!

MADAME TORTOISE: He could not understand that I took him, just as I select a new pin every day. He came back again and could not understand why the door was barred to him. He was such a fool.

WARRIOR: I have no wish to hear.

MADAME TORTOISE: Your soldiers gave me my name. It is one I revel in. You may call me by that name.
[*The soldier shuts his eyes fiercely, tries to stop his ears but his hands are chained together.*]

MADAME TORTOISE: Mata Kharibu is a fool. You are a man and a leader, Soldier. Have you no wish to sit where Mata Kharibu sits?

WARRIOR: I cannot hear you Madame, I cannot hear you!

MADAME TORTOISE: Call me by my name. Madame Tortoise. I

am the one who outlasts you all. Madame Tortoise. You are
a man, I swear I must respect you.

WARRIOR: Guard! Guard!

MADAME TORTOISE: I can save you. I can save you alone, or with
your men. Choose. Choose. Why should a man be wasted?
Why must you waste yourself for a fool like Kharibu? Choose,
and let me be with you.

SOLDIER: Guard! Guard!

MADAME TORTOISE: What are you? Men have killed for me. Men
have died for me. Have you flints in your eye? Fool, have you
never lived?

WARRIOR [*desperately.*]: Guard!

[*A woman, dishevelled, rushes in, followed by a guard, who clutches
her shawl. They come to a stop as the queen turns on them, face
contorted with fury. The woman is pregnant. (She is the Dead
Woman.)*]

WARRIOR [*turning slowly, nearly breaking down.*]: Go home, in
heaven's name, go home.

MADAME TORTOISE [*her face breaks into fiendishness.*]: I knew it was
incredible. It could not be. I, Madame Tortoise, spurned by a
common soldier. For that! Was it for that?

[*The wife moves towards the queen, falls on her knees.*]

WOMAN [*very faintly.*]: Mercy!

MADAME TORTOISE: Guard. Pay close attention to my words. Do
eunuchs not fetch a good price at the market?

GUARD: Madame?

WOMAN: Have pity. Have pity.

MADAME TORTOISE [*to the Warrior.*]: You are lost. But have your
wish. Warriors are sold as men but eunuchs guard the harems
of other Mata Kharibus, drooling on wares that they cannot
taste. Choose!

[*The Captain looks at his wife, who turns her face to the ground.*]

MADAME TORTOISE: I am impatient. I will not be trifled with!

[*The Captain continues to look at his wife.*]

MADAME TORTOISE: Guard. You know my sentence. See that you
carry it out.

[*The woman clasps her womb, gasps and collapses. Sudden black-out.
Immediate light to reveal Aroni and Forest Head, who continue to
stare into the spectacle. They remain so for several moments.*]

ESHUORO [*striding in, with his jester at his heels.*]: The soldier was a fool.

ARONI: Eshuoro!

ESHUORO: The soldier was a fool. A woman. He was a woman. What have you proved?

ARONI: I see you could not be kept away.

ESHUORO: I was not invited. Once again, I was marked down to be slighted. Aroni, I warn you beware. You walk close to the Father of Forests and I suspect you do me an ill turn at every word.

FOREST HEAD: Be silent then and do not harm yourself with your every word.

ESHUORO: When is the gentle admonishment? The spectacle is over and not a word of the ills wreaked on me. Have I not lodged complaint? I hear no word of redress. I have been assaulted and my follower murdered—yes, I know it now—murdered. Must I be minced and ground in the dust before Forest Head deigns to look my way?

FOREST HEAD: I forget nothing. There is still the welcome of the dead. I omit nothing.

[*Enter Ogun.*]

OGUN: Face to face at last Eshuoro. Do you come here with your loud words and empty boasts? Soulless one, Demoke is no empty nut that fell, motherless from the sky. In all that he did, he followed my bidding. I will speak for him.

ESHUORO: I have suffered this too long. Perhaps the master must first be taught and then he can teach his minions to be humble.

OGUN: Minion? This minion of mine Eshuoro—is it not rumoured that he has done you service lately as a barber?

ESHUORO [*between his teeth.*]: I have borne too much already to take your taunts lightly. Ogun, I warn you beware . . .

OGUN: Eshuoro, what news of Oremole?

ESHUORO: Take care . . .

OGUN: What news of Oremole, slave to my servant. Did you sleep when your butcher frightened earth with his screams and his legs opened foolishly on his downward way to hell?

ESHUORO: You can hear him. Do you all bear with this against me?

OGUN: You look shaven on the skull Eshuoro. And I think once, there were more hairs on your chest. Have not I seen you at the gathering of the tribes, wet and naked by my servants' hands?

[*Eshuoro takes a sudden leap at him. Thunderclap. Blackout.*
Forest Head is next seen holding them apart, without touching them.]

FOREST HEAD: Soon, I will not tell you from the humans, so closely
have their habits grown on you. Did I summon this welcoming
for your prowess or for ends of my own? Take care how you
tempt my vanity. Eshuoro, you came here to bathe in blood,
Ogun, you to defend the foibles of your ward. Let this night
alone, when I lay out the rites of the dead or my anger will
surpass your spleen. Aroni, you know my will. Proceed.

ESHUORO: What will you achieve?

ARONI: It is enough that they discover their own regeneration.

ESHUORO: Another trick. I came here for vengeance.

FOREST HEAD: I know.

ESHUORO: And I will not leave without it.

ARONI: You have your case. Let the future judge them by reversal
of its path or by stubborn continuation.

OGUN: Will you foresee the many confusions Eshuoro hatches in
his mind? Aroni, let my servant go. He has suffered enough.

ARONI: I need him most of all.

OGUN: He has no guilt. I, Ogun, swear that his hands were mine
in every action of his life.

FOREST HEAD: Will you all never rid yourselves of these conceits!

ESHUORO: I am impatient.

ARONI: You must wait, like us. In any case the Forest Spirits have
gone to the gathering of the tribes. Or did you not know that—
Eshuoro?

ESHUORO: And so the future will not be chorused. I know it.
I have seen through your tricks of delay.

ARONI: I said you must wait. Forest Head has provided for the
default of your brothers. The living ones will themselves speak
for the future. For the event, they will be, like you, of the
Forest. Have you a better suggestion, brother fiend?

ESHUORO [*slowly.*]: Why? Why are you so ready with a solution?

FOREST HEAD: Was it not the same remedy with which you boldly
and with confidence approached us? Was it not to this end that
you frightened away all those who would not attend the
welcome to speak on your behalf? Since when was I smitten
with deafness or blindness, Eshuoro?

ESHUORO: I threatened none.

FOREST HEAD: Enough. Do not deny that all goes as you planned it. [*Eshuoro goes out.*] But only because it is my wish. And so we all must be content. Call the questioner and let no one foully intervene for the furthering of his cause.

[*Back-scene lights up gradually to reveal a dark, wet, atmosphere, dripping moisture, and soft, moist soil. A palm-tree sways at a low angle, broken but still alive. Seemingly lightning-reduced stumps. Rotting wood all over the ground. A mound or two here and there. Footfalls are muffled. First, there is total stillness, emphasized by the sound of moisture dripping to the ground. Forest Head is sitting on a large stone, statuesque, the Questioner stands beside him. Aroni is no longer to be seen. The Dead Woman enters, dead as on first appearance. She behaves exactly as before, hesitant, seemingly lost.*]

QUESTIONER: Who sent you?

DEAD WOMAN: I am certain she had no womb, but I think
It was a woman.

QUESTIONER: Before your time?
Was it before your time?

DEAD WOMAN: I have come to ask that of
The knowing ones. My knowledge is
The hate alone. The little ball of hate
Alone consumed me. Wet runnels
Of the earth brought me hither.
Call Forest Head. Say someone comes
For all the rest. Say someone asks—
Was it for this, for this,
Children plagued their mothers?

QUESTIONER: A mother, and in haste?
Were there no men? No barren women,
Aged and toothless women?
What called you forth beyond the backyard fence?
Beyond the cooking pots? What made you deaf
To the life that begged within you?
Had he no claim?

DEAD WOMAN: For him. It was for him.

QUESTIONER: You should have lived for him. Did you dare
Snatch death from those that gasped for breath?

DEAD WOMAN: My weakness, Forest Head. I was a woman
I was weak.

QUESTIONER: And the other. The one who sent you.
　　The one you call a wombless woman
　　Was she weak?
　　[*The woman is silent.*]
FOREST HEAD: Every day. Every hour. Where will it end?
　　Child, there is no choice but one of suffering
　　And those who tread the understreams
　　Add ashes to the hairs
　　Of Forest Father. Rest awhile.
　　The beings of the Forest have been called
　　To dance the welcome, to quiet your spirit
　　Torn loosely by the suddenness. And roots
　　Have brought us news of another son
　　And he has come a longer way, almost
　　They murmur, from quite another world.
　　[*The Dead Man, after a still silence, enters.*]
DEAD MAN: Three lives I led since first I went away
　　But still my first possesses me
　　The pattern is unchanged.
QUESTIONER: You who enter sleek and well fed
　　Have you, at least, a tale of
　　Pleasure and content?
DEAD MAN: My father said, and his great father
　　Before him, if you find no rest, go home
　　And they will know you.
　　Kind friends, take me to Forest Head.
FOREST HEAD: I knew you, Mulieru ...
DEAD MAN: Then you are Forest Head. When I died
　　And still they would not let my body rest;
　　When I lived, and they would not let me be
　　The man I felt, cutting my manhood, first
　　With a knife, next with words and the dark
　　Spit of contempt, the voice at my shoulder said,
　　Go seek out Forest Head. If I am home, then
　　I have come to sleep.
QUESTIONER: When the fattened calf complains of hunger
　　May one not fear his brain is seized
　　With fever?
FOREST HEAD: Hush! Mulieru, I knew you

In the days of pillaging, in the days
Of sudden slaughter, and the parting
Of child and brother. I knew you
In the days of grand destroying
And you a part of the waste.
Mulieru, you were one of those who journeyed
In the market-ships of blood.
You were sold Mulieru, for . . .

QUESTIONER [*who has been consulting his barks.*]: . . . a flask of rum.

DEAD MAN: Then I am home
If it was I Mulieru, who
Rowed the slave-ship to the beating
Of the lash, the sea has paid its debt.

QUESTIONER: Your wise men, casting bones of oracle
Promised peace and profit.
New knowledge, new beginnings after toil
Mulieru, sleek and fat, and skin-mellowed Mulieru
Was there not fruit and corn-wine at the end?

DEAD MAN: Flesh there is upon my bones
As the skin is flesh-filled on the bones
Of every gelded pig.
[*The Questioner approaches, touches him, presses his skin and withdraws his hand in sudden disgust, wiping it on the soil.*]

QUESTIONER: Three hundred rings have formed
Three hundred rings within that bole
Since Mulieru went away, was sold away
And the tribe was scattered
Three hundred moultings of
The womb-snake of the world
And does the son return now
Empty-handed?

FOREST HEAD: Enough. Enough.
The priest was burnt, and do you ask
What became of his beard?

QUESTIONER: Three lives he boasted of, and each
A certain waste, foolishly cast aside.
Has he learnt the crime of laziness?
What did he prove, from the first when,
Power at his grasp, he easily

Surrendered his manhood. It was surely
The action of a fool. What did he prove?
And does he come whining here for sleep?
Let him wander a hundred further ...
[*Enter Aroni, looking puzzled.*
*Reaches suddenly and rips off the Questioner's mask. It is Eshuoro,
and he immediately rushes off. There is only amusement on the face
of Forest Head.*]

ARONI: I was sure I recognized a similarity in venom, but I did not
think even Eshuoro would dare.

OGUN [*entering.*]: For my part I have played fairly.

FOREST HEAD: I know it. Nothing is affected. But where is my
Questioner? No, it matters no longer. It is time we had the
welcome. Let the earthly protagonists be called, and see that
the Interpreter is present.
[*Low music of Ibo flutes in the background. Enter the Interpreter
leading Demoke, Rola, Adenebi, resignation on each face as they
were last seen following Obaneji.*]
Let the one whose incompletion denies him rest be patient
till the Forest has chorused the Future through lips of
earth-beings.
[*At this, the Dead Man makes a dumb distressed protest, but Aroni
leads him off.*
Forest Head subjects the Interpreter to severe scrutiny.]

FOREST HEAD [*eventually.*]: You are not the Interpreter I knew.

INTERPRETER: Like the others, he went to ...

FOREST HEAD: The gathering of the tribes, do I not know it?

INTERPRETER: I am his acolyte. I shall do my best.

FOREST HEAD: Note that I have my eyes on you. If Eshuoro sent
you ...
[*Eshuoro enters, sulkily.*]

ESHUORO: Eshuoro needs no slaves to fulfil his designs.

FOREST HEAD: Then mind you do not do your own slaving—at
my bidding. I am the rock of patience, but my bosom is hard.
[*Re-enter Aroni.*]

FOREST HEAD: Aroni, relieve this woman of her burden and let
the tongue of the unborn, stilled for generations, be loosened.
[*Dead Woman is led off by Aroni.*
Soft rhythmic drumming accompanies Forest Head's last instruction.

*The Interpreter moves and masks the three protagonists. The
mask-motif is as their state of mind—resigned passivity. Once
masked, each begins to move round in a slowly widening circle, but
they stop to speak, and resume their sedate pace as they chorus the
last words.]*

FOREST HEAD [*When the three are masked.*]:
   I take no part, but listen. If shadows,
   Future shadows form in rain-water
   Held in hollow leaves, this is the moment
   For the welcome of the dead.
   [*Goes to his seat, impassive.*
   *Enter the Dead Woman, unpregnant, leading the Half-Child by
   the hand. As each spirit is summoned, one of the human three
   becomes agitated, possessed and then pronounces.]*

INTERPRETER [*calls.*]: Spirit of the Palm!
SPIRIT OF THE PALM: White skeins wove me, I, Spirit of the Palm
   Now course I red.
   I who suckle blackened hearts, know
   Heads will fall down,
   Crimson in their red!
   [*The Half-Child, startled, tries to find out which of them it was that
   spoke. Failing, he lets go of the Dead Woman's hand, leaves her
   side. A Figure in Red appears, and begins to walk deliberately in his
   footprints. The Half-Child crosses to the opposite side, digs a little
   hole in the ground, and begins to play a game of 'sesan'. He has no
   sooner flicked the first seed than the Figure in Red squats behind
   him and leans over to join in the game. The Half-Child immediately
   gets up, the Figure in Red following. The Half-Child seems to
   appeal for help mutely from those around him, but they stand silent.
   The Figure in Red keeps close behind him. Downcast, the Half-Child
   returns to his game, speaking as he goes.]*

HALF-CHILD: I who yet await a mother
   Feel this dread,
   Feel this dread,
   I who flee from womb
   To branded womb, cry it now
   I'll be born dead
   I'll be born dead.
INTERPRETER: Spirit of the Dark!

SPIRIT OF DARKNESS: More have I seen, I, Spirit of the Dark,
 Naked they breathe within me, foretelling now
 How, by the dark of peat and forest
 They'll be misled
 And the shutters of the leaves
 Shall close down on the doomed
 And naked head.

HALF-CHILD [*softly, without detracting from the intensity of his game.*]:
 Branded womb, branded womb . . .

SPIRIT OF THE PALM: White skeins wove me.

SPIRIT OF DARKNESS: Peat and forest.

INTERPRETER: Spirit of Precious Stones!

SPIRIT OF PRECIOUS STONES: Still do I draw them, down
 Into the pit that glitters, I
 Spirit of gold and diamonds
 Mine is the vain light courting death
 A-ah! Blight this eye that threaded
 Rocks with light, earth with golden lodes
 Traitor to the guardian tribe, turn
 Turn to lead!

HALF-CHILD: Branded womb, branded womb.

SPIRIT OF THE PALM: White skeins wove me.

SPIRIT OF DARKNESS: Peat and forest.

SPIRIT OF PRECIOUS STONES: Courting death.

INTERPRETER: The Pachyderms!

SPIRIT OF THE PACHYDERMS: Blood that rules the sunset, bathe
 This, our ivory red
 Broken is the sleep of giants
 Wanton raiders, ivory has a point
 Thus, thus we bled.

HALF-CHILD: Branded womb, branded womb.

SPIRIT OF THE PALM: White skeins wove me.

SPIRIT OF DARKNESS: Peat and forest.

SPIRIT OF PRECIOUS STONES: Courting death.

SPIRIT OF THE PACHYDERMS: Thus we bled.

INTERPRETER: Spirit of the Rivers!

SPIRIT OF THE RIVERS: From Limpopo to the Nile coils but one
 snake.
 On mudbanks, and sandy bed

I who mock the deserts, shed a tear
Of pity to form palm-ringed oases
Stain my bowels red!

[*Silence. All movement stops except for the Half-Child and the Figure in Red playing out their game. The Figure in Red flicks all the seeds into the hole, the Half-Child scoring none. Triumphantly he scoops up the seeds in his hand, rises fully. Forest Head rises, Aroni with him. There is some measure of consternation from the forest spirits. He looks round to where Eshuoro was last seen. Eshuoro is no longer there. Aroni makes a move towards the Figure in Red, bur Forest Head restrains him. From a distance, a slow rumble, gathering force.*]

CHORUS OF THE WATERS: Let no man then lave his feet
In any stream, in any lake
In rapids or in cataracts
Let no woman think to bake
Her cornmeal wrapped in leaves
With water gathered of the rain
He'll think his eye deceives
Who treads the ripples where I run
In shallows. The stones shall seem
As kernels, his the presser's feet
Standing in the rich, and red, and cloying stream . . .

SPIRIT OF THE RIVERS: Then shall men say that I the Mother
Have joined veins with the Palm my Brothers.

CHORUS OF THE WATERS: Let the Camel mend his leaking hump
Let the squirrel guard the hollows in the Stump.

[*The distant noise grows more insistent. What appears to be a cloud of dust begins to rise steadily, darkening the scene. Aroni moves with sudden determination towards the Figure in Red, but the Interpreter begins a sudden dance which comes between them, and Aroni is forced to retreat.*]

INTERPRETER: Spirit of the Sun! Spirit of the Sun!

SPIRIT OF THE SUN: Red is the pit of the sun's entrails, and I
Who light the crannies of the bole
Would speak, but shadows veil the eye
That pierces with the thorn. I know the stole
That warms the shoulders of the moon.
But this is not its shadow. And I trace

No course that leaves a cloud. The Sun cries Noon
Whose hand is it that covers up his face!
[*The forest spirits murmur together on one side, Aroni and Forest
Head confer on the other.*]

FOREST HEAD: Who are you?
Why do you blanket earth and swarm
Like molten rocks?

SPIRIT OF VOLCANOES: Nipples I engender, scattered
Through the broad breast of the earth,
I, Spirit of erupting mountains
But I am not now winded. I have not belched
These twenty hours or more. I have spat
No hot ashes in the air.

FOREST HEAD: If the hills are silent, who are these,
If the sun is full and the winds are still
Whose hand is this that reaches from the grave?

ANT LEADER: We take our colour from the loam
And blindness hits them, and they tread us
Underfoot.

FOREST HEAD: Are you my sons?

ANT LEADER: We are the blazers of the trail
If you are Forest Father, we think
We are your sons.

FOREST HEAD: But who are you?

ANT LEADER: We take our colour from the fertile loam
Our numbers from the hair-roots of the earth
And terror blinds them. They know
We are the children of earth. They
Break our skin upon the ground, fearful
That we guard the wisdom of Earth,
Our Mother.

FOREST HEAD: Have you a grievance?

ANT LEADER: None Father, except great clods of earth
Pressed on our feet. The world is old
But the rust of a million years
Has left the chains unloosened.

FOREST HEAD: Are you not free?

ANT LEADER: Freedom we have
Like the hunter on a precipice

And the horns of a rhinoceros
Nuzzling his buttocks.

FOREST HEAD: Do you not walk? Talk? Bear
And suckle children by the gross?

ANT LEADER: Freedom indeed we have
To choose our path
To turn to the left or the right
Like the spider in the sand-pit
And the great ball of eggs
Pressing on his back.

FOREST HEAD: But who are you?

[*The leader retreats, and another takes his place.*]

ANT: I thought, staying this low,
They would ignore me. I am the one
That tried to be forgotten.

ANOTHER: I am the victim of the careless stride.

ANOTHER: I know the path was thin, a trickle
In the marsh. Yet we mowed the roots
Our bellies to the ground.

FOREST HEAD: Have you a Cause, or shall I
Preserve you like a riddle?

ANT LEADER: We are the ones remembered
When nations build ...

ANOTHER: ... with tombstones.

ANOTHER: We are the dried leaves, impaled
On one-eyed brooms.

ANOTHER: We are the headless bodies when
The spade of progress delves.

ANOTHER: The ones that never looked up when
The wind turned suddenly, erupting
In our heads.

ANOTHER: Down the axis of the world, from
The whirlwind to the frozen drifts,
We are the ever legion of the world,
Smitten, for—'the good to come'.

ANT LEADER: Once my eyes were earthworms
Dragging in my tears.

ARONI [*shouting.*]: What is this? For what cursed future
Do you rise to speak?

ANT LEADER: Then the ring of scourges was complete
And my hair rose on its tail
Like scorpions.
[*They vanish. The Figure in Red goes resolutely to Forest Head and confronts him. Forest Head appears hesitant, even reluctant. Eventually, he gestures brusquely to the Interpreter.*]

FOREST HEAD: Unmask them. The Half-Child has played out his game and lost. Let them see the rest with their natural eyes, their human sight.
[*The Interpreter unmasks all three. Enter the first of the Triplets. It is the lower trunk of a body, with arms. Loose, uncontrolled manner.*]

FIRST TRIPLET [*speaking as he comes in.*]: Has anyone found the Means? I am the End that will justify it.
[*The Interpreter turns quickly and does a round of 'ampe'[1] with him. Enter Second Triplet. An over-blown head, drooling.*]

SECOND TRIPLET: I am the Greater Cause, standing ever ready, excusing the crimes of today for tomorrow's mirage. Hungry I come, hearing there was a feast for the dead . . .
Am I expected?
[*The Interpreter and the Second Triplet 'ampe', then the Interpreter with the First, and then the two Triplets together.*]

SECOND TRIPLET [*stops suddenly. Goes to where Demoke, etc., stand huddled together. Sniffs them, turns them to the Interpreter.*]: But who are these?

FOREST HEAD: They are the lesser criminals, pursuing the destructive path of survival. Weak, pitiable criminals, hiding their cowardice in sudden acts of bluster. And you obscenities . . .
[*Waves his hand towards the Triplets, who shriek and dance in delight.*] You perversions are born when they acquire power over one another, and their instincts are fulfilled a thousandfold, a hundred thousandfold. But wait, there is still the third triplet to come. You have as always decided your own fates. Today is no different from your lives. I merely sit and watch.
[*Enter the Third Triplet, fanged and bloody.*]

THIRD TRIPLET: I find I am Posterity. Can no one see on what milk I have been nourished?

1. A children's foot-slipping game.

[*The Figure in Red rips off his head-cover. It is Eshuoro.
Reaches a hand for the Half-child. Ogun steps forward.*]

OGUN: You fooled no one.

ESHUORO: Beware. I won him fairly.

OGUN: You play too many roles Eshuoro. Watch out for the mask
that is lined with scorpions. [*Goes out.*]

[*Eshuoro again stretches a hand towards the Half-Child, who tries
to go to the Dead Woman.*]

HALF-CHILD: I found an egg, smooth as a sea-pebble.

ESHUORO [*gleefully.*]: Took it home with him,
Warmed it in his bed of rushes
And in the night the egg was hatched
And the serpent came and swallowed him.

[*The Half-Child begins to spin round and round, till he is quite
giddy. Stops suddenly.*]

HALF-CHILD: Still I fear the fated bearing
Still I circle yawning wombs.

DEAD WOMAN: Better not to know the bearing
Better not to bear the weaning
I who grow the branded navel
Shudder at the visitation
Shall my breast again be severed
Again and yet again be severed.
From its right of sanctity?
Child, your hand is pure as sorrow
Free me of the endless burden,
Let this gourd, let this gourd
Break beyond my hearth . . .

[*The Half-Child continues slowly towards the Mother, Eshuoro
imperiously offering his hand, furious as each step takes the child
nearer her. Looks up sharply and finds Ogun on the other side of the
woman, with hand similarly outstretched. Snaps his fingers suddenly
at the Interpreter. A clap of drums, and the Interpreter begins another
round of 'ampe' with the Third Triplet. The Woman's hand and
the Half-Child's are just about to meet when this happens, and the
child turns instantly, attracted by the game. The 'ampe' gradually
increases tempo among the three Triplets. The Interpreter throws
off his mask, reveals himself as Eshuoro's Jester. He draws the child
into a game of 'ampe'. When the Half-Child is totally disarmed by*]

*the Jester, Eshuoro picks him up suddenly and throws him towards
the Third Triplet who makes to catch him on the point of two knives
as in the dance of the child acrobats. Rola screams, the child is tossed
up by the Third Triplet who again goes through the same motion,
the other two Triplets continuing the furious 'ampe' round him and
yelling at the top of their voices. Demoke, Rola and Adenebi again
cluster together. The Half-Child is now tossed back to Eshuoro, and
suddenly Demoke dashes forward to intercept. Eshuoro laughs,
pretends to throw the child back, Demoke dashes off only to find
that he still retains the child. The Interpreter, Eshuoro and the Third
Triplet all evading the knife-points at the last moment and catching
the Half-Child in the crook of their elbows.*

*They keep up this game for a brief period, with Demoke running
between them, until Ogun appears behind the Interpreter, pulls him
aside just as the child is thrown towards him, makes the catch himself
passing it instantly to Demoke who has come running as before.
All action stops again, including the first and second Triplets who
have never ceased to 'ampe'. They all look at Demoke, who stands
confused, not knowing what the next step should be. He decides
eventually to restore the child to the Dead Woman, and attempts
to do so. Eshuoro partially blocks his way and appeals to Forest Head.
Ogun appeals against him.]*

FOREST HEAD [*more to himself.*]: Trouble me no further. The
fooleries of beings whom I have fashioned closer to me weary
and distress me. Yet I must persist, knowing that nothing is ever
altered. My secret is my eternal burden—to pierce the
encrustations of soul-deadening habit, and bare the mirror of
original nakedness—knowing full well, it is all futility. Yet I
must do this alone, and no more, since to intervene is to be
guilty of contradiction, and yet to remain altogether unfelt
is to make my long-rumoured ineffectuality complete; hoping
that when I have tortured awareness from their souls, that
perhaps, only perhaps, in new beginnings ... Aroni, does
Demoke know the meaning of his act?

ARONI: Demoke, you hold a doomed thing in your hand. It is no
light matter to reverse the deed that was begun many lives ago.
The Forest will not let you pass.

[*The Woman appeals, mutely to Demoke. All eyes are intent upon
Demoke until he makes up his mind; gives the child to the Dead*

Woman. Immediately, Aroni leads out the Dead Woman with the Half-Child. Forest Head takes a final look at the gathering, goes off. Eshuoro gives a loud yell of triumph, rushes offstage, accompanied by his Jester. The Triplets follow gleefully.

A silhouette of Demoke's totem is seen. The village people dancing round it, also in silhouette, in silence. There is no contact between them and the Forest ones. The former in fact are not aware of the other beings. Eshuoro's Jester leaps on stage, bearing the sacrificial basket which he clamps on to Demoke's head; performing a wild dance in front of him. Eshuoro re-enters, bearing a heavy club. Dance of the Unwilling Sacrifice, in which Eshuoro and his Jester head Demoke relentlessly towards the totem and the silent dancing figures. Rola and Adenebi are made to sprinkle libation on the scene, continuously as in a trance. Demoke, headed towards his handiwork is faded away, and re-appears at the foot of the totem, the crowd parting in silence. He begins to climb, hampered further by the load on his head. There are only the drums, Eshuoro and his Jester have stopped dancing. Slowly, Demoke disappears from view, and the crowd cheer wildly, without sound. Eshuoro rushes out in a frenzy. Returns at the totem with a fire-brand; sets fire to the tree. Enter Ogun, catches Demoke as he falls. Blackout. Then the front gets increasingly lighter as Eshuoro returns and dances out his frenzy, lashing his Jester with a branch.

Noise of the beaters from a distance. Dawn is breaking. Ogun enters bearing Demoke, eyeing the sky anxiously. He is armed with a gun and cutlass. The sun creeps through; Ogun gently lays down Demoke, leaves his weapons beside him, flees. Eshuoro is still dancing as the foremost of the beaters break on the scene and then he flees after his Jester. It is now fully dawn. Agboreko and the Old Man enter, Murete, very drunk, dragging them on. The sound of the main body of beaters with the drummers continues in the distance.]

MURETE: Here, I said it was here.

AGBOREKO: I will not forget my promise.

[*The Old Man rushes towards Demoke, lying inert, raises him to a sitting position. Demoke opens his eyes.*]

OLD MAN: Safe! What did you see? What did you see?

AGBOREKO: Let them be, old man. When the crops have been gathered it will be time enough for the winnowing of the grains. Prov . . .

MURETE [*drunkenly*.]: Proverbs to bones and silence.

AGBOREKO: It is time to think of the fulfilment of vows.

OLD MAN [*to Demoke*.]: We searched all night. Knowing who your companion was ...

AGBOREKO: Madame Tortoise ... the one who never dies ... never ...

OLD MAN: And then I was troubled by the mystery of the fourth. The council orator I knew. And Madame Tortoise. But the fourth ... [*he looks round*.] You are back to three. Did the other reveal himself?

DEMOKE: The father of ghommids. Forest Head himself.

AGBOREKO: At first we thought it would be Eshuoro, tricking you onwards like the echo in the woods. And then I thought, Murete cannot be silent only from fear. It must be Forest Head himself.

OLD MAN: Forest Head! And did you see the lame one?
[*Demoke nods*.]
Fools we were to pit our weakness against the cunning of Aroni, chasing souls whom he was resolved to welcome.

AGBOREKO: We paid dearly for this wisdom newly acquired.

OLD MAN: Cruelly. Look, look at me. Behind every sapling, there was the sudden hand of Aroni, and he aims well.
[*Gingerly feels a weal across his face*.]

DEMOKE: There was a path that brought us here. Could not Murete find it?

OLD MAN: We would have done better without him. Sometimes I suspect his drunkenness. We have tasted the night thickness of the forest like the nails of a jealous wife.
[*Agboreko nudges the Old Man. He becomes suddenly uncomfortable, hems and coughs*.]

OLD MAN: Demoke, we made sacrifice and demanded the path of expiation ...

DEMOKE: Expiation? We three who lived many lives in this one night, have we not done enough? Have we not felt enough for the memory of our remaining lives?

OLD MAN: What manner of a night was it? Can you tell us that? In this wilderness, was there a kernel of light?
[*Rola comes forward. She looks chastened*.]

AGBOREKO: I did not think to find her still alive, this one who outlasts them all. Madame Tortoise ...

DEMOKE: Not any more. It was the same lightning that seared us
    through the head.
AGBOREKO [*snorts.*]: Does that mean something wise, child?
    [*Sneaking up to Demoke.*] Of the future, did you learn anything?
OLD MAN [*comes up and pulls him away.*]: 'When the crops have
    been gathered . . .'
AGBOREKO [*reproved. With ponderous finality.*]: Proverb to bones
    and silence.

THE END

The 'Dance for the Half-Child' as it was performed in the 1960 production.

DEAD WOMAN: Better not to know the bearing
    Better not to bear the weaning
    I who grow the branded navel
    Shudder at the visitation
    Shall my breast again be severed
    Again and yet again be severed
    From its right and sanctity?
    Child, your hand is pure as sorrow
    Free me of the endless burden,
    Let this gourd, let this gourd
    Break beyond my hearth . . .
    [*The Half-Child continues slowly towards the Mother, Eshuoro imperiously offering his hand, furious as each step takes the child nearer her. Looks up sharply and finds Ogun on the other side of the woman, with hand similarly outstretched. Snaps his fingers suddenly at the Interpreter. A clap of drums, and the Interpreter begins another round of 'ampe' with the Third Triplet. The Woman's hand and the Half-Child's are just about to meet when this happens, and the child turns instantly, attracted by the game. Hanging carelessly from the hand of the Half-Child is the wood figure of an 'ibeji'*[1] *which he has clutched from his first appearance. Eshuoro waits until he is totally mesmerized by the Jester's antics, snatches it off him and throws it to the Third Triplet. It jerks the Half-Child awake and he runs after it. Third Triplet, the Interpreter and Eshuoro toss the 'ibeji' to one another while the child runs between them trying to recover it, but they only taunt him with it and throw it over his head. The First and Second Triplets keep up their incessant 'ampe'. The Interpreter is standing near Demoke, and suddenly he pulls the Interpreter aside, catches the 'ibeji'. Eshuoro moves at once to the Half-Child but he runs to Demoke and clings to him. Everything stops. Eshuoro silently appeals to Forest Head, Ogun appeals against him.*]

1. Twin or twin figurine.

FOREST HEAD [*more to himself.*]: Trouble me no further. The
fooleries of beings whom I have fashioned closer to me weary
and distress me. Yet I must persist, knowing that nothing is
ever altered. My secret is my eternal burden—to pierce the
encrustations of soul-deadening habit, and bare the mirror of
original nakedness—knowing full well, it is all futility. Yet I
must do this alone, and no more, since to intervene is to be
guilty of contradiction, and yet to remain altogether unfelt is
to make my long-rumoured ineffectuality complete; hoping
that when I have tortured awareness from their souls, that
perhaps, only perhaps, in new beginnings . . . Aroni, does
Demoke know the meaning of his act?

[*Exit Forest Head, displaying a long-suffering irritation.*]

ARONI: Demoke, you hold a doomed thing in your hand. It is no
light matter to reverse the deed that was begun many lives ago.
The Forest will not let you pass.

[*The Dead Woman appeals, mutely to Demoke. All eyes are intent
on Demoke until he makes up his mind. Restores the 'ibeji' to the
Half-Child. Again Eshuoro turns to Forest Head but he is no longer
there. He looks to Aroni for interference but Aroni refuses to notice
any more, sits down where Forest Head sat earlier. The Interpreter
signals urgently offstage, and immediately a group of forest creatures
enter, all replicas of the Jester, do an 'atilogwu'-ordered dance[1]
towards the Half-Child. Ogun snatches a cutlass, Eshuoro a Club,
and they clash briefly, across the dancers. As the Jesters stamp towards
the Half-Child again, Demoke picks him up and seats him on one
shoulder, tries to move towards the Dead Woman standing with eager
arms outstretched. They manoeuvre Demoke away at every attempt
he makes. On one side Eshuoro swinging his club, prowling,
trembling from head to foot in elemental fury. Ogun on the other,
watchful, cutlass at the ready. Both are kept apart by the dancers only,
and from time to time they clash, always briefly, and they spring
apart again.*

*It begins to lighten. In the distance, faint sounds of the beaters come
over the music of the forest drums. Demoke gets wearier and wearier,
begins to sag. At every falter the Jesters move towards him to snatch
their quarry but he recovers. The scene brightens. The Triplets*

1. A vigorous dance of the Ibos. *Atilogwu* means literally 'putting in the
medicine'.

*scatter. Aroni looks at the sky, slips off. Ogun and Eshuoro lose
control, fly at each other, seemingly blind. They miss, begin to feel
for the other's position, flailing wildly. Coming suddenly on each
other, they lock together, bear each other out of sight.*

*The Forest rhythm becomes thoroughly confused with the beaters'
music and shortly after, the Jesters stop totally, bewildered. The
First Jester looks at the sky flees, and they follow. Demoke sags to
his knees, the Dead Woman runs to him, snatches the falling
Half-Child and is swallowed by the forest. Demoke collapses on
the ground.*

It is now fully dawn.

Entry of Agboreko and the Old Man, led by Murete.]

—*al Fin.*

THE
SWAMP DWELLERS

Characters

ALU   an old woman
MAKURI   her husband
A BEGGAR
KADIYE   priest

IGWEZU   son to Alu
A DRUMMER
ATTENDANTS TO KADIYE

A village in the swamps.

Frogs, rain and other swamp noises.

The scene is a hut on stilts, built on one of the scattered semi-firm islands in the swamps. Two doors on the left lead into other rooms, and the one on the right leads outside. The walls are marsh stakes plaited with hemp ropes.

The room is fairly large, and is used both as the family workshop and as the 'parlour' for guests. About the middle of the right half of the stage is a barber's swivel chair, a very ancient one. On a small table against the right wall is a meagre row of hairdressing equipment—a pair of clippers, scissors, local combs, lather basin and brush, razor—not much else. A dirty white voluminous agbada serves for the usual customer's sheet.

Makuri, an old man of about sixty, stands by the window, looking out. Near the left downstage are the baskets he makes from the rushes which are strewn in front of him. Upstage left, his equally aged wife, Alu, sits on a mat, busy at her work, unravelling the patterns in dyed 'adire' cloths. Alu appears to suffer more than the normal viciousness of the swamp flies. She has a flick by her side which she uses frequently, yelling whenever a bite has caught her unawares.

It is near dusk, and there is a gentle wash of rain outside.

ALU: Can you see him?

MAKURI: See who?

ALU: My son Igwezu. Who else?

MAKURI: I did not come to look for him. Came only to see if the rain looks like stopping.

ALU: Well, does it?

MAKURI [*grunts.*]

ALU [*goes back to her work. Then—*]: It is time he was back. He went hours and hours ago.

MAKURI: He knows the way. He's a grown-up man, with a wife.

ALU [*flaring up with aged lack of heat.*]: If you had any good at all in you, you'd go and look for him.

MAKURI: And catch my death of cramp? Not likely . . . And anyway, [*getting warmer*] what's preventing you from going?

ALU: I want to be here when he gives me the news. I don't want to fall down dead out in the open.

MAKURI: The older you get, the more of a fraud you become. Every day for the past ten years, you've done nothing but swear that your son was dead in the marshes. And now you sit there like a crow and tell me that you're waiting for news about him.

ALU [*stubbornly*.]: I know he's dead.

MAKURI: Then what do you want Igwezu to tell you?

ALU: I only want to know if ... I only want to ask him ... I ... I ... He shouldn't have rushed off like that ... dashing off like a madman before anyone could ask him a thing.

MAKURI [*insistently*.]: Before anyone could ask him WHAT?

ALU [*flares up again*.]: You're always trying to make me a liar.

MAKURI: I don't have to make you one.

ALU: Bah! Frog-face! [*Resumes her work*.] ... Dropped his bundle and rushed off before I could ask him a thing ... And to think he could have found him after all. To think he could have found him in the city ...

MAKURI: Dead men don't go to the city. They go to hell.

ALU: I know one dead man who is sitting right here instead of going quietly to hell.

MAKURI: Now see who is calling who ...

ALU: You're so useless now that it takes you nearly a whole week to make one basket ... and to think you don't even cut your own rushes!

MAKURI: If you had to get up so often to shave the heads of the whole village ... and most of them crusted with kraw-kraw so that a man has to scrape and scrape until ...

ALU [*yells suddenly and slaps herself on the arm*.]

MAKURI [*looks at her for a moment*.]: Ha! Don't tell me now that a fly has been trying to suck blood from your dried-up veins.

ALU: If you had enough blood to hold you up, you'd prove it by going to look for your own son, and bring him home to supper.

MAKURI: He'll come home when he's hungry.

ALU: Suppose he's lost his way? Suppose he went walking in the swamps and couldn't find his way back?

MAKURI [*in bewilderment*.]: Him? Get lost? Woman, isn't it your son we're speaking of? The one who was born here, and has lived here all his life?

ALU: But he has been away now for some time. You cannot expect him to find his way about so quickly.

MAKURI: No, no. Of course not. The poor child has been away for eight ... whole ... months ...! Tch, tch. You'd drive a man to drown himself in the swamps—just to get away from your fussing.

ALU [*puts aside her work and rises.*]: I'm going after him. I don't want to lose him too. I don't want him missing his foothold and vanishing without a cry, without a chance for anyone to save him.

MAKURI: Stay where you are.

[*Alu crosses to doorpost and looks out.*]

ALU: I'm going out to shout his name until he hears me. I had another son before the mire drew him into the depths. I don't want Igwezu going the same way.

MAKURI [*follows her.*]: You haven't lost a son yet in the slough, but you will soon if you don't stop calling down calamities on their heads.

ALU: It's not what I say. The worst has happened already. Awuchike was drowned.

MAKURI: You're a blood-thirsty woman. Awuchike got sick of this place and went into the city. That's where you'll find him, fadding it out with the gentlemen. But you'll be satisfied with nothing less than a festering corpse beneath the mire ...

ALU: It's the truth.

MAKURI: It's a lie. All the young men go into the big town to try their hand at making money ... only some of them remember their folk and send word once in a while.

ALU: You'll see. When Igwezu returns, you'll find that he never saw a trace of him.

MAKURI: And if he didn't? The city is a large place. You could live there all your life and never meet half the people in it.

ALU: They are twins. Their close birth would have drawn them together even if they were living at the opposite ends of the town.

MAKURI: Bah!

ALU: Bah to yourself. Nobody has ever seen him. Nobody has ever heard of him, and yet you say to me ...

MAKURI: Nobody? Did you say nobody?

ALU: No one that really knew him. No one that could swear it was he.

MAKURI [*despairingly.*]: No one. No one that could swear . . . Ah, what a woman you are for deceiving yourself.

ALU: No one knows. Only the Serpent can tell. Only the Serpent of the swamps, the Snake that lurks beneath the slough.

MAKURI: The serpent be . . . ! Bah! You'll make me voice a sacrilege before I can stop my tongue. The traders came. They came one year, and they came the next. They looked at Igwezu and asked, Has he a twin? Has he a twin brother who lives in the town?

ALU: There are many people who look alike.

MAKURI [*sits down and takes up his work.*]: Well, I'll not perform the death rites for a son I know to be living.

ALU: If you felt for him like a true father, you'd know he was dead. But you haven't any feelings at all. Anyone would think they weren't your own flesh and blood.

MAKURI: Well, I have only your own word for that.

ALU: Ugh! You always did have a dirty tongue.

MAKURI [*slyly.*]: The land is big and wide, Alu, and you were often out by yourself, digging for crabs. And there were all those shifty-eyed traders who came to hunt for crocodile skins . . . Are you sure they didn't take your own skin with them . . . you old crocodile!

ALU: And if they did?

MAKURI: Poor luck to them. They couldn't have minded much which crocodile they took.

ALU: You're asking . . . Ayi! [*Slaps off a fly and continues more furiously.*] You're asking to have your head split and the wind let out.

MAKURI: And to think . . .

ALU [*makes a move to rise.*]: And I'll do it for you if you carry on the same . . .

MAKURI: Now, now, Alu. You know I didn't mean a word of that.
[*Alu tightens her lips and resumes her work.*]
[*In a hurriedly placating tone.*] There wasn't a woman anywhere more faithful than you, Alu; I never had a moment of worry in the whole of my life . . . [*His tone grows more sincere.*] Not every man can look his wife in the face and make that boast,

Alu. Not every man can do it. [*Alu remains inflexible.*]
And the chances you could have taken. Those traders—
every one of them wanted you to go back with him; promised
he'd make you live like a lady, clothe you in silks and have
servants to wait on your smallest wants . . . You don't belong
here, they used to tell you. Come back with us to the city
where men know the value of women . . . No, there was no
doubt about it. You could have had your choice of them. You
turned their heads like a pot of cane brew.
[*Alu begins to smile in spite of herself.*]

MAKURI: And the way I would go walking with you, and I could
hear their heads turning round, and one tongue hanging out
and saying to the other, Now I wonder what she sees in him . . .
Poor fools . . . if only they knew. If only they could see me
take you out into the mangrove, and I so strong that I could
make you gripe and sweat and sink your teeth into my cheeks.

ALU: You were always one for boasting.

MAKURI: And you with your eyes shut so tight that I thought the
skin would tear itself. Your eyes always shut, so that up till
this day, you cannot tell what I looked like when the spirit took
me, and I waxed as hot as the devil himself.

ALU: Be quiet.

MAKURI: You never feared the swamp then. You could walk across
it day and night and go to sleep in the middle of it . . . Alu, do
you remember our wedding night?

ALU [*pleased just the same.*]: We're past that kind of talk now. Have
you no shame?

MAKURI: Come on, my own Alu. Tell old Makuri what you did
on the night of our wedding.

ALU: No.

MAKURI: You're a stubborn old hen . . . Won't you even tell how
you dragged me from the house and we went across the swamps,
though it was so dark that I could not see the whites of your eyes?

ALU [*stubbornly.*]: I do not remember.

MAKURI: And you took me to the point where the streams meet,
and there you said . . . [*Pauses.*]

ALU [*shyly.*]: Well, it was my mother who used to say it.

MAKURI: Tell me just the same . . . just as you said it that night
when I thought they were your own words.

ALU: My memory is not so good . . . but . . .

MAKURI: It will come. Think slowly.

ALU [*with a shy smile.*]: She said I had to say it on my bridal bed.

MAKURI: Just where we stood. Go on, say it again.

ALU: 'Where the rivers meet, there the marriage must begin. And the river bed itself is the perfect bridal bed.'

MAKURI [*thoughtfully.*]: Ay–ii . . . The bed of the river itself . . . the bed of the river . . . [*Bursts suddenly into what appears to be illogical laughter.*]

ALU: Eh? Why? What are you laughing at now?

MAKURI [*futile effort to control himself.*]: Ay—ya-ya! The river bed . . . [*Bursts out laughing again.*]

ALU: Are you well Makuri?

MAKURI: Ay—ii! You must be really old, Alu. If you don't remember this, you're too old to lie on another river bed.

ALU: I don't . . . What are you . . . ?

MAKURI: Think hard woman. Do you not remember? We did not know that the swamp came up as far as that part of the stream . . . The ground . . . gave . . . way beneath us!

ALU [*beginning to laugh.*]: It is all beginning to come back . . . yes, yes, so it did. So it did!

MAKURI: And can you remember that you were left kicking in the mire . . . ha ha!

ALU [*no longer amused.*]: I was? I suppose you never even got your fingers muddy?

MAKURI: Well, I jumped up in time, didn't I? But you went down just as you were, flat on your back. And there I stood looking at you . . .

ALU: Ay. Gawking and yelling your head off with laughter. I can remember now.

MAKURI: You'd have laughed too if you had stood where I did and seen what could be seen of you.

ALU: Call yourself a man? And all my ribs bruised because you stood on me trying to get me out.

MAKURI: If you hadn't been thrashing about so much, I'd have got you out much quicker . . .

[*Alu has tightened her lips again. Bends rigidly over her work. Pause.*]

MAKURI: The whole village said that the twins were the very

colour of the swamp . . . . eh . . . Alu?

[*Alu remains deaf to him.*]

MAKURI: Ah well . . . Those were the days . . . those days were really good. Even when times were harsh and the swamp overran the land, we were able to laugh with the Serpent . . . [*Continues to work.*] . . . but these young people . . . They are no sooner born than they want to get out of the village as if it carried a plague . . . [*Looks up suddenly.*] I bet none of them has ever taken his woman into the swamps.

ALU: They have more sense than that. [*She says this with an effort and immediately resumes her frigidity.*]

MAKURI: It is not sense they have . . . not sense at all. Igwezu was hardly joined to his wife before he took her off into the city. What would a girl like Desala do in a place like that, I ask you. What would she find to do in the city?

ALU [*primly.*]: If you'd kept your eyes about you, you would have known that she made him promise to take her there before she would wed him.

MAKURI: It ruins them. The city ruins them. What do they seek there except money? They talk to the traders, and then they cannot sit still . . . There was Gonushi's son for one . . . left his wife and children . . . not a word to anyone.

ALU [*almost between her teeth.*]: It was the swamp . . . He went the same way as my son . . .

MAKURI [*throwing down his basket.*]: Woman . . . !

[*He is interrupted by the sound of footsteps on the planks outside.*]

MAKURI: That must be Igwezu now.

ALU: Thank heavens. It will soon be dark.

MAKURI: You'd better make the most of him. He might be going back tomorrow.

ALU: Why should he?

MAKURI: He came for his crops. Now that he knows they've been ruined by the floods, he'll be running back to the city.

ALU: He will stay a few days at least.

MAKURI [*licking his lips.*]: With a full-bosomed woman like Desala waiting for him in the city . . . ? You must be getting old.

ALU: It's a let-down for him—coming all the way back and finding no harvest.

MAKURI: Now don't you start. We've had worse years before this.

ALU [*flaring.*]: But you haven't journeyed three days only to be cheated of your crops . . .

[*The footsteps are right at the door. There is a knock on the wall.*]

ALU: That's a queer mood he's in. Why is he knocking?

MAKURI: It's not Igwezu . . . I didn't think they were his footsteps. [*Goes towards the door and pulls aside the door matting.*] A good evening to you, stranger.

VOICE OFFSTAGE: Allah protect you.

MAKURI: Were you sent to me? Come in. Come into the house. [*The caller enters, feeling his way with a staff.*]

MAKURI [*picks up the bundle from the floor.*]: Alu, take this bundle out of here . . . And bring some light. It is too dark in here.

BEGGAR: No, no. Not on my account. It makes no difference whatever to me.

MAKURI [*in a bewildered manner.*]: Oh . . . oh . . . I understand. [*Takes hold of the other end of the staff and leads him to the swivel chair.*] Sit here . . . Ah. [*Touches the stranger's forehead, and then his, saying devoutly—*] Blessed be the afflicted of the gods.

BEGGAR: Allah grant everlasting peace to this house.

[*The blind man is tall and straight. It is obvious from his dress that he is a stranger to these parts. He wears a long, tubular gown, white, which comes below his calf, and a little skull cap. Down one ear hangs a fairly large ear-ring, and he wears a thick ring on one of his fingers. He has a small beard, which, with the skull cap, accentuates the length of his face and emphasizes its ebony-carving nature. His feet are muddy above the ankles. The rest of him is lightly wet. His bearing is of quiet dignity.*]

MAKURI: You have journeyed far?

BEGGAR: Very far. I came all the way down the river.

MAKURI: Walking?

BEGGAR: Most of the way. Wherever it was possible, I walked. But sometimes, I was forced to accept a lift from the ferries.

MAKURI [*looks rapidly down his legs.*]: Alu! Some water for the man to wash his feet.

ALU [*coming in with the taper.*]: Give me time. I can't do everything at once, can I? [*Lights the oil lamps which are hanging from the rafters. Goes back again.*]

MAKURI: Have you met anyone in the village? Were you directed here?

BEGGAR: No. This happened to be the first house on my way ...
Are you the head of this house?

MAKURI: Y-yes, yes I am.

BEGGAR: Then it is with you I must speak.

MAKURI: We haven't much, but you can have shelter for the night,
and food for ...

BEGGAR: I have not come to beg for alms.

MAKURI: Oh? Do you know anyone here?

BEGGAR: No. I come from far away in the North. Have you ever
heard of Bukanji?

MAKURI: Bukanji? Bukan ... ? Ah, is that not the village of
beggars?

BEGGAR: So it is known by the rest of the world ... the village of
beggars ... but I have not come to beg.

MAKURI: Bukanji! That is a march of several weeks!

BEGGAR: I have been journeying for longer than that. I resolved
to follow the river as far as it went, and never turn back. If I
leave here, it will be to continue in the same direction.

MAKURI: But this is the end—this is where the river ends!

BEGGAR: No, friend. There are many more miles left of this river.

MAKURI: Yes, yes ... But the rest is all swamp. Between here and
the sea, you'll not find a human soul.

BEGGAR: I must stay here or walk on. I have sworn to tread only
where the soil is moist.

MAKURI: You'll not get far in that direction. This is the end. This
is as far as human beings can go, even those who have the use
of their sight.

BEGGAR: Then I must stay here.

MAKURI: What do you want?

BEGGAR: Work.

MAKURI: Work?

BEGGAR: Yes, work. I wish to work on the soil. I wish to knead it
between my fingers.

MAKURI: But you're blind. Why don't you beg like others? There
is no true worshipper who would deny you this charity.

BEGGAR: I want a home, and I wish to work with my hands.

MAKURI [*in utter bewilderment.*]: You ... the afflicted of the gods!
Do you really desire to work, when even the least devout
lives under the strict injunction of hospitality towards you?

BEGGAR [*getting up.*]: No more, no more. All the way down the river the natives read me the code of the afflicted, according to their various faiths. Some fed and clothed me. Others put money in my hands, food and drink in my bag. With some, it was the children and their stones, and sometimes the dogs followed me and whetted their teeth on my ankles . . . Good-bye. I shall follow the river to the end.

MAKURI: Wait. You are very hasty. Did you never learn that the blind man does not hurry for fear he out-walks his guide? Sit down again . . . Alu! Alu! When is that supper coming?

ALU [*from inside.*]: What supper? The last time it was water for washing his feet.

MAKURI: Well, hurry . . . [*Helps the blind man back into the chair.*] There . . . Now tell me all about your journey . . . Did you come through any of the big cities?

BEGGAR: One or two, but I did not stop there. I walked right through them without a halt.

MAKURI: And you have been on the road for . . . how long did you say?

BEGGAR: I have lost all count of time. To me, one day is just like another . . . ever since my sight became useless.

MAKURI: It must be strange . . . living in perpetual dark.

BEGGAR: I did not have many years to enjoy the benefit of the eyes. Four or five years at the most, and then . . . You have heard of the fly sickness?

MAKURI [*shaking his head.*]: Who hasn't? Who hasn't?

BEGGAR: It is fatal to cattle. The human beings fall ill and suffer agonies. When the sickness is over, the darkness begins . . . At first, it is mystifying and then . . . [*smiles*]. When it happened to me, I thought I was dead and that I had gone to a paradise where my earthly eyes were unsufficing.

MAKURI: You did? If it had been old Makuri, he would have thought that he was in the darkest corner of hell.

BEGGAR [*smiling still.*]: But I was only a child, and I knew that I had committed no sins. Moreover, my faith promises paradise for all true believers—paradise in the company of Muhammad and all the prophets . . . [*Becoming serious.*] Those few moments were the happiest in my life. Any moment, I thought, and my eyes would be opened to the wonders around me. I heard familiar voices, and I rejoiced, because I thought that they were dead also, and were in paradise with me ... And then slowly, the truth came to me, and I knew that I was living—but blind.

MAKURI: The gods be merciful.

BEGGAR: Even before anyone told me, I knew exactly what I had to do to live. A staff, a bowl, and I was out on the roads begging for alms from travellers, singing my prayers, pouring out blessings upon them which were not mine to give ...

MAKURI: No, my friend. The blessings were yours. My faith teaches me that every god shakes a beggar by the hand, and his gifts are passed into his heart so that every man he blesses ...

BEGGAR: Ah, but did I bless them from the heart? Were they not so many that I blessed without thought, and took from whatever hand was willing, however vile it was? Did I know if the alms came from a pure heart or from a robber and taker of lives, from the devout or the profane ... ? I thanked and blessed them equally, even before I had the time to discover the size of their bounty ... [*Begins to nod his head in time to his chanting.*] [*His chanting is tonal. No clear words.*
Faint drumming can now be heard offstage. The Beggar hears it and stops abruptly, listening hard for the sound.]

BEGGAR: Have you a festivity in the village tonight?

MAKURI: No. Why?

BEGGAR: I can hear drumming.

MAKURI [*after listening for a moment.*]: It must be the frogs. There is a whole city of them in the marshes.

BEGGAR: No, this is drumming. And it is coming this way ... yes, it is drawing nearer.

MAKURI: Y—yes ... I think I can hear it now ... Alu!

ALU [*from inside*]: What now?

MAKURI: Can you hear the drumming?

ALU: What drumming?

MAKURI : That means you can't. [*Confidentially.*] She was deaf the day she was born. [*Goes to the door and looks out.*] They are not within sight yet, whoever it is ... Ah, I know who it must be ... My son.

BEGGAR: You have a son?

MAKURI: Yes. He only came back today. He has been in the city making money.

BEGGAR: So he is wealthy?

MAKURI: We don't know yet. He hardly said a word to anyone before he rushed off again to see what the floods had done to his farm . . . The man is a fool. I told him there wasn't a thing to see except the swamp water, but he rushed out like a madman, dropping his bundle on the floor. He said he had to see for himself before he would believe it.

BEGGAR: Was there much damage to the farm?

MAKURI: Much damage? Not a grain was saved, not one tuber in the soil . . . And what the flood left behind was poisoned by the oil in the swamp water. [Shakes his head.] . . . It is hard for him, coming back for a harvest that isn't there.

BEGGAR: But it is possible then. It is possible to plant on this land in spite of the swamp?

MAKURI [straining his eyes into the dark outside.]: Oh yes. There are little bits of land here and there where a man can sow enough to keep his family, and even take to the market . . . Not much, but . . . I can't see them . . . But I'm sure it is he. He must have run into one of the drummers and been merry-making all afternoon. You can trust Luyaka to drum him back to his own house in welcome.

BEGGAR: Is there land here which a man can till? Is there any land to spare for a man who is willing to give his soul to the soil?

MAKURI [shakes his head.]: No, friend. All the land that can take the weight of a hoe is owned by someone in the village. Even the few sheep and goats haven't any land on which to graze. They have to be fed on cassava and other roots.

BEGGAR: But if a man is willing to take a piece of the ground and redeem it from the swamp—will they let him? If a man is willing to drain the filth away and make the land yield coco-yams and lettuce—will they let him?

MAKURI [stares wildly.]: Mind what you are saying, son. Mind what profanities you utter in this house.

BEGGAR [surprised.]: I merely ask to be given a little of what land is useless to the people.

MAKURI: You wish to rob the Serpent of the Swamps? You wish to take the food out of his mouth?

BEGGAR: The Serpent? The Serpent of the Swamps?

MAKURI: The land that we till and live on has been ours from the beginning of time. The bounds are marked by ageless iroko trees that have lived since the birth of the Serpent, since the birth of the world, since the start of time itself. What is ours is ours. But what belongs to the Serpent may never be taken away from him.

BEGGAR: I beg your forgiveness. [*Rises.*] I have not come to question your faith. Allah reward you for your hospitality ... I must continue my journey ...

MAKURI: Wait. [*He listens for a moment to the drumming which is now just outside the door.*] That is the drummer of the priest ... [*Enter Alu running.*] Alu, is that not the priest's salutations coming from the drums?

ALU: Yes. It must be the Kadiye.

MAKURI: It is. It is ... Well, don't stand there. Get the place fit to receive him ... Clear away all the litter ...
[*Alu begins to tidy the room hastily. She takes away Makuri's baskets and rushes, returns to fetch her own things and takes them out of the room. She trims the lamp wicks and takes away any oddments lying around.*]

MAKURI: And see if there is any brew in the attic. The Kadiye might like some.

ALU [*grumbling.*]: Take this away ... Prepare supper ... See if there is any brew in the ... Why don't you try and do something to help ... !

MAKURI: Do you want me to be so ill-mannered as to leave my guest by himself? ... [*Takes the blind man by the arm and leads him towards his stool.*] ... You mustn't pay any attention to that ill-tempered hen ... She always gets in a flutter when the Kadiye honours our house. [*Picks up his stool and moves off towards Alu's corner.*] ... He's probably come to offer prayers of thanks for the safe return of our son ... He's our holy man, the Servant and Priest of the Serpent of the Swamp ... [*Puts down the stool.*] Here. Sit down here. We must continue our talk when he is gone.
[*The drummer is now at the door, and footsteps come up the gangway.*
The drummer is the first to enter. He bows in backwards, drumming praises of the Kadiye. Next comes the Kadiye himself,

C.P.I—6

*a big, voluminous creature of about fifty, smooth-faced except for
little tufts of beard around his chin. His head is shaved clean. He
wears a kind of loin-cloth, white, which comes down to below his
knees and a flap of which hangs over his left arm. He is bare above
the waist. At least half of the Kadiye's fingers are ringed. He is
followed by a servant, who brushes the flies off him with a horse-tail
flick.]*

MAKURI [*places his arm across his chest and bows.*]: My house is open
to you, Kadiye. You are very welcome.

[*The Kadiye places a hand on his head.*]

[*Alu hurries into the room and kneels. The Kadiye blesses her also.*]

KADIYE [*looks at the Beggar who remains sitting. Signs to the drummer
to stop.*]: Did Igwezu bring a friend with him?

MAKURI: No Kadiye. This is a stranger who called at my house
for charity. He is blind.

KADIYE: The gods protect you, friend.

BEGGAR: Allah shield you from all evil.

KADIYE [*startled.*]: Allah? is he from the North?

MAKURI: He is. He journeyed all the way from Bukanji.

KADIYE: Ah, from Bukanji. [*To the servant.*] Kundigu, give the man
something.

[*The servant brings out a purse and approaches the Beggar. When
he is about a foot away, the Beggar, without a change of expression
turns his bowl upside down. The servant stands puzzled and looks
to his master for further instructions. Kadiye looks quickly away, and
the servant tries to turn the bowl inside up. But the Beggar keeps it
firmly downwards. The servant looks backwards at the Kadiye—
who by now has hemmed and begun to talk to Makuri—slips the
money into his own pocket, pulls the strings shut and returns to his
place.*]

KADIYE: Ahem . . . Where is your son? I hear he has returned.

MAKURI: Yes he has. He went out in the afternoon to see his . . .
He must have been detained by old friends and their sympathizing.

KADIYE: Yes, it is a pity. But, then, he is not the only one. Others
lost even more than he did . . . And anyway, he has probably
made himself a fortune in the city . . . Hasn't he?

MAKURI: I don't know. He hasn't told us . . . Won't you sit
here . . . ?

KADIYE [*sits in the swivel chair.*]: They all do. They all make money.

MAKURI: Well, I only hope he has. He'll need something on which he can fall back.

KADIYE [*patting the arm of the chair.*]: Didn't he send you this chair within a few weeks of his arriving in the city?

MAKURI: Yes, he did. He's a man for keeping his word. Before he left, he said to me, With the first money I make, I am going to buy you one of those chairs which spin like a top. And you can put your customers in it and spin them until they are giddy.

KADIYE [*pushing his toes into the ground to turn the chair.*]: Ay—It is comfortable.

MAKURI: It is. When I have no customers, I sit in it myself. It is much better than a rocking chair ... Alu!

ALU: Coming.

MAKURI: When are we having something to drink? Are you going to keep us waiting all night ... ? [*Back to the Kadiye—*] And when they were bringing it over the water, it knocked a hole in the bottom of the canoe and nearly sank it ... But that wasn't all. The carrier got stuck in the swamps and they had to dig him out ... Alu!

ALU [*comes out with a gourd and a number of calabash-cups.*]: Here it is ... There is no need to split your guts with shouting.

MAKURI [*takes the gourd from her and serves the drinks. Alu takes it round. She curtseys to the Kadiye when she hands him his cup. Makuri takes a smell at the liquor before he begins to pour it out.*] A-a-ah! You'll find this good, Kadiye ...

KADIYE: Has it been long fermenting?

MAKURI: Months and months. I pulped the canes nearly ...

ALU: *You* did?

MAKURI: If you'd only give me a chance, woman! ... I was going to say that my son pulped the canes before he left for the city.

ALU [*looking out of the door in between serving the drinks.*]: I wish he'd come. I wish he'd hurry up and come home. It is so dark and the swamps are ...

MAKURI [*impatiently.*]: Here, here, take this to the drummer and stop your cackling. It will be his own fault if he doesn't come and we finish the lot. Pah! He's probably used to drinking bottled beer by now, instead of thriving on good wholesome cane brew, fermented in the froth of the swamp itself.

[*Everyone now has a drink, except the Beggar, who, in spite of a dumb persuasive attempt by Alu, refuses a cup. The Kadiye waits for Makuri to come and taste his drink.*]

MAKURI [*takes the cup from the Kadiye.*]: If my face belies my thoughts, may the venom grip at once. [*Drinks a mouthful and hands it back.*]

KADIYE: The protection of the heavens be on us all. [*Drinks and smacks his lips. Then he looks round the room and announces gravely—*] The rains have stopped.

MAKURI [*shakes his head in distrust.*]: They have stopped too often Kadiye. It is only a lull.

KADIYE: No. They have stopped finally. My soothsayers have confirmed it. The skies are beginning to open: what few clouds there are, are being blown along the river.

MAKURI [*shrugs, without much enthusiasm.*]: The gods be praised.

KADIYE: The floods are over . . . The river will recede and we can plant again . . . I am now released of my vow.

MAKURI: Your vow, Kadiye?

KADIYE: Yes, When the floods began and the swamps overran the land, I vowed to the Serpent that I would neither shave nor wash until the rains ceased altogether . . .

MAKURI [*drops his cup.*]: I had no idea . . . is that the reason for your visit?

KADIYE: Yes, of course. Did you not guess?

MAKURI [*getting out the lather.*]: I will only be a moment . . .

KADIYE: No, old man. I shall wait for your son.

MAKURI: For Igwezu? . . . As you please, Kadiye . . . I hope he still remembers his trade. It must be a long time since he last wielded a razor.

KADIYE: Be it as it may, his hand is steadier than yours.

MAKURI [*replacing the lather.*]: True. True . . . We must all get old some time.

KADIYE: Has he been out long?

MAKURI: All day . . . But he should be back any moment now. He must be drinking with his friends . . . they haven't seen him for a whole season, and they won't let him go in a hurry . . .

ALU: He ought to be back by now. Who of his friends could have kept him so long?

KADIYE: Did he bring his wife?

ALU: No. He wouldn't want to expose her to the flooded roads and other discomforts of the journey.

MAKURI [*disgustedly.*]: Ah! They're soft. This younger generation is as soft as ...

ALU: Aw, shut up in a while. Igwezu himself was lucky to get here at all. He would have had to turn back at the river if it wasn't for old Wazuri who is still ferrying travellers across the swollen stream. All the other fishermen have hung up their boats with their nets. [*Goes into the house.*]

MAKURI: And isn't that what I am telling you? As soon as the floods came, the younger men ran home to their wives. But not Wazuri! He's as old as the tortoise himself, but he keeps the paddle in his hand.

[*The servant comes up and whispers in Kadiye's ear.*]

KADIYE: Ah yes ... I nearly forgot. [*Drains his cup and gives it to Makuri.*] I must go first to Daruga. His son is going to be circumcised tonight and he wants me to say the usual prayers ... I'll call again on my way back. [*Rises, the servant helping him.*]

MAKURI: Just as you please, Kadiye. And if Igwezu returns I shall tell him to prepare for you.

KADIYE: I shall send a man to find him out ... [*Rubs his chin.*] This nest is beginning to attract the swamp flies. I must get it off tonight.

[*Goes out, preceded by his drummer who drums him out as before, bowing backwards.*]

MAKURI [*who has held the matting aside for them. Looks after them as the drumming dies away. Sighs.*]: What a day! What a day! The whole world seems to have picked the same day to drop into my house ... [*Stops suddenly as he is smitten by a recollection ...*] The pot-bellied pig! So I am too old to shave him now, am I? Too old! Why he's nearly as old as the Serpent himself ... Bah! I hope Igwezu has been celebrating with his friends and comes home drunk. He-he! We'll see who has the steady hand then. We'll see who goes from here with his chin all slashed and bleeding ... He-he ... [*Stops again, thinking hard ...*] Now where was I before ...? Alu!

ALU [*enters simultaneously with a bowl of warm water.*]: If you want to bellow, go out into the swamp and talk to the frogs.

MAKURI: Aha, is that the water? No, no, bring it over here . . .
   Come on, my friend . . . come over here. It will be easier to
   wash your feet sitting in this chair . . . [*Leading him to the swivel
   chair* . . .] Do you realize it? You've brought good luck with you.

BEGGAR: Have I?

MAKURI: Well, didn't you hear what the Kadiye said? The rains
   have stopped . . . the floods are over. You must carry luck with
   your staff.

BEGGAR: Yes, I could feel the air growing lighter, and the clouds
   clearing over my head. I think the worst of your season is over.

MAKURI: I hope so. Only once or twice in my whole lifetime have
   we had it so bad.

BEGGAR: How thankful we would have been for the excess that you
   had here. If we had had the hundredth part of the fall you had,
   I would not be sitting under your roof this moment.

MAKURI: Is it really dry up country?

BEGGAR [*Smiles indulgently.*]: A little worse than that.

MAKURI: Drought? Did you have a drought?

   [*While the Beggar is speaking, Alu squats down and washes his feet.
   When this is finished, she wipes them dry, takes a small jar from
   one of the shelves, and rubs his feet with some form of ointment.*]

BEGGAR: We are used to droughts. Our season is one long
   continuous drought . . . But we were used to it. Even when
   it rained, the soil let the water run right through it and join
   some stream in the womb of the earth. All that we knew,
   and were content to live on alms . . . Until one day, about a
   year or more ago . . .

   [*There is only the gentle lapping of the water in the bowl. Makuri
   has brought his stool and is sitting on the left side of the chair,
   looking up at the Beggar.*]

   . . . then we had more rain than I had ever known in my life.
   and the soil not only held the water, but it began to show off
   a leaf here and there . . . even on kola trees which had been
   stunted from birth. Wild millet pushed its way through the
   soil, and little tufts of elephant grass appeared from seeds which
   had lain forgotten season upon season . . . Best of all, hope
   began to spring in the heart of everyone . . . It is true that
   the land had lain barren for generations, that the fields had
   yielded no grain for the lifetime of the eldest in the village.

We had known nothing but the dryness of the earth. Dry soil.
Dry crumbs of dust. Clouds of dust even when there was no
wind, but only a vulture flying low and flapping its wings over
the earth ... But now ... we could smell the sweetness of
lemon leaves, and the feel of the fronds of desert palm was a
happiness which we had never known ... The thought was no
sooner born than we set to work before the soil changed its
mind and released its moisture. We deserted the highways and
marched on this land, hoes and mattocks in hand—and how
few of these there were! The village had been long unused to
farming, and there was no more than a handful of hoes. But
we took our staffs and drove them into the earth. We
sharpened stakes and picked the sand and the pebble until they
bled ... And it seemed as if the heavens rejoiced in our
labour, for their blessings were liberal, and their good will
on our side. The rains came when we wanted it. And the sun
shone and the seeds began to ripen.
[*Igwezu enters quietly, and remains by the door, unobserved.*]
Nothing could keep us from the farms from the moment that
the shoots came through the surface, and all through the months
of waiting. We went round the plantains and rubbed our skins
against them, lightly, so that the tenderest bud could not be
hurt. This was the closest that we had ever felt to one another.
This was the moment that the village became a clan, and the
clan a household, and even that was taken by Allah in one of his
large hands and kneaded together with the clay of the earth.
We loved the sound of a man's passing footsteps as if the rustle
of his breath it was that gave life to the sprouting wonder
around us. We even forgot to beg, and lived on the marvel
of this new birth of the land, and the rich smell of its
goodness ... But it turned out to have been an act of spite.
The feast was not meant for us—but for the locusts.

MAKURI [*involuntarily*.]: Locusts!

BEGGAR: They came in hordes, and squatted on the land. It only
took an hour or two, and the village returned to normal.

ALU [*moaning*.]: Ay-ii, Ay-ii ...
[*Makuri buries his head in his hands.*]

BEGGAR: I headed away from my home, and set my face towards
the river. When I said to the passing stranger, Friend, set my

face towards the river, he replied, which river? But I only said to him, Towards any river, towards any stream; set my face towards the seas itself. But let there be water, because I am sick of the dryness.

MAKURI: Ay-ii, the hands of the gods are unequal. Their gifts become the burden of . . .

[*Alu, who has now finished her task, takes the bowl and rises. She is startled by suddenly seeing Igwezu, and she drops the bowl in her fright.*]

ALU: My son!

MAKURI: Hm? Oh, he's back at last . . . [*Wakes suddenly to the dropped bowl, shouts—*] But was that a reason for you to be drowning the whole house? Now go and wipe it up instead of gawking at the man . . . Come on here, Igwezu. Come and sit down.

BEGGAR [*rising.*]: Your son? Is that the son you spoke of?

MAKURI: Yes . . . Now hurry up. Hurry up and dry the place.

[*The Beggar feels for his staff and moves out of the chair. Igwezu sits down. He appears indifferent to his surroundings.*]

MAKURI: What held you? Have you been carousing?

IGWEZU: No. I went for a walk by myself.

MAKURI: All afternoon?

[*Igwezu nods.*]

Do you mean to tell me . . .? [*anxiously.*] Son, are you feeling well?

ALU [*coming into the room with a piece of rag, overhears the last question.*]: Is he unwell? What is the matter with him?

MAKURI: He is not unwell. I merely asked him how he felt.

ALU [*on her knees, begins to wipe the floor.*]: Well, how does he feel?

IGWEZU [*without any kind of feeling.*]: Glad to be home. Glad to be once again with my own people . . . Is that not what every home-coming son should feel?

MAKURI [*after watching him for a moment.*]: Have you seen the farm?

[*Igwezu is silent.*]

Son, you mustn't take it so hard. There is nothing that . . .

[*Shakes his head in energetic despair and sees Alu still wiping the floor.*] Hurry up, woman! Is the man not to get any supper after walking around by himself all day?

[*Alu gasps.*]

IGWEZU: No, don't give yourself the trouble. I want no supper.

MAKURI: But you've eaten nothing all day.

IGWEZU: I have had my feast of welcome. I found it on the farm where the beans and the corn had made an everlasting pottage with the mud.

BEGGAR [coming forward.]: Master, it will thrive again.

IGWEZU [He looks up at the Beggar, as if seeing him for the first time.]: Who are you? And why do you call me master?

BEGGAR: I am a wanderer, a beggar by birth and fortunes. But you own a farm. I have stood where your soil is good and cleaves to the toes like the clay of bricks in the mixing; but it needs the fingers of drought whose skin is parchment. I shall be your bondsman. I shall give myself to you and work the land for your good. I feel I can make it yield in my hands like an obedient child.

IGWEZU [looks from Alu to Makuri, who only shrugs his shoulders.]: Where do you come from?

BEGGAR: Bukanji.

IGWEZU [relapsing into his former manner.]: Bukanji. Yes, I have heard of it, I have heard of it . . .

[The Kadiye's drum has begun again to sound offstage.]

MAKURI: The Kadiye! I had forgotten. Son, the Kadiye has been here. I think I can hear him returning now. He wants you to shave him tonight.

IGWEZU: Does he?

MAKURI: Yes. Now that the rains have ceased, his vow is come to an end. He wanted me to do it, but I said, No, Kadiye; I am still strong and healthy, but my fingers shake a little now and then, and your skin is tender.

IGWEZU: Yes. Is it not strange that his skin is tender? Is it not strange that he is smooth and well-preserved?

BEGGAR [eagerly.]: Is he fat, master? When he spoke, I detected a certain bulk in his voice.

IGWEZU: Ay, he is fat. He rolls himself like a fat and greasy porpoise.

ALU: Son, you must speak better of the holy man.

MAKURI [tut-tutting.]: The city has done him no good. No good at all.

BEGGAR: Master, is it true what they say? Do you speak ill of the holy man because your heart is in the city?

IGWEZU: Why? What does it matter to you?

BEGGAR: The bondsman must know the heart of the master; then
he may serve him well.

[*Igwezu continues to stare at the Beggar, puzzled.*]

BEGGAR: Do you serve the Serpent, master? Do you believe with
the old man—that the land may not be redeemed? That the
rotting swamps may not be purified?

IGWEZU: You make a strange slave with your questioning? What
is all this to you?

BEGGAR: Even a slave may know the bounds of his master's
kingdom.

IGWEZU: You know that already.

BEGGAR: Perhaps. I know that the Serpent has his share, but not
who sets the boundaries ... Is is the priest, or is it the master?

IGWEZU: What does it matter?

BEGGAR: I am a free bondsman. I give myself willingly. I gave
without the asking. But I must know whom I serve, for then
I will not stint my labour.

IGWEZU: Serve whom you please. It does not matter to Igwezu.

BEGGAR: Does the priest live well? Is the Serpent well kept and
nourished?

IGWEZU: You may see for yourself. His thighs are like skinfuls of
palm oil ...

[*The beggar throws back his head and laughs. It is the first time
he has done so, and the effect is immediate on Makuri and Alu, who
stare at him in wonder. Igwezu looks up ordinarily.*]

IGWEZU: It is a careless bondsman who laughs before his master.

BEGGAR: How does the Serpent fare in times of dearth? Does he
thrive on the poisonous crabs? Does he drink the ooze of the
mire?

MAKURI [*trembling with anger.*]: Beware. That borders upon sacrilege.
That trespasses on the hospitality of this house.

BEGGAR [*with dignity.*]: I beg your forgiveness. It is for the master to
question not the slave. [*He feels his way to the far corner, and
remains there, standing.*]

IGWEZU [*thoughtfully.*]: Ay. So it is ... So it is ... and yet, I saw
him come into this house; but I turned and went away again,
back to the Serpent with whom I'd talked all afternoon.

MAKURI: You did what? Who are you talking about?

IGWEZU: The Kadiye. I saw him when he entered this house, but I went away and continued my walk in the swamps.

MAKURI: You did?

IGWEZU: Yes, I did not trust myself.

MAKURI: You did not trust yourself. Why? What has the Kadiye ever done to you?

IGWEZU: I do not know. At this moment, I do not know. So perhaps it is as well that he comes. Perhaps he can explain. Perhaps he can give meaning to what seems dark and sour ... When I met with harshness in the city, I did not complain. When I felt the nakedness of its hostility, I accepted it. When I saw its knife sever the ties and the love of kinship, and turn brother against brother ...

ALU [quickly.]: You met him then. You found your brother in the city.

IGWEZU: Did I?

ALU: Your silence has deceived no one, Igwezu. Do you think I did not know all the time?

IGWEZU: He is dead. You've said so yourself. You have said it often enough.

ALU: Which death did he die—that is all I want to know. Surely a mother may say that much, and be forgiven the sin of lying to herself—even at the moment of the asking. And he is still my son, Igwezu; he is still your own twin.

[Igwezu remains silent.]

ALU: I am too old to be a pilgrim to his grave. I am too weak to seek to bring him back to life ... I only seek to know ... Igwezu, did you find my son?

[After a moment, Igwezu nods slowly.]

ALU: Let me hear it through your lips, and then I will know it is no trick of my eyes. Does my son live?

IGWEZU [wearily.]: He lives.

ALU [nodding.]: He lives. What does it matter that he breathes a foreign air. Perhaps there is something in the place that makes men forget. [Going.] What if he lives sufficient only to himself. He lives. One cannot ask too much. [Goes into the house.]

MAKURI [ordinarily.]: Was he well?

[Igwezu nods.]

MAKURI [obviously uncertain how to proceed. He keeps his eyes on the

*ground, from where he spies on Igwezu. Slowly, and with
hesitation ...*] Did you ... did you often ... meet?

IGWEZU: I lived under his roof—for a while.

MAKURI [*shouting at the departed Alu.*]: Did you hear that? Did you
hear that you stubborn old crow? ... Was he ... Did ... er ...?
You did say he was in good health?

IGWEZU: Healthier than you or I. And a thousand times as wealthy.

MAKURI: There! [*shouting out again.*] Did you hear? Did I not
always say so? [*more confidently now.*] How did he make his
money?

IGWEZU: In timber. He felled it and floated it over the seas ... He
is wealthy, and he is big.

MAKURI: Did he ever talk of his father? Does he remember his
own home?

IGWEZU: Awuchike is dead to you and to this house. Let us not
raise his ghost.

MAKURI [*stands bewildered for a moment. Then, with a sudden
explosiveness ...*]: What did he do son? What happened in the
city?

IGWEZU: Nothing but what happens to a newcomer to the race.
The city reared itself in the air, and with the strength of its
legs of brass kicked the adventurer in the small of his back.

MAKURI: And Awuchike? Was he on the horse that kicked?
[*Igwezu is silent.*]

MAKURI: Did your own brother ride you down, Igwezu? ... Son,
talk to me. What took place between you two? [*Igwezu is silent
again, and then*]

IGWEZU: The wound heals quicker if it is left unopened. What
took place is not worth the memory ... Does it not suffice that
in the end I said to myself ... I have a place, a home, and
though it lies in the middle of the slough, I will go back to it.
And I have a little plot of land which has rebelled against the
waste that surrounds it, and yields a little fruit for the asking.
I sowed this land before I went away. Now is the time for
harvesting, and the cocoa-pods must be bursting with fullness ...
I came back with hope, with consolation in my heart. I came
back with the assurance of one who has lived with his land and
tilled it faithfully ...

MAKURI: It is the will of the heavens ...

IGWEZU: It was never in my mind . . . the thought that the farm could betray me so totally, that it could drive the final wedge into this growing loss of touch . . .

[*The Kadiye's drum has become more audible.*]

BEGGAR: Master, I think the Serpent approaches.

IGWEZU: I can hear him, bondsman. I can hear him.

[*The Kadiye's party arrives at the door. Makuri runs to hold the matting aside, and the party enters as before. Alu comes out again and curtseys.*]

KADIYE: Is he back? Ah Igwezu, it is good to see you again.

[*Igwezu rises unhurriedly. The Kadiye tries to bless him but Igwezu avoids this, as if by accident.*] I am glad to see you safe and well . . . [*Seats himself in the chair.*] Ah, what an affair that was. The child was crying loud enough to drown all the frogs in the swamp . . .

MAKURI: [*leaning down to him. With fiendishness on his face—*] Did it happen, Kadiye? Did the child take his revenge?

KADIYE: Oh yes, he did. He drenched the healer with a sudden gush!

[*Makuri dances delightedly, laughing in his ghoulish manner.*]

KADIYE: And that wasn't all. The foolish mother! She heard the cries and tried to get to her son from where she has been locked.

MAKURI: And pollute her own son!

KADIYE: Amazing, is it not? The mothers can never be trusted . . . And to think that she did succeed in the end!

MAKURI [*snapping his fingers over his head.*]: The gods forbid it!

KADIYE: She did. I had to purify the boy and absolve him from the crime of contamination. That is the fourth circumcision where I have known it to happen.

MAKURI: The best thing is to send the mother out of the house.

KADIYE: Do you think that hasn't been tried? It is harder to shift them than to get the child to stay still.

MAKURI: Ay. That is true enough. All women are a blood-thirsty lot. They love to hear the child wailing and crying out in pain. Then they can hug themselves and say, Serve you right, you little brat. Now you'll know what pains I went through, giving birth to you.

KADIYE: Ah, that is the truth of it . . . Anyway, it is all over now

... all over and done with ... [*Hems with pomposity and turns to Igwezu.*] And how is the city gentleman? Have you been making a lot of money, Igwezu?

IGWEZU: None ... where must I shave, Kadiye?

KADIYE [*puzzled.*]: Where?

IGWEZU: Is it the head or the chin?

MAKURI [*gasps. Then tries to force a casualness in his tone.*]: Pay no attention, Kadiye. It is only the humour of the townsmen.

KADIYE: A-ah ... The chin, Igwezu. Shave off the beard.

IGWEZU [*begins to prepare the instruments.*]: Did you make other vows, Kadiye? Were there other pleasures from which you abstained until the rains abated?

KADIYE: Oh, yes. Oh, yes indeed. I vowed that my body would remain unwashed.

IGWEZU: Ah. Did you keep within doors?

KADIYE: No. I had my duties ... People still die, you know. And mothers give birth to children.

IGWEZU: And it rained throughout? Almost without a stop?

KADIYE: Yes, it did.

IGWEZU: Then perhaps once or twice you were out in the rain ... ?

MAKURI [*quickly.*]: Igwezu ... you ... you ... you were going to tell Kadiye about the big town.

IGWEZU: Was I?

KADIYE: Ah, yes. Tell me about the place. Was business as good as they say?

IGWEZU: For some people.

KADIYE: And you? Did your business thrive?

IGWEZU: No more than my farming has done.

KADIYE: Come now, Igwezu. I am not trying to obtain the promise of an ox for sacrifice ... You did make some money?

IGWEZU: No.

KADIYE: I see he must be coaxed ... Admit you've made enough to buy this village—men, livestock and all.

IGWEZU [*slips the agbada over the Kadiye's head.*]: No, Kadiye. I made none at all.

KADIYE: A-ah, they are all modest ... Did you make a little then?

IGWEZU: No I made none at all.

KADIYE: [*looks hard at him. He is obviously disturbed by Igwezu's manner. Speaks nervously.*] Well, never mind, never mind.

To some it comes quickly; to others a little more slowly.
But your own turn will come soon, Igwezu; it will come
before long.

IGWEZU: I'm afraid I have had my turn already. I lost everything;
my savings, even my standing as a man. I went into debt.

KADIYE: Impossible!

IGWEZU: Shall I tell you what I offered as security? Would you like
to know, Kadiye?

KADIYE: Not your pretty wife, I hope. [*guffawing.*] I notice you
had to come without her.

IGWEZU: No, holy one. It was not my wife. But what I offered
had a lot in common with her. I put down the harvest from
my farm.

MAKURI: Ha?

ALU: Igwezu. My poor Igwezu.

KADIYE [*laughing.*]: Now what do you take us for? As if anyone
in the city would lend money on a farm which he had never
even seen. Are they such fools—these business men of yours?

IGWEZU: No. They are not fools; my brother least of all. He is
anything but a fool.

ALU: Awuchike!

MAKURI: My own son? Your own flesh and blood?

[*Alu remains staring at Igwezu for several moments. Then, shaking
her head in complete and utter bewilderment, she turns round slowly
and goes into the house, more slouched than ever before.*]

IGWEZU [*in the same calm relentlessness.*]: Wait, mother . . . I have
not told you all. [*He begins to lather the Kadiye's face.*]

ALU: I know enough. [*She has stopped but does not turn round.*] But
I no longer understand. I feel tired, son. I think I'll go to sleep.

IGWEZU: Don't you want news of my wife? Have you no interest
in the simple and unspoilt child whom you wooed on my
behalf?

[*Alu goes slowly out of the room.*
Igwezu begins to shave the Kadiye. There is silence.]

IGWEZU [*without stopping.*]: Father. Tell me, father, is my brother
a better man than I?

MAKURI: No, son. His heart is only more suited to the city.

IGWEZU: And yet we are twins. And in spite of that, he looked at
my wife, and she went to him of her own accord . . . Tell me

father, are women so easily swayed by wealth? Are all women the same?

MAKURI: Alu was different. She turned their heads but she kept her own.

IGWEZU: Thank you, father. Now where is the stranger who would be my bondsman?

BEGGAR: Here, master.

IGWEZU: You sightless ones are known to be gifted with more than human wisdom. You detected from the Kadiye's voice that he was fat . . . Keep still, priest of the swamps; this razor is keen and my hand is unsettled . . . Have I still your attention, bondsman? You have listened to me. It there anything in my voice which tells you what is lacking? Does something in my voice tell you why the bride of less than a season deserts her husband's side?

BEGGAR: I must seek that answer in the voice of the bride.

IGWEZU: That was wisely spoken. You have all the makings of a true bondsman.

MAKURI: You talk strangely, Igwezu. What is running in your head?

IGWEZU: It is only a game of children, father. Only a game of riddles and you have answered yours. So has my bondsman. Now it is the turn of the Kadiye.

KADIYE: I am prepared.

IGWEZU: With you, holy one, my questions must be roundabout. But you will unravel them, because you speak with the voice of gods . . . ?

KADIYE: As I said before, I am ready.

IGWEZU: Who must appease the Serpent of the Swamps?

KADIYE: The Kadiye.

IGWEZU: Who takes the gifts of the people, in order that the beast may be gorged and made sleepy-eyed with the feast of sacrifice.

KADIYE: The Kadiye.

IGWEZU [*His speech is increasing in speed and intensity*.]: On whom does the land depend for the benevolence of the reptile? Tell me that, priest. Answer in one word.

KADIYE: Kadiye.

IGWEZU: Can you see my mask, priest? Is it of this village?

KADIYE: Yes.

IGWEZU: Was the wood grown in this village?

KADIYE: Yes.

IGWEZU: Does it sing with the rest? Cry with the rest? Does it till the swamps with the rest of the tribe?

KADIYE: Yes.

IGWEZU: And so that the Serpent might not vomit at the wrong season and drown the land, so that He might not swallow at the wrong moment and gulp down the unwary traveller, do I not offer my goats to the priest?

KADIYE: Yes.

MAKURI: Igwezu, sometimes the guardians of the air are hard to please ...

IGWEZU: Be quiet, father! ... and did he offer them in turn to the Serpent?

KADIYE: He did.

IGWEZU: Everything which he received, from the grain to the bull?

KADIYE: Everything.

IGWEZU: The goat and the white cockerel which I gave before I left?

KADIYE: Every hair and feather of them.

IGWEZU: And he made it clear—that the offering was from me? That I demanded the protection of the heavens on me and my house, on my father and my mother, on my wife, land and chattels?

KADIYE: All the prayers were repeated.

IGWEZU: And ever since I began to till the soil, did I not give the soil his due? Did I not bring the first of the lentils to the shrine, and pour the first oil upon the altar?

KADIYE: Regularly.

IGWEZU: And when the Kadiye blessed my marriage, and tied the heaven-made knot, did he not promise a long life? Did he not promise children? Did he not promise happiness?

[*Igwezu has shaved off all except a last smear of lather. He remains standing with one hand around the Kadiye's jowl, the other retaining an indifferent hold on the razor, on the other side of his face.*]

KADIYE [*Does not reply this time.*]

IGWEZU [*slowly and disgustedly.*]: Why are you so fat, Kadiye?

[*The drummer stares, hesitates, and runs out. The servant moves nearer the door.*]

MAKURI [*snapping his fingers round his head.*]: May heaven forgive
what has been uttered here tonight. May earth reject the folly,
spoken by my son.

IGWEZU: You lie upon the land, Kadiye, and choke it in the folds
of a serpent.

MAKURI: Son, listen to me . . .

IGWEZU: If I slew the fatted calf, Kadiye, do you think the land
might breathe again? If I slew all the cattle in the land and
sacrificed every measure of goodness, would it make any
difference to our lives, Kadiye? Would it make any
difference to our fates?
[*The servant runs out also.*]

KADIYE [*in a choking voice.*]: Makuri, speak to your son . . .

BEGGAR: Master . . . master . . .
[*Igwezu suddenly shaves off the final smear of lather with a rapid
stroke which makes the Kadiye flinch. Releases him and throws
the razor on the table.
Kadiye scrambles up at once, tearing the cloth from his neck.
Makes for the door.*]

KADIYE [*panting.*]: You shall pay for this . . . I swear I shall make
you pay for this . . . Do you think that you can make an ass
of the Kadiye? . . . Do you think that you can pour your
sacrilege into my ears with impunity?

IGWEZU: Go quickly, Kadiye. [*Sinks into the chair.*] And the next
time that you wish to celebrate the stopping of the rains, do
not choose a barber whose harvest rots beneath the mire.

KADIYE: You will pay, I swear it . . . You will pay for this.
[*Flings off the sheet and goes out.*]

MAKURI: Son, what have you done?

IGWEZU: I know that the floods can come again. That the swamp
will continue to laugh at our endeavours. I know that we can
feed the Serpent of the Swamp and kiss the Kadiye's feet—but
the vapours will still rise and corrupt the tassels of the corn.

MAKURI: I must go after him or he'll stir up the village against us.
[*Stops at the door.*] This is your home, Igwezu, and I would not
drive you from it for all the world. But it might be best for
you if you went back to the city until this is forgotten.
[*Exit.*]
[*Pause.*]

BEGGAR [*softly.*]: Master . . . master . . . slayer of serpents.

IGWEZU [*in a tired voice.*]: I wonder what drove me on.

BEGGAR: What, master?

IGWEZU: Do you think that my only strength was that of despair?
Or was there something of a desire to prove myself?
[*The Beggar remains silent.*]

IGWEZU: Your fat friend is gone. But will he stay away?

BEGGAR: I think that the old man was right. You should go back
to the city.

IGWEZU: Is it of any earthly use to change one slough for another?

BEGGAR: I will come and keep you company. If necessary, I will
beg for you.

IGWEZU [*stares at him, slowly shaking his head.*]: What manner of
man are you? How have I deserved so much of you that you
would beg for me?

BEGGAR: I made myself your bondsman. This means that I must
share your hardships.

IGWEZU: I am too tired to see it all. I think we all ought to go to
bed. Have they given you a place to sleep?

BEGGAR: Will I return with you to the city?

IGWEZU: No, friend. You like this soil. You love to scoop it up
in your hands. You dream of cleaving ridges under the flood
and making little balls of mud in which wrap your seeds.
Is that not so?

BEGGAR: Yes, master.

IGWEZU: And you have faith, have you not? Do you not still
believe in what you sow? That it will sprout and see the
harvest sun?

BEGGAR: It must. In my wanderings, I think that I have grown a
healer's hand.

IGWEZU: Then stay. Stay here and take care of the farm. I must
go away.
[*He crosses the room as if to go into the house.
Hesitates at the door, then turns round and walks slowly away.*]
Tell my people I could not stop to say good-bye.

BEGGAR: You are not going now, master?

IGWEZU: I must not be here when the people call for blood.

BEGGAR: But the water is high. You should wait until the floods
subside.

IGWEZU: No I want to paddle as I go.

BEGGAR: Is it not night? Is it not dark outside?

IGWEZU: It is.

BEGGAR: Then I shall come with you. I know the dark. Let me come with you over the swamp, as far as the river's edge.

IGWEZU: Two blind men groping in the dark? No.

BEGGAR: And how would you cross the river? There is no ferryman to be found after dark.

IGWEZU [*still looking out of the window. Pauses. He walks away, picks up the old man's work in absent movements. He drops it and looks up.*]:
Only the children and the old stay here, bondsman. Only the innocent and the dotards. [*Walks slowly off.*]

BEGGAR: But you will return, master?

[*Igwezu checks briefly, but does not stop.*]

BEGGAR: The swallows find their nest again when the cold is over. Even the bats desert dark holes in the trees and flap wet leaves with wings of leather. There were wings everywhere as I wiped my feet against your threshold. I heard the cricket scratch himself beneath the armpit as the old man said to me . . .
[*The door swings to. The Beggar sighs, gestures a blessing and says.*]
I shall be here to give account.
[*The oil lamps go out slowly and completely. The Beggar remains on the same spot, the moonlight falling on him through the window.*]

THE END

THE
STRONG BREED

Characters

EMAN   a stranger

SUNMA   Jaguna's daughter

IFADA   an idiot

A GIRL

JAGUNA

OROGE

Attendant Stalwarts.   The villagers

from Eman's past—

OLD MAN   his father

OMAE   his betrothed

TUTOR

PRIEST

Attendants.   The villagers

The scenes are described briefly, but very often a darkened stage with lit areas will not only suffice but is necessary. Except for the one indicated place, there can be no break in the action. A distracting scene-change would be ruinous.

A mud house, with space in front of it. Eman, in light buba and trousers stands at the window, looking out. Inside, Sunma is clearing the table of what looks like a modest clinic, putting the things away in a cupboard. Another rough table in the room is piled with exercise books, two or three worn text-books, etc. Sunma appears agitated. Outside, just below the window crouches Ifada. He looks up with a shy smile from time to time, waiting for Eman to notice him.

SUNMA [*hesitant.*]: You will have to make up your mind soon Eman. The lorry leaves very shortly.
 [*As Eman does not answer, Sunma continues her work, more nervously. Two villagers, obvious travellers, pass hurriedly in front of the house, the man has a small raffia sack, the woman a cloth-covered basket, the man enters first, turns and urges the woman who is just emerging to hurry.*]

SUNMA [*seeing them, her tone is more intense.*]: Eman, are we going or aren't we? You will leave it till too late.

EMAN [*quietly.*]: There is still time—if you want to go.

SUNMA: If I want to go . . . and you?
 [*Eman makes no reply.*]

SUNMA [*bitterly.*]: You don't really want to leave here. You never want to go away—even for a minute.
 [*Ifada continues his antics. Eman eventually pats him on the head and the boy grins happily. Leaps up suddenly and returns with a basket of oranges which he offers to Eman.*]

EMAN: My gift for today's festival enh?
 [*Ifada nods, grinning.*]

EMAN: They look ripe—that's a change.

SUNMA [*she has gone inside the room. Looks round the door.*]: Did you call me?

EMAN: No. [*She goes back.*] And what will you do tonight Ifada? Will you take part in the dancing? Or perhaps you will mount your own masquerade?
 [*Ifada shakes his head, regretfully.*]

EMAN: You won't? So you haven't any? But you would like to own one.

[*Ifada nods eagerly.*]

EMAN: Then why don't you make your own?

[*Ifada stares, puzzled by this idea.*]

EMAN: Sunma will let you have some cloth you know. And bits of wool. . .

SUNMA [*coming out.*]: Who are you talking to Eman?

EMAN: Ifada. I am trying to persuade him to join the young maskers.

SUNMA [*losing control.*]: What does he want here? Why is he hanging round us?

EMAN [*amazed.*]: What . . . ? I said Ifada, Ifada.

SUNMA: Just tell him to go away. Let him go and play somewhere else!

EMAN: What is this? Hasn't he always played here?

SUNMA: I don't want him here. [*Rushes to the window.*] Get away idiot. Don't bring your foolish face here any more, do you hear? Go on, go away from here . . .

EMAN [*restraining her.*]: Control yourself Sunma. What on earth has got into you?

[*Ifada, hurt and bewildered, backs slowly away.*]

SUNMA: He comes crawling round here like some horrible insect. I never want to lay my eyes on him again.

EMAN: I don't understand. It *is* Ifada you know. Ifada! The unfortunate one who runs errands for you and doesn't hurt a soul.

SUNMA: I cannot bear the sight of him.

EMAN: You can't do what? It can't be two days since he last fetched water for you.

SUNMA: What else can he do except that? He is useless. Just because we have been kind to him . . . Others would have put him in an asylum.

EMAN: You are not making sense. He is not a madman, he is just a little more unlucky than other children. [*Looks keenly at her.*] But what is the matter?

SUNMA: It's nothing. I only wish we had sent him off to one of those places for creatures like him.

EMAN: He is quite happy here. He doesn't bother anyone and he makes himself useful.

SUNMA: Useful! Is that one of any use to anybody? Boys of his age are already earning a living but all he can do is hang around and drool at the mouth.

EMAN: But he does work. You know he does a lot for you.

SUNMA: Does he? And what about the farm you started for him! Does he ever work on it? Or have you forgotten that it was really for Ifada you cleared that bush. Now you have to go and work it yourself. You spend all your time on it and you have no room for anything else.

EMAN: That wasn't his fault. I should first have asked him if he was fond of farming.

SUNMA: Oh, so he can choose? As if he shouldn't be thankful for being allowed to live.

EMAN: Sunma!

SUNMA: He does not like farming but he knows how to feast his dumb mouth on the fruits.

EMAN: But I want him to. I encourage him.

SUNMA: Well keep him. I don't want to see him any more.

EMAN [*after some moments.*]: But why? You cannot be telling all the truth. What has he done?

SUNMA: The sight of him fills me with revulsion.

EMAN [*goes to her and holds her.*]: What really is it?
[*Sunma avoids his eyes.*] It is almost as if you are forcing yourself to hate him. Why?

SUNMA: That is not true. Why should I?

EMAN: Then what is the secret? You've even played with him before.

SUNMA: I have always merely tolerated him. But I cannot any more. Suddenly my disgust won't take him any more. Perhaps . . . perhaps it is the new year. Yes, yes, it must be the new year.

EMAN: I don't believe that.

SUNMA: It must be. I am a woman, and these things matter. I don't want a mis-shape near me. Surely for one day in the year, I may demand some wholesomeness.

EMAN: I do not understand you.
[*Sunma is silent.*]
It was cruel of you. And to Ifada who is so helpless and alone. We are the only friends he has.

SUNMA: No, just you. I have told you, with me it has always been only an act of kindness. And now I haven't any pity left for him.

EMAN: No. He is not a wholesome being.

[*He turns back to looking through the window.*]

SUNMA [*half-pleading.*]: Ifada can rouse your pity. And yet if anything, I need more kindness from you. Every time my weakness betrays me, you close your mind against me . . . Eman . . . Eman . . .

[*A Girl comes in view, dragging an effigy by a rope attached to one of its legs. She stands for a while gazing at Eman. Ifada, who has crept back shyly to his accustomed position, becomes somewhat excited when he sees the effigy. The girl is unsmiling. She possesses in fact, a kind of inscrutability which does not make her hard but is unsettling.*]

GIRL: Is the teacher in?

EMAN [*smiling.*]: No.

GIRL: Where is he gone?

EMAN: I don't really know. Shall I ask?

GIRL: Yes, do.

EMAN [*turning slightly.*]: Sunma, a girl outside wants to know . . .

[*Sunma turns away, goes into the inside room.*]

EMAN: Oh. [*Returns to the girl, but his slight gaiety is lost.*] There is no one at home who can tell me.

GIRL: Why are you not in?

EMAN: I don't really know. Maybe I went somewhere.

GIRL: All right. I will wait until you get back.

[*She pulls the effigy to her, sits down.*]

EMAN [*slowly regaining his amusement.*]: So you are all ready for the new year.

GIRL [*without turning round.*]: I am not going to the festival.

EMAN: Then why have you got that?

GIRL: Do you mean my carrier? I am unwell you know. My mother says it will take away my sickness with the old year.

EMAN: Won't you share the carrier with your playmates?

GIRL: Oh, no. Don't you know I play alone? The other children won't come near me. Their mothers would beat them.

EMAN: But I have never seen you here. Why don't you come to the clinic?

GIRL: My mother said No.

[*Gets up, begins to move off.*]

EMAN: You are not going away?

GIRL: I must not stay talking to you. If my mother caught me . . .

EMAN: All right, tell me what you want before you go.

GIRL [*stops. For some moments she remains silent.*]: I must have some clothes for my carrier.

EMAN: Is that all? You wait a moment.

[*Sunma comes out as he takes down a buba from the wall. She goes to the window and glares almost with hatred at the girl. The girl retreats hastily, still impassive.*]

By the way Sunma, do you know who that girl is?

SUNMA: I hope you don't really mean to give her that.

EMAN: Why not? I hardly ever use it.

SUNMA: Just the same don't give it to her. She is not a child. She is as evil as the rest of them.

EMAN: What has got into you today?

SUNMA: All right, all right. Do what you wish.

[*She withdraws. Baffled, Eman returns to the window.*]

EMAN: Here . . . will this do? Come and look at it.

GIRL: Throw it.

EMAN: What is the matter? I am not going to eat you.

GIRL: No one lets me come near them.

EMAN: But I am not afraid of catching your disease.

GIRL: Throw it.

[*Eman shrugs and tosses the buba. She takes it without a word and slips it on the effigy, completely absorbed in the task. Eman watches for a while, then joins Sunma in the inner room.*]

GIRL: [*after a long, cool survey of Ifada.*]: You have a head like a spider's egg, and your mouth dribbles like a roof. But there is no one else. Would you like to play?

[*Ifada nods eagerly, quite excited.*]

GIRL: You will have to get a stick.

[*Ifada rushes around, finds a big stick and whirls it aloft, bearing down on the carrier.*]

GIRL: Wait. I don't want you to spoil it. If it gets torn I shall drive you away. Now, let me see how you are going to beat it.

[*Ifada hits it gently.*]

GIRL: You may hit harder than that. As long as there is something left to hang at the end.

[*She appraises him up and down.*]

You are not very tall . . . will you be able to hang it from a tree?

[*Ifada nods, grinning happily.*]

GIRL: You will hang it up and I will set fire to it. [*Then, with surprising venom.*] But just because you are helping me, don't think it is going to cure you. I am the one who will get well at midnight, do you understand? It is my carrier and it is for me alone.

[*She pulls at the rope to make sure that it is well attached to the leg.*]

Well don't stand there drooling. Let's go.

[*She begins to walk off, dragging the effigy in the dust. Ifada remains where he is for some moments, seemingly puzzled. Then his face breaks into a large grin and he leaps after the procession, belabouring the effigy with all his strength. The stage remains empty for some moments. Then the horn of a lorry is sounded and Sunma rushes out. The hooting continues for some time with a rhythmic pattern. Eman comes out.*]

EMAN: I am going to the village . . . I shan't be back before nightfall.

SUNMA [*blankly.*]: Yes.

EMAN [*hesitates.*]: Well what do you want me to do?

SUNMA: The lorry was hooting just now.

EMAN: I didn't hear it.

SUNMA: It will leave in a few minutes. And you did promise we could go away.

EMAN: I promised nothing. Will you go home by yourself or shall I come back for you?

SUNMA: You don't even want me here?

EMAN: But you have to go home haven't you?

SUNMA: I had hoped we would watch the new year together—in some other place.

EMAN: Why do you continue to distress yourself?

SUNMA: Because you will not listen to me. Why do you continue to stay where nobody wants you?

EMAN: That is not true.

SUNMA: It is. You are wasting your life on people who really want you out of their way.

EMAN: You don't know what you are saying.

SUNMA: You think they love you? Do you think they care at all for what you—or I—do for them?

EMAN: *Them*? These are your own people. Sometimes you talk as if you were a stranger too.

SUNMA: I wonder if I really sprang from here. I know they are
   evil and I am not. From the oldest to the smallest child, they
   are nourished in evil and unwholesomeness in which I have no
   part.

EMAN: You knew this when you returned?

SUNMA: You reproach me then for trying at all?

EMAN: I reproach you with nothing? But you must leave me out
   of your plans. I can have no part in them.

SUNMA [nearly pleading.]: Once I could have run away. I would have
   gone and never looked back.

EMAN: I cannot listen when you talk like that.

SUNMA: I swear to you, I do not mind what happens afterwards.
   But you must help me tear myself away from here. I can no
   longer do it by myself ... It is only a little thing. And we have
   worked so hard this past year ... surely we can go away for a
   week ... even a few days would be enough.

EMAN: I have told you Sunma...

SUNMA [desperately.]: Two days Eman. Only two days.

EMAN [distressed.]: But I tell you I have no wish to go.

SUNMA [suddenly angry.]: Are you so afraid then?

EMAN: Me? Afraid of what?

SUNMA: You think you will not want to come back.

EMAN [pitying.]: You cannot dare me that way.

SUNMA: Then why won't you leave here, even for an hour? If
   you are so sure that your life is settled here, why are you afraid
   to do this thing for me? What is so wrong that you will not
   go into the next town for a day or two?

EMAN: I don't want to. I do not have to persuade you, or myself
   about anything. I simply have no desire to go away.

SUNMA [his quiet confidence appears to incense her.]: You are afraid.
   You accuse me of losing my sense of mission, but you are afraid
   to put yours to the test.

EMAN: You are wrong Sunma. I have no sense of mission. But I
   have found peace here and I am content with that.

SUNMA: I haven't. For a while I thought that too, but I found there
   could be no peace in the midst of so much cruelty. Eman,
   tonight at least, the last night of the old year ...

EMAN: No Sunma. I find this too distressing; you should go home
   now.

SUNMA: It is the time for making changes in one's life Eman. Let's breathe in the new year away from here.

EMAN: You are hurting yourself.

SUNMA: Tonight. Only tonight. We will come back tomorrow, as early as you like. But let us go away for this one night. Don't let another year break on me in this place ... you don't know how important it is to me, but I will tell you, I will tell you on the way ... but we must not be here today, Eman, do this one thing for me.

EMAN [*sadly*.]: I cannot.

SUNMA [*suddenly calm*.]: I was a fool to think it would be otherwise. The whole village may use you as they will but for me there is nothing. Sometimes I think you believe that doing anything for me makes you unfaithful to some part of your life. If it was a woman then I pity her for what she must have suffered.
[*Eman winces and hardens slowly. Sunma notices nothing.*]
Keeping faith with so much is slowly making you inhuman.
[*Seeing the change in Eman.*] Eman. Eman. What is it?
[*As she goes towards him, Eman goes into the house.*]

SUNMA [*apprehensive, follows him*.]: What did I say? Eman. forgive me, forgive me please.
[*Eman remains facing into the slow darkness of the room. Sunma, distressed, cannot decide what to do.*]
I swear I didn't know ... I would not have said it for all the world.
[*A lorry is heard taking off somewhere nearby. The sound comes up and slowly fades away into the distance. Sunma starts visibly, goes slowly to the window.*]

SUNMA [*as the sound dies off, to herself.*]: What happens now?

EMAN [*joining her at the window.*]: What did you say?

SUNMA: Nothing.

EMAN: Was that not the lorry going off?

SUNMA: It was.

EMAN: I am sorry I couldn't help you.
[*Sunma, about to speak, changes her mind.*]

EMAN: I think you ought to go home now.

SUNMA: No, don't send me away. It's the least you can do for me. Let me stay here until all the noise is over.

EMAN: But are you not needed at home? You have a part in the festival.

SUNMA: I have renounced it; I am Jaguna's eldest daughter only in name.

EMAN: Renouncing one's self is not so easy—surely you know that.

SUNMA: I don't want to talk about it. Will you at least let us be together tonight?

EMAN: But . . .

SUNMA: Unless you are afraid my father will accuse you of harbouring me.

EMAN: All right, we will go out together.

SUNMA: Go out? I want us to stay here.

EMAN: When there is so much going on outside?

SUNMA: Some day you will wish that you went away when I tried to make you.

EMAN: Are we going back to that?

SUNMA: No. I promise you I will not recall it again. But you must know that it was also for your sake that I tried to get us away.

EMAN: For me? How?

SUNMA: By yourself you can do nothing here. Have you not noticed how tightly we shut out strangers? Even if you lived here for a lifetime, you would remain a stranger.

EMAN: Perhaps that is what I like. There is peace in being a stranger.

SUNMA: For a while perhaps. But they would reject you in the end. I tell you it is only I who stand between you and contempt. And because of this you have earned their hatred. I don't know why I say this now, except that somehow, I feel that it no longer matters. It is only I who have stood between you and much humiliation.

EMAN: Think carefully before you say any more. I am incapable of feeling indebted to you. This will make no difference at all.

SUNMA: I ask for nothing. But you must know it all the same. It is true I hadn't the strength to go by myself. And I must confess this now, if you had come with me, I would have done everything to keep you from returning.

EMAN: I know that.

SUNMA: You see, I bare myself to you. For days I had thought it over, this was to be a new beginning for us. And I placed my fate wholly in your hands. Now the thought will not leave me, I have a feeling which will not be shaken off, that in some way, you have tonight totally destroyed my life.

EMAN: You are depressed, you don't know what you are saying.

SUNMA: Don't think I am accusing you. I say all this only because I cannot help it.

EMAN: We must not remain shut up here. Let us go and be part of the living.

SUNMA: No. Leave them alone.

EMAN: Surely you don't want to stay indoors when the whole town is alive with rejoicing.

SUNMA: Rejoicing! Is that what it seems to you? No, let us remain here. Whatever happens I must not go out until all this is over.

[*There is silence. It has grown much darker.*]

EMAN: I shall light the lamp.

SUNMA [*eager to do something.*]: No, let me do it.

[*She goes into the inner room.*

Eman paces the room, stops by a shelf and toys with the seeds in an 'ayo' board, takes down the whole board and places it on a table, playing by himself.

The girl is now seen coming back, still dragging her 'carrier'. Ifada brings up the rear as before. As he comes round the corner of the house two men emerge from the shadows. A sack is thrown over Ifada's head, the rope is pulled tight rendering him instantly helpless. The girl has reached the front of the house before she turns round at the sound of scuffle. She is in time to see Ifada thrown over the shoulders and borne away. Her face betraying no emotion at all, the girl backs slowly away, turns and flees, leaving the 'carrier' behind. Sunma enters, carrying two kerosene lamps. She hangs one up from the wall.]

EMAN: One is enough.

SUNMA: I want to leave one outside.

[*She goes out, hangs the lamp from a nail just above the door. As she turns she sees the effigy and gasps. Eman rushes out.*]

EMAN: What is it? Oh, is that what frightened you?

SUNMA: I thought . . . I didn't really see it properly.

[*Eman goes towards the object, stoops to pick it up.*]

EMAN: It must belong to that sick girl.

SUNMA: Don't touch it.

EMAN: Let's keep it for her.

SUNMA: Leave it alone. Don't touch it Eman.

EMAN [*shrugs and goes back.*]: You are very nervous.

SUNMA: Lets go in.

EMAN: Wait. [*He detains her by the door, under the lamp.*] I know there is something more than you've told me. What are you afraid of tonight?

SUNMA: I was only scared by that thing. There is nothing else.

EMAN: I am not blind Sunma. It is true I would not run away when you wanted me to, but that doesn't mean I do not feel things. What does tonight really mean that it makes you so helpless?

SUNMA: It is only a mood. And your indifference to me ... let's go in.

[*Eman moves aside and she enters; he remains there for a moment and then follows.*

She fiddles with the lamp, looks vaguely round the room, then goes and shuts the door, bolting it. When she turns, it is to meet Eman's eyes, questioning.]

SUNMA: There is a cold wind coming in.

[*Eman keeps his gaze on her.*]

SUNMA: It *was* getting cold.

[*She moves guiltily to the table and stands by the 'ayo' board, rearranging the seeds. Eman remains where he is a few moments, then brings a stool and sits opposite her. She sits down also and they begin to play in silence.*]

SUNMA: What brought you here at all, Eman? And what makes you stay?

[*There is another silence.*]

SUNMA: I am not trying to share your life. I know you too well by now. But at least we have worked together since you came. Is there nothing at all I deserve to know?

EMAN: Let me continue a stranger—especially to you. Those who have much to give fulfil themselves only in total loneliness.

SUNMA: Then there is no love in what you do.

EMAN: There is. Love comes to me more easily with strangers.

SUNMA: That is unnatural.

EMAN: Not for me. I know I find consummation only when I have spent myself for a total stranger.

SUNMA: It seems unnatural to me. But then I am a woman. I have a woman's longings and weaknesses. And the ties of blood are very strong in me.

EMAN [*smiling.*]: You think I have cut loose from all these—ties of blood.

SUNMA: Sometimes you are so inhuman.

EMAN: I don't know what that means. But I am very much my father's son.

[*They play in silence. Suddenly Eman pauses listening.*]

EMAN: Did you hear that?

SUNMA [*quickly.*]: I heard nothing . . . it's your turn.

EMAN: Perhaps some of the mummers are coming this way.

[*Eman about to play, leaps up suddenly.*]

SUNMA: What is it? Don't you want to play any more?

[*Eman moves to the door.*]

SUNMA: No. Don't go out Eman.

EMAN: If it's the dancers I want to ask them to stay. At least we won't have to miss everything.

SUNMA: No, no. Don't open the door. Let us keep out everyone tonight.

[*A terrified and disordered figure bursts suddenly round the corner, past the window and begins hammering at the door. It is Ifada. Desperate with terror, he pounds madly at the door, dumb-moaning all the while.*]

EMAN: Isn't that Ifada?

SUNMA: They are only fooling about. Don't pay any attention.

EMAN [*looks round the window.*]: That is Ifada. [*Begins to unbolt the door.*]

SUNMA [*pulling at his hands.*]: It is only a trick they are playing on you. Don't take any notice Eman.

EMAN: What are you saying? The boy is out of his senses with fear.

SUNMA: No, no. Don't interfere Eman. For God's sake don't interfere.

EMAN: Do you know something of this then?

SUNMA: You are a stranger here Eman. Just leave us alone and go your own way. There is nothing you can do.

EMAN [*he tries to push her out of the way but she clings fiercely to him.*]: Have you gone mad? I tell you the boy must come in.

SUNMA: Why won't you listen to me Eman? I tell you it's none of your business. For your own sake do as I say.

[*Eman pushes her off, unbolts the door. Ifada rushes in, clasps Eman round the knees, dumb-moaning against his legs.*]

EMAN [*manages to re-bolt the door.*]: What is it Ifada? What is the matter?

[*Shouts and voices are heard coming nearer the house.*]

SUNMA: Before it's too late, let him go. For once Eman, believe what I tell you. Don't harbour him or you will regret it all your life.

[*Eman tries to calm Ifada who becomes more and more abject as the outside voices get nearer.*]

EMAN: What have they done to him? At least tell me that. What is going on Sunma?

SUNMA [*with sudden venom.*]: Monster! Could you not take yourself somewhere else?

EMAN: Stop talking like that.

SUNMA: He could have run into the bush couldn't he? Toad! Why must he follow us with his own disasters!

VOICES OUTSIDE: It's here . . . Round the back . . . Spread, spread . . . this way . . . no, head him off . . . use the bush path and head him off . . . get some more lights . . .

[*Eman listens. Lifts Ifada bodily and carries him into the inner room. Returns at once, shutting the door behind him.*]

SUNMA [*slumps into a chair, resigned.*]: You always follow your own way.

JAGUNA [*comes round the corner followed by Oroge and three men, one bearing a torch.*]: I knew he would come here.

OROGE: I hope our friend won't make trouble.

JAGUNA: He had better not. You, recall all the men and tell them to surround the house.

OROGE: But he may not be in the house after all.

JAGUNA: I know he is here . . . [*to the men.*] . . . go on, do as I say.

[*He bangs on the door.*]

Teacher, open your door . . . you two stay by the door. If I need you I will call you.

[*Eman opens the door.*]

JAGUNA [*speaks as he enters.*]: We know he is here.

EMAN: Who?

JAGUNA: Don't let us waste time. We are grown men, teacher. You understand me and I understand you. But we must take back the boy.

EMAN: This is my house.

JAGUNA: Daughter, you'd better tell your friend. I don't think he quite knows our ways. Tell him why he must give up the boy.

SUNMA: Father, I . . .

JAGUNA: Are you going to tell him or aren't you?

SUNMA: Father, I beg you, leave us alone tonight . . .

JAGUNA: I thought you might be a hindrance. Go home then if you will not use your sense.

SUNMA: But there are other ways . . .

JAGUNA [turning to the men.]: See that she gets home. I no longer trust her. If she gives trouble carry her. And see that the women stay with her until all this is over.

[Sunma departs, accompanied by one of the men.]

JAGUNA: Now teacher . . .

OROGE [restrains him.]: You see, Mister Eman, it is like this. Right now, nobody knows that Ifada has taken refuge here. No one except us and our men—and they know how to keep their mouths shut. We don't want to have to burn down the house you see, but if the word gets around, we would have no choice.

JAGUNA: In fact, it may be too late already. A carrier should end up in the bush, not in a house. Anyone who doesn't guard his door when the carrier goes by has himself to blame. A contaminated house should be burnt down.

OROGE: But we are willing to let it pass. Only, you must bring him out quickly.

EMAN: All right. But at least you will let me ask you something.

JAGUNA: What is there to ask? Don't you understand what we have told you?

EMAN: Yes. But why did you pick on a helpless boy. Obviously he is not willing.

JAGUNA: What is the man talking about? Ifada is a godsend. Does he have to be willing?

EMAN: In my home, we believe that a man should be willing.

OROGE: Mister Eman, I don't think you quite understand. This is not a simple matter at all. I don't know what you do, but here, it is not a cheap task for anybody. No one in his senses would do such a job. Why do you think we give refuge to idiots like him? We don't know where he came from. One morning, he is simply there, just like that. From nowhere at all. You see, there is a purpose in that.

JAGUNA: We only waste time.

OROGE: Jaguna, be patient. After all, the man has been with us

for some time now and deserves to know. The evil of the old
year is no light thing to load on any man's head.

EMAN: I know something about that.

OROGE: You do? [*Turns to Jaguna who snorts impatiently.*] You see
I told you so didn't I? From the moment you came I saw you
were one of the knowing ones.

JAGUNA: Then let him behave like a man and give back the boy.

EMAN: It is you who are not behaving like men.

JAGUNA [*advances aggressively.*]: That is a quick mouth you have . . .

OROGE: Patience Jaguna . . . if you want the new year to cushion
the land there must be no deeds of anger. What did you mean
my friend?

EMAN: It is a simple thing. A village which cannot produce its own
carrier contains no men.

JAGUNA: Enough. Let there be no more talk or this business will
be ruined by some rashness. You . . . come inside. Bring the
boy out, he must be in the room there.

EMAN: Wait.

[*The men hesitate.*]

JAGUNA [*hitting the nearer one and propelling him forward.*]: Go on.
Have you changed masters now that you listen to what he says?

OROGE [*sadly.*]: I am sorry you would not understand Mister
Eman. But you ought to know that no carrier may return to
the village. If he does, the people will stone him to death. It has
happened before. Surely it is too much to ask a man to give up
his own soil.

EMAN: I know others who have done more.

[*Ifada is brought out, abjectly dumb-moaning.*]

EMAN: You can see him with your own eyes. Does it really have
meaning to use one as unwilling as that.

OROGE [*smiling.*]: He shall be willing. Not only willing but actually
joyous. I am the one who prepares them all, and I have
seen worse. This one escaped before I began to prepare him for
the event. But you will see him later tonight, the most joyous
creature in the festival. Then perhaps you will understand.

EMAN: Then it is only a deceit. Do you believe the spirit of a new
year is so easily fooled?

JAGUNA: Take him out. [*The men carry out Ifada.*] You see, it is so
easy to talk. You say there are no men in this village because

they cannot provide a willing carrier. And yet I heard Oroge
tell you we only use strangers. There is only one other stranger
in the village, but I have not heard him offer himself [*spits.*]
It is so easy to talk is it not?
[*He turns his back on him.*
*They go off, taking Ifada with them, limp and silent. The only sign
of life is that he strains his neck to keep his eyes on Eman till the
very moment that he disappears from sight. Eman remains where
they left him, staring after the group.*]

[*A black-out lasting no more than a minute. The lights come up
slowly and Ifada is seen returning to the house. He stops at the
window and looks in. Seeing no one, he bangs on the sill. Appears
surprised that there is no response. He slithers down on his favourite
spot, then sees the effigy still lying where the girl had dropped it
in her flight. After some hesitation, he goes towards it, begins to
strip it of the clothing. Just then the girl comes in.*]

GIRL: Hey, leave that alone. You know it's mine.

[*Ifada pauses, then speeds up his action.*]

GIRL: I said it is mine. Leave it where you found it.

[*She rushes at him and begins to struggle for possession of the carrier.*]

GIRL: Thief! Thief! Let it go, it is mine. Let it go. You animal,
just because I let you play with it. Idiot! Idiot!

[*The struggle becomes quite violent. The girl is hanging to the effigy
and Ifada lifts her with it, flinging her all about. The girl hangs on
grimly.*]

GIRL: You are spoiling it . . . why don't you get your own?
Thief! Let it go you thief!

[*Sunma comes in walking very fast, throwing apprehensive glances
over her shoulder. Seeing the two children, she becomes immediately
angry. Advances on them.*]

SUNMA: So you've made this place your playground. Get away
you untrained pigs. Get out of here.

[*Ifada flees at once, the girl retreats also, retaining possession of the
'carrier'.*
*Sunma goes to the door. She has her hand on the door when the
significance of Ifada's presence strikes her for the first time. She
stands rooted to the spot, then turns slowly round.*]

SUNMA: Ifada! What are you doing here?

[*Ifada is bewildered. Sunma turns suddenly and rushes into the house, flying into the inner room and out again.*]

Eman! Eman! Eman!

[*She rushes outside.*]

Where did he go? Where did they take him?

[*Ifada distressed, points. Sunma seizes him by the arm, drags him off.*]

Take me there at once. God help you if we are too late. You loathsome thing, if you have let him suffer. . .

[*Her voice fades into other shouts, running footsteps, banged tins, bells, dogs, etc., rising in volume.*]

[*It is a narrow passage-way between two mud-houses. At the far end one man after another is seen running across the entry, the noise dying off gradually.*

About half-way down the passage, Eman is crouching against the wall, tense with apprehension. As the noise dies off, he seems to relax, but the alert hunted look is still in his eyes which are ringed in a reddish colour. The rest of his body has been whitened with a floury substance. He is naked down to the waist, wears a baggy pair of trousers, calf-length, and around both feet are bangles.]

EMAN: I will simply stay here till dawn. I have done enough.

[*A window is thrown open and a woman empties some slop from a pail. With a startled cry Eman leaps aside to avoid it and the woman puts out her head.*]

WOMAN: Oh, my head. What have I done! Forgive me neighbour. . . . . Eh, it's the carrier!

[*Very rapidly she clears her throat and spits on him, flings the pail at him and runs off, shouting.*]

He's here. The carrier is hiding in the passage. Quickly, I have found the carrier!

[*The cry is taken up and Eman flees down the passage. Shortly afterwards his pursuers come pouring down the passage in full cry. After the last of them come Jaguna and Oroge.*]

OROGE: Wait, wait. I cannot go so fast.

JAGUNA: We will rest a little then. We can do nothing anyway.

OROGE: If only he had let me prepare him.

JAGUNA: They are the ones who break first, these fools who think they were born to carry suffering like a hat. What are we to do now?

OROGE: When they catch him I must prepare him.

JAGUNA: He? It will be impossible now. There can be no joy left in that one.

OROGE: Still, it took him by surprise. He was not expecting what he met.

JAGUNA: Why then did he refuse to listen? Did he think he was coming to sit down to a feast. He had not even gone through one compound before he bolted. Did he think he was taken round the people to be blessed? A woman, that is all he is.

OROGE: No, no. He took the beating well enough. I think he is the kind who would let himself be beaten from night till dawn and not utter a sound. He would let himself be stoned until he dropped dead.

JAGUNA: Then what made him run like a coward?

OROGE: I don't know. I don't really know. It is a night of curses Jaguna. It is not many unprepared minds will remain unhinged under the load.

JAGUNA: We must find him. It is a poor beginning for a year when our own curses remain hovering over our homes because the carrier refused to take them.

[*They go. The scene changes. Eman is crouching beside some shrubs, torn and bleeding.*]

EMAN: They are even guarding my house ... as if I would go there, but I need water ... they could at least grant me that ... I can be thirsty too ... [*he pricks his ears.*] ... there must be a stream nearby ... [*as he looks round him, his eyes widen at a scene he encounters.*]

[*An old man, short and vigorous looking is seated on a stool. He also is wearing calf-length baggy trousers, white. On his head, a white cap. An attendant is engaged in rubbing his body with oil. Round his eyes, two white rings have already been marked.*]

OLD MAN: Have they prepared the boat?

ATTENDANT: They are making the last sacrifice.

OLD MAN: Good. Did you send for my son?

ATTENDANT: He's on his way.

OLD MAN: I have never met the carrying of the boat with such a heavy heart. I hope nothing comes of it.

ATTENDANT: The gods will not desert us on that account.

OLD MAN: A man should be at his strongest when he takes the boat my friend. To be weighed down inside and out is not a wise thing. I hope when the moment comes I shall have found my strength.

[*Enter Eman, a wrapper round his waist and a 'danski'*[1] *over it.*]

OLD MAN: I meant to wait until after my journey to the river, but my mind is so burdened with my own grief and yours I could not delay it. You know I must have all my strength. But I sit here, feeling it all eaten slowly away by my unspoken grief. It helps to say it out. It even helps to cry sometimes.

[*He signals to the attendant to leave them.*]

Come nearer ... we will never meet again son. Not on this side of the flesh. What I do not know is whether you will return to take my place.

EMAN: I will never come back.

OLD MAN: Do you know what you are saying? Ours is a strong breed my son. It is only a strong breed that can take this boat to the river year after year and wax stronger on it. I have taken down each year's evils for over twenty years. I hoped you would follow me.

EMAN: My life here died with Omae.

OLD MAN: Omae died giving birth to your child and you think the world is ended. Eman, my pain did not begin when Omae died. Since you sent her to stay with me son, I lived with the burden of knowing that this child would die bearing your son.

EMAN: Father ...

OLD MAN: Don't you know it was the same with you? And me? No woman survives the bearing of the strong ones. Son, it is not the mouth of the boaster that says be belongs to the strong breed. It is the tongue that is red with pain and black with sorrow. Twelve years you were away my son, and for those twelve years I knew the love of an old man for his daughter and the pain of a man helplessly awaiting his loss.

EMAN: I wish I had stayed away. I wish I never came back to meet her.

OLD MAN: It had to be. But you know now what slowly ate away my strength. I awaited your return with love and fear. Forgive me then if I say that your grief is light. It will pass. This grief may drive you now from home. But you must return.

1. A brief Yoruba attire.

EMAN: You do not understand. It is not grief alone.

OLD MAN: What is it then? Tell me, I can still learn.

EMAN: I was away twelve years. I changed much in that time.

OLD MAN: I am listening.

EMAN: I am unfitted for your work father. I wish to say no more. But I am totally unfitted for your call.

OLD MAN: It is only time you need son. Stay longer and you will answer the urge of your blood.

EMAN: That I stayed at all was because of Omae. I did not expect to find her waiting. I would have taken her away, but hard as you claim to be, it would have killed you. And I was a tired man. I needed peace. Because Omae was peace, I stayed. Now nothing holds me here.

OLD MAN: Other men would rot and die doing this task year after year. It is strong medicine which only we can take. Our blood is strong like no other. Anything you do in life must be less than this, son.

EMAN: That is not true father.

OLD MAN: I tell you it is true. Your own blood will betray you son, because you cannot hold it back. If you make it do less than this, it will rush to your head and burst it open. I say what I know my son.

EMAN: There are other tasks in life father. This one is not for me. There are even greater things you know nothing of.

OLD MAN: I am very sad. You only go to give to others what rightly belongs to us. You will use your strength among thieves. They are thieves because they take what is ours, they have no claim of blood to it. They will even lack the knowledge to use it wisely. Truth is my companion at this moment my son. I know everything I say will surely bring the sadness of truth.

EMAN: I am going father.

OLD MAN: Call my attendant. And be with me in your strength for this last journey. A-ah, did you hear that? It came out without my knowing it; this is indeed my last journey. But I am not afraid.

[*Eman goes out. A few moments later, the attendant enters.*]

ATTENDANT: The boat is ready.

OLD MAN: So am I.

[*He sits perfectly still for several moments. Drumming begins somewhere in the distance, and the old man sways his head almost imperceptibly. Two men come in bearing a miniature boat, containing an indefinable mound. They rush it in and set it briskly down near the old man, and stand well back. The old man gets up slowly, the attendant watching him keenly. He signs to the men, who lift the boat quickly onto the old man's head. As soon as it touches his head, he holds it down with both hands and runs off, the men give him a start, then follow at a trot.*

As the last man disappears Oroge limps in and comes face to face with Eman—as carrier—who is now seen still standing beside the shrubs, staring into the scene he has just witnessed. Oroge, struck by the look on Eman's face, looks anxiously behind him to see what has engaged Eman's attention. Eman notices him then, and the pair stare at each other. Jaguna enters, sees him and shouts, 'Here he is', rushes at Eman who is whipped back to the immediate and flees, Jaguna in pursuit. Three or four others enter and follow them. Oroge remains where he is, thoughtful.]

JAGUNA [*re-enters.*]: They have closed in on him now, we'll get him this time.

OROGE: It is nearly midnight.

JAGUNA: You were standing there looking at him as if he was some strange spirit. Why didn't you shout?

OROGE: You shouted didn't you? Did that catch him?

JAGUNA: Don't worry. We have him now. But things have taken a bad turn. It is no longer enough to drive him past every house. There is too much contamination about already.

OROGE [*not listening.*]: He saw something. Why may I not know what it was?

JAGUNA: What are you talking about?

OROGE: Hm. What is it?

JAGUNA: I said there is too much harm done already. The year will demand more from this carrier than we thought.

OROGE: What do you mean?

JAGUNA: Do we have to talk with the full mouth?

OROGE: S-sh . . . look!

[*Jaguna turns just in time to see Sunma fly at him, clawing at his face like a crazed tigress.*]

SUNMA: Murderer! What are you doing to him. Murderer! Murderer!

[*Jaguna finds himself struggling really hard to keep off his daughter, he succeeds in pushing her off and striking her so hard on the face that she falls to her knees. He moves on her to hit her again.*]

OROGE [*comes between.*]: Think what you are doing Jaguna, she is your daughter.

JAGUNA: My daughter! Does this one look like my daughter? Let me cripple the harlot for life.

OROGE: That is a wicked thought Jaguna.

JAGUNA: Don't come between me and her.

OROGE: Nothing in anger—do you forget what tonight is?

JAGUNA: Can you blame me for forgetting?

[*Draws his hand across his cheek—it is covered with blood.*]

OROGE: This is an unhappy night for us all. I fear what is to come of it.

JAGUNA: Let's go. I cannot restrain myself in this creature's presence. My own daughter . . . and for a stranger . . .

[*They go off, Ifada, who came in with Sunma and had stood apart, horror-stricken, comes shyly forward. He helps Sunma up. They go off, he holding Sunma bent and sobbing.*]

[*Enter Eman—as carrier. He is physically present in the bounds of this next scene, a side of a round thatched hut. A young girl, about fourteen runs in, stops beside the hut. She looks carefully to see that she is not observed, puts her mouth to a little hole in the wall.*]

OMAE: Eman . . . Eman . . .

[*Eman—as carrier—responds, as he does throughout the scene, but they are unaware of him.*]

EMAN [*from inside.*]: Who is it?

OMAE: It is me, Omae.

EMAN: How dare you come here!

[*Two hands appear at the hole and pushing outwards, create a much larger hole through which Eman puts out his head. It is Eman as a boy, the same age as the girl.*]

Go away at once. Are you trying to get me into trouble!

OMAE: What is the matter?

EMAN: You. Go away.

OMAE: But I came to see you.

EMAN: Are you deaf? I say I don't want to see you. Now go before my tutor catches you.

OMAE: All right. Come out.

EMAN: Do what!

OMAE: Come out.

EMAN: You must be mad.

OMAE [*sits on the ground.*]: All right, if you don't come out I shall simply stay here until your tutor arrives.

EMAN [*about to explode, thinks better of it and the head disappears. A moment later he emerges from behind the hut.*] What sort of a devil has got into you?

OMAE: None. I just wanted to see you.

EMAN [*his mimicry is nearly hysterical.*]: 'None. I just wanted to see you.' Do you think this place is the stream where you can go and molest innocent people?

OMAE [*coyly.*]: Aren't you glad to see me?

EMAN: I am not.

OMAE: Why?

EMAN: Why? Do you really ask me why? Because you are a woman and a most troublesome woman. Don't you know anything about this at all. We are not meant to see any woman. So go away before more harm is done.

OMAE [*flirtatious.*]: What is so secret about it anyway? What do they teach you.

EMAN: Nothing any woman can understand.

OMAE: Ha ha. You think we don't know eh? You've all come to be circumcised.

EMAN: Shut up. You don't know anything.

OMAE: Just think, all this time you haven't been circumcised, and you dared make eyes at us women.

EMAN: Thank you—woman. Now go.

OMAE: Do they give you enough to eat?

EMAN [*testily.*]: No. We are so hungry that when silly girls like you turn up, we eat them.

OMAE [*feigning tears.*]: Oh, oh, oh, he's abusing me. He's abusing me.

EMAN [*alarmed.*]: Don't try that here. Go quickly if you are going to cry.

OMAE: All right, I won't cry.

EMAN: Cry or no cry, go away and leave me alone. What do you think will happen if my tutor turns up now.

OMAE: He won't.

EMAN [*mimicking.*]: 'He won't.' I suppose you are his wife and he tells you where he goes. In fact this is just the time he comes round to our huts. He could be at the next hut this very moment.

OMAE: Ha-ha. You're lying. I left him by the stream, pinching the girls' bottoms. Is that the sort of thing he teaches you?

EMAN: Don't say anything against him or I shall beat you. Isn't it you loose girls who tease him, wiggling your bottoms under his nose?

OMAE [*going tearful again.*]: A-ah, so I am one of the loose girls eh?

EMAN: Now don't start accusing me of things I didn't say.

OMAE: But you said it. You said it.

EMAN: I didn't. Look Omae, someone will hear you and I'll be in disgrace. Why don't you go before anything happens.

OMAE: It's all right. My friends have promised to hold your old rascal tutor till I get back.

EMAN: Then you go back right now. I have work to do. [*Going in.*]

OMAE [*runs after and tries to hold him. Eman leaps back, genuinely scared.*]: What is the matter? I was not going to bite you.

EMAN: Do you know what you nearly did? You almost touched me!

OMAE: Well?

EMAN: Well! Isn't it enough that you let me set my eyes on you? Must you now totally pollute me with your touch? Don't you understand anything?

OMAE: Oh, that.

EMAN [*nearly screaming.*]: It is not 'oh that'. Do you think this is only a joke or a little visit like spending the night with your grandmother? This is an important period of my life. Look, these huts, we built them with our own hands. Every boy builds his own. We learn things, do you understand? And we spend much time just thinking. At least, I do. It is the first time I have had nothing to do except think. Don't you see, I am becoming a man. For the first time, I understand that I have a life to fulfil. Has that thought ever worried you?

OMAE: You are frightening me.

EMAN: There. That is all you can say. And what use will that be when a man finds himself alone—like that? [*Points to the hut.*] A man must go on his own, go where no one can help him, and test his strength. Because he may find himself one day sitting alone in a wall as round as that. In there, my mind could hold no other thought. I may never have such moments again to myself. Don't dare to come and steal any more of it.

OMAE [*this time, genuinely tearful*]: Oh, I know you hate me. You only want to drive me away.

EMAN [*impatiently.*]: Yes, yes, I know I hate you—but go.

OMAE [*going, all tears. Wipes her eyes, suddenly all mischief.*]: Eman.

EMAN: What now?

OMAE: I only want to ask one thing ... do you promise to tell me?

EMAN: Well, what is it?

OMAE [*gleefully.*]: Does it hurt?

[*She turns instantly and flees, landing straight into the arms of the returning tutor.*]

TUTOR: Te-he-he ... what have we here? What little mouse leaps straight into the beak of the wise old owl eh?

[*Omae struggles to free herself, flies to the opposite side, grimacing with distaste.*]

TUTOR: I suppose you merely came to pick some fruits eh? You did not sneak here to see any of my children.

OMAE: Yes, I came to steal your fruits.

TUTOR: Te-he-he ... I thought so. And that dutiful son of mine over there. He saw you and came to chase you off my fruit trees didn't he? Te-he-he ... I'm sure he did, isn't that so my young Eman?

EMAN: I was talking to her.

TUTOR: Indeed you were. Now be good enough to go into your hut until I decide your punishment. [*Eman withdraws.*] Te-he-he ... now now my little daughter, you need not be afraid of me.

OMAE [*spiritedly.*]: I am not.

TUTOR: Good. Very good. We ought to be friendly. [*His voice becomes leering.*] Now this is nothing to worry you my daughter ... a very small thing indeed. Although of course if I were to let it slip that your young Eman had broken a strong taboo, it might go hard on him you know. I am sure you would not like that to happen, would you?

OMAE: No.

TUTOR: Good. You are sensible my girl. Can you wash clothes?

OMAE: Yes.

TUTOR: Good. If you will come with me now to my hut, I shall give you some clothes to wash, and then we will forget all about this matter eh? Well, come on.

OMAE: I shall wait here. You go and bring the clothes.

TUTOR: Eh? What is that? Now now, don't make me angry. You should know better than to talk back at your elders. Come now.

[*He takes her by the arm, and tries to drag her off.*]

OMAE: No no, I won't come to your hut. Leave me. Leave me alone you shameless old man.

TUTOR: If you don't come I shall disgrace the whole family of Eman, and yours too.

[*Eman re-enters with a small bundle.*]

EMAN: Leave her alone. Let us go Omae.

TUTOR: And where do you think you are going?

EMAN: Home.

TUTOR: Te-he-he . . . As easy as that eh? You think you can leave here any time you please? Get right back inside that hut!

[*Eman takes Omae by the arm and begins to walk off.*]

TUTOR: Come back at once.

[*He goes after him and raises his stick. Eman catches it, wrenches it from him and throws its away.*]

OMAE [*hopping delightedly.*]: Kill him. Beat him to death.

TUTOR: Help! Help! He is killing me! Help!

[*Alarmed, Eman clamps his hand over his mouth.*]

EMAN: Old tutor, I don't mean you any harm, but you mustn't try to harm me either. [*He removes his hand.*]

TUTOR: You think you can get away with your crime. My report shall reach the elders before you ever get into town.

EMAN: You are afraid of what I will say about you? Don't worry. Only if you try to shame me, then I will speak. I am not going back to the village anyway. Just tell them I have gone, no more. If you say one word more than that I shall hear of it the same day and I shall come back.

TUTOR: You are telling me what to do? But don't think to come back next year because I will drive you away. Don't think to come back here even ten years from now. And don't send your children.

[*Goes off with threatening gestures.*]

EMAN: I won't come back.

OMAE: Smoked vulture! But Eman, he says you cannot return next year. What will you do?

EMAN: It is a small thing one can do in the big towns.

OMAE: I thought you were going to beat him that time. Why didn't you crack his dirty hide?

EMAN: Listen carefully Omae . . . I am going on a journey.

OMAE: Come on. Tell me about it on the way.

EMAN: No, I go that way. I cannot return to the village.

OMAE: Because of that wretched man? Anyway you will first talk to your father.

EMAN: Go and see him for me. Tell him I have gone away for some time. I think he will know.

OMAE: But Eman . . .

EMAN: I haven't finished. You will go and live with him till I get back. I have spoken to him about you. Look after him!

OMAE: But what is this journey? When will you come back?

EMAN: I don't know. But this is a good moment to go. Nothing ties me down.

OMAE: But Eman, you want to leave me.

EMAN: Don't forget all I said. I don't know how long I will be. Stay in my father's house as long as you remember me. When you become tired of waiting, you must do as you please. You understand? You must do as you please.

OMAE: I cannot understand anything Eman. I don't know where you are going or why. Suppose you never came back! Don't go Eman. Don't leave me by myself.

EMAN: I must go. Now let me see you on your way.

OMAE: I shall come with you.

EMAN: Come with me! And who will look after you? Me? You will only be in my way, you know that! You will hold me back and I shall desert you in a strange place. Go home and do as I say. Take care of my father and let him take care of you.

[*He starts going but Omae clings to him.*]

OMAE: But Eman, stay the night at least. You will only lose your way. Your father Eman, what will he say? I won't remember what you said . . . come back to the village . . . I cannot return alone Eman . . . come with me as far as the crossroads.

[*His face set, Eman strides off and Omae loses balance as he increases*

*his pace. Falling, she quickly wraps her arms around his ankle, but
Eman continues unchecked, dragging her along.*]

OMAE: Don't go Eman ... Eman, don't leave me, don't leave
me ... don't leave your Omae ... don't go Eman ... don't
leave your Omae ...

[*Eman—as carrier—makes a nervous move as if he intends to go
after the vanished pair. He stops but continues to stare at the point
where he last saw them. There is stillness for a while. Then the
Girl enters from the same place and remains looking at Eman.
Startled, Eman looks apprehensively round him. The Girl goes
nearer but keeps beyond arm's length.*]

GIRL: Are you the carrier?

EMAN: Yes. I am Eman.

GIRL: Why are you hiding?

EMAN: I really came for a drink of water ... er ... is there anyone
in front of the house?

GIRL: No.

EMAN: But there might be people in the house. Did you hear voices?

GIRL: There is no one here.

EMAN: Good. Thank you. [*He is about to go, stops suddenly.*] Er ...
would you ... you will find a cup on the table. Could you
bring me the water out here? The water-pot is in a corner.
[*The Girl goes. She enters the house, then, watching Eman
carefully, slips out and runs off.*]

EMAN [*sitting.*]: Perhaps they have all gone home. It will be good
to rest. [*He hears voices and listens hard.*] Too late. [*Moves
cautiously nearer the house.*] Quickly girl, I can hear people
coming. Hurry up. [*Looks through the window.*] Where are you?
Where is she? [*The truth dawns on him suddenly and he moves off,
sadly.*]

[*Enter Jaguna and Oroge, led by the Girl.*]

GIRL [*pointing.*]: He was there.

JAGUNA: Ay, he's gone now. He is a sly one is your friend. But it
won't save him for ever.

OROGE: What was he doing when you saw him?

GIRL: He asked me for a drink of water.

JAGUNA, }
OROGE   }: Ah! [*They look at each other.*]

OROGE: We should have thought of that.

JAGUNA: He is surely finished now. If only we had thought of it earlier.

OROGE: It is not too late. There is still an hour before midnight.

JAGUNA: We must call back all the men. Now we need only wait for him—in the right place.

OROGE: Everyone must be told. We don't want anyone heading him off again.

JAGUNA: And it works so well. This is surely the help of the gods themselves Oroge. Don't you know at once what is on the path to the stream?

OROGE: The sacred trees.

JAGUNA: I tell you it is the very hand of the gods. Let us go.

[*An overgrown part of the village. Eman wanders in, aimlessly, seemingly uncaring of discovery. Beyond him, an area lights up, revealing a group of people clustered round a spot, all the heads are bowed. One figure stands away and separate from them. Even as Eman looks, the group breaks up and the people disperse, coming down and past him. Only three people are left, a man (Eman) whose back is turned, the village priest and the isolated one. They stand on opposite sides of the grave, the man on the mound of earth. The priest walks round to the man's side and lays a hand on his shoulder.*]

PRIEST: Come.

EMAN: I will. Give me a few moments here alone.

PRIEST: Be comforted.

[*They fall silent.*]

EMAN: I was gone twelve years but she waited. She whom I thought had too much of the laughing child in her. Twelve years I was a pilgrim, seeking the vain shrine of secret strength. And all the time, strange knowledge, this silent strength of my child-woman.

PRIEST: We all saw it. It was a lesson to us; we did not know that such goodness could be found among us.

EMAN: Then why? Why the wasted years if she had to perish giving birth to my child? [*They are both silent.*] I do not really know for what great meaning I searched. When I returned, I could not be certain I had found it. Until I reached my home and I found her a full-grown woman, still a child at heart. When I grew to believe it, I thought, this, after all, is what I sought. It was here all the time. And I threw away my new-gained knowledge. I buried the part of me that was formed in strange places. I made a home in my birthplace.

PRIEST: That was as it should be.

EMAN: Any truth of that was killed in the cruelty of her brief happiness.

PRIEST [*looks up and sees the figure standing away from them, the child in his arms. He is totally still.*] Your father—he is over there.

EMAN: I knew he would come. Has he my son with him?

PRIEST: Yes.

EMAN: He will let no one take the child. Go and comfort him priest. He loved Omae like a daughter, and you all know how well she looked after him. You see how strong we really are. In his heart of hearts the old man's love really awaited a daughter. Go and comfort him. His grief is more than mine.

[*The priest goes. The old man has stood well away from the burial group. His face is hard and his gaze unswerving from the grave. The priest goes to him, pauses, but sees that he can make no dent in the man's grief. Bowed, he goes on his way.*]

[*Eman, as carrier, walking towards the graveside, the other Eman having gone. His feet sink into the mound and he breaks slowly on to his knees, scooping up the sand in his hands and pouring it on his head. The scene blacks out slowly.*]

[*Enter Jaguna and Oroge.*]

OROGE: We have only a little time.

JAGUNA: He will come. All the wells are guarded. There is only the stream left him. The animal must come to drink.

OROGE: You are sure it will not fail—the trap I mean.

JAGUNA: When Jaguna sets the trap, even elephants pay homage— their trunks downwards and one leg up in the sky. When the carrier steps on the fallen twigs, it is up in the sacred trees with him.

OROGE: I shall breathe again when this long night is over.

[*They go out.*]

[*Enter Eman—as carrier—from the same direction as the last two entered. In front of him is a still figure, the old man as he was, carrying the dwarf boat.*]

EMAN [*joyfully.*]: Father.

[*The figure does not turn round.*]

EMAN: It is your son. Eman. [*He moves nearer.*] Don't you want to look at me? It is I, Eman. [*He moves nearer still.*]

OLD MAN: You are coming too close. Don't you know what I carry on my head?

EMAN: But Father, I am your son.

OLD MAN: Then go back. We cannot give the two of us.

EMAN: Tell me first where you are going.

OLD MAN: Do *you* ask that? Where else but to the river?

EMAN [*visibly relieved.*]: I only wanted to be sure. My throat is burning. I have been looking for the stream all night.

OLD MAN: It is the other way.

EMAN: But you said . . .

OLD MAN: I take the longer way, you know how I must do this. It is quicker if you take the other way. Go now.

EMAN: No, I will only get lost again. I shall go with you.

OLD MAN: Go back my son. Go back.

EMAN: Why? Won't you even look at me?

OLD MAN: Listen to your father. Go back.

EMAN: But father!

[*He makes to hold him. Instantly the old man breaks into a rapid trot. Eman hesitates, then follows, his strength nearly gone.*]

EMAN: Wait father. I am coming with you . . . wait . . . wait for me father . . .

[*There is a sound of twigs breaking, of a sudden trembling in the branches. Then silence.*]

[*The front of Eman's house. The effigy is hanging from the sheaves. Enter Sunma, still supported by Ifada, she stands transfixed as she sees the hanging figure. Ifada appears to go mad, rushes at the object and tears it down. Sunma, her last bit of will gone, crumbles against the wall. Some distance away from them, partly hidden, stands the Girl, impassively watching. Ifada hugs the effigy to him, stands above Sunma. The Girl remains where she is, observing.*
Almost at once, the villagers begin to return, subdued and guilty. They walk across the front, skirting the house as widely as they can. No word is exchanged. Jaguna and Oroge eventually appear. Jaguna who is leading, sees Sunma as soon as he comes in view. He stops at once, retreating slightly.]

OROGE [*almost whispering.*]: What is it?

JAGUNA: The viper.

[*Oroge looks cautiously at the woman.*]

OROGE: I don't think she will even see you.

JAGUNA: Are you sure? I am in no frame of mind for another meeting with her.

OROGE: Let's go home.

JAGUNA: I am sick to the heart of the cowardice I have seen tonight.

OROGE: That is the nature of men.

JAGUNA: Then it is a sorry world to live in. We did it for them. It was all for their own common good. What did it benefit me whether the man lived or died. But did you see them? One and all they looked up at the man and words died in their throats.

OROGE: It was no common sight.

JAGUNA: Women could not have behaved so shamefully. One by one they crept off like sick dogs. Not one could raise a curse.

OROGE: It was not only him they fled. Do you see how unattended we are?

JAGUNA: There are those who will pay for this night's work!

OROGE: Ay, let us go home.

[*They go off. Sunma, Ifada and the Girl remain as they are, the light fading slowly on them.*]

THE END

THE ROAD

Characters

MURANO	*personal servant to Professor*
KOTONU	*driver, lately of 'No Danger No Delay'*
SAMSON	*passenger tout and driver's mate to Kotonu*
SALUBI	*driver-trainee*
PROFESSOR	*proprietor etc. of the drivers' haven. Formerly Sunday-school teacher and lay-reader*
CHIEF-IN-TOWN	*a politician*
SAY TOKYO KID	*driver and captain of thugs*
PARTICULARS JOE	*a policeman*
SEVERAL LAY-ABOUTS	
A CROWD	

Translations of the Yoruba songs and a glossary of pidgin words will be found after p. 229.

For the Producer

Since the mask-idiom employed in *The Road* will be strange to many, the preface poem Alagemo should be of help. Agemo is simply, a religious cult of flesh dissolution.

The dance is the movement of transition; it is used in the play as a visual suspension of death—in much the same way as Murano, the mute, is a dramatic embodiment of this suspension. He functions as an arrest of time, or death, since it was in his 'agemo' phase that the lorry knocked him down. Agemo, the mere phase, includes the passage of transition from the human to the divine essence (as in the festival of Ogun in this play), as much as the part psychic, part intellectual grope of Professor towards the essence of death.

Alagemo

I heard! I felt their reach
And heard my naming named.
The pit is there, the digger fell right through
My roots have come out in the other world.
Make away. Agemo's hoops
Are pathways of the sun.
Rain-reeds, unbend to me, Quench
The burn of cartwheels at my waist!
Pennant in the stream of time—Now,
Gone, and Here the Future
Make way. Let the rivers woo
The thinning, thinning Here and
Vanished Leap that was the Night
And the split that snatched the heavy-lidded
She-twin into Dawn.
No sweat-beads droop beneath
The plough-wings of the hawk.
No beetle finds a hole between Agemo's toes.
When the whirlwind claps his feet
It is the sundering of the . . . name no ills . . .
Of . . . the Not-to-be
Of the moistening moment of a breath . . .
Approach. Approach and feel
Did I not speak? Is there not flesh
Between the dead man's thumbs?

PART ONE

Dawn is barely breaking on a road-side shack, a ragged fence and a corner of a church with a closed stained-glass window. Above this a cross-surmounted steeple tapers out of sight. Thrusting downstage from a corner of the shack is the back of a 'bolekaja' (mammy waggon), lop-sided and minus its wheels. It bears the inscription—AKSIDENT STORE—ALL PART AVAILEBUL. In the opposite corner, a few benches and empty beer-cases used as stools. Downstage to one side, a table and chair, placed in contrasting tidiness.

Kotonu is asleep on a mat against the tailboard, Samson stretched a few feet away, a small bundle under his head. In the other corner the motor-park lay-abouts are sprawled on the floor and on benches, Salubi on two benches placed together, his driver's uniform neatly folded beside his head. Murano lies coiled under the Professor's table.

Murano gets up. Goes and washes his face from a pot just showing among rubble of worn tyres, hubs, twisted bumpers etc. Picks up his climbing rope, his gourd and his 'osuka' and sets off. Samson wakes half-way through his ablutions and watches him furtively. As Murano disappears he considers following him but thinks better of it, returns to his mat.

The tower clock strikes five. Samson stretches, tosses about restlessly. Eventually he gets up, scratching. Goes outside and tries to follow Murano with his eyes. Gives up. He ambles around aimlessly, stopping to pick up crumbs from a plate lying on a table. Then he goes out and urinates against the wall, stretching like a practised idler. About to re-enter, a thought strikes him and he turns and with some trepidation, goes towards the churchyard. Goes through a gap in the fence, and eggs himself further and further inside. Startling him, the tower clock strikes the half-hour and he belts back, flinging himself through the gap before he realizes what the noise is. Shakes his fist at the tower and returns to the shack.

He sees all the others sleeping peacefully and this incenses him. Gives Salubi a kick in the leg but Salubi only draws it back on the bench. He pushes another off the bench. The man continues his sleep on the floor. All round them are the empty cups used at the last carousing; Samson picks up a tin mug, flings it up in the air and lets it drop. Only one or two react, but this does not go beyond turning on the other side. Disgusted he goes over to a spider's web in the corner, pokes it with a stick. He soon wearies of this.

In frustration, Samson flings himself on the mat only to be flung up again by the clock suddenly striking the hour.

Salubi stirs, gets up.

SALUBI: Six o'clock I bet. I don't know how it is, but no matter when I go to sleep, I wake up when it strikes six. Now that is a miracle.

[*He gets out his chewing stick, begins to chew on it.*]

SAMSON: There is a miracle somewhere but not what you say. Maybe the sight of you using a chewing stick.

SALUBI: Look Samson, it's early in the morning. Go back to sleep if you're going to start that again.

[*He starts to put on his chauffeur's uniform.*]

SAMSON: Who lend you uniform?

SALUBI: I buy it with my own money.

[*Samson goes over, feels the cloth.*]

SAMSON: Second-hand.

SALUBI: So what?

SAMSON: At least you might have washed it. Look at that blood-stain—has someone been smashing your teeth?

SALUBI: Rubbish. Na palm-oil.

SAMSON: All right all right. But you are a funny person. Funny like one of those street idiots. How can anyone buy a uniform when he hasn't got a job?

SALUBI: Impression. I take uniform impress all future employer.

SAMSON: With that smear on the front?

SALUBI: Go mind your own business you jobless tout.

SAMSON: Me a jobless tout? May I ask what you are?

SALUBI: A uniformed private driver—temporary unemploy.

[*Straightens his outfit.*]

SAMSON: God almighty! You dey like monkey wey stoway inside sailor suit.

SALUBI: Na common jealousy dey do you. I know I no get job, but I get uniform.

[*Starts to shine his brass buttons.*]

SAMSON [*shakes his head.*]: Instead of using all that labour to shine your buttons you should spare some for your teeth, you know, and your body—a little soap and sponge would do it. After all, new uniform deserves new body. White coat deserves white teeth.

SALUBI [*desperately.*]: Wes matter? Na me you take dream last night or na wetin? Why you no mind your own business for heaven's sake!

SAMSON: Because I have no business to mind you dirty pig. Why am I sitting here at this time of the morning? Every self-respecting tout is already in the motor park badgering passengers. Look at all these touts still sleeping. They have no pride in their job. Part-time tout part-time burglar. In any case they are the pestilence of the trade. No professional dignity. Hear them snoring as if their exhaust has dropped off. Now that is what Kotonu expects me to do—start touting for any lorry which happens to come along. Is that the sort of life for the Champion Tout of Motor Parks?

SALUBI: I think say beggar no get choice.

SAMSON: Is that so? Of course you should know. You are ready to crawl on your belly and beg for anything. As for me, I am a proud man. I tout for my own driver, not for anyone else. I'm a one-driver tout, no more no less.

SALUBI: You say you get pride and still yet you are a conductor on bolekaja.

SAMSON: Nonsense, we run a bus. The seats face where you are going, just like the driver himself and the first-class passengers. In a common bolekaja you turn your side or your back to where you are going.

SALUBI: Anyway, the matter is that you are going with passenger lorry. You and these ruffians, you are the same. Me, I don't drive lorry. I drive only private owner—no more no less.

SAMSON: Private wey no get licence. Go siddon my friend.
[*Salubi gives the last button a flourish, straightens himself and looks satisfied.*]

SALUBI: As I am standing so, I fit to drive the Queen of England.

SAMSON: One look at you and she will abdicate.

SALUBI: All I need now is a licence. It is only a matter of getting Professor to forge one for me.

SAMSON: Ask him.

SALUBI: I have asked him a hundred times, but he always says . . .

SAMSON [*mimicking.*]: Go away. Come back when you have a job.

SALUBI: You see. And a man can't get a job without a licence.

SAMSON: And you can't get a licence without a job. So why don't you just go and hang yourself.

SALUBI: I no sabbe do am. You fit show me?

SAMSON: When Professor returns and I will tell him you tried to hang yourself.

SALUBI [*jumping.*]: You can't frighten me you hear. Who do you think is afraid of that madman. [*Looking towards the churchyard.*] I wonder if he is still asleep.

[*Progressively during the scene, the sleeping forms get up, give their faces a wash, go round the back-yard, hang on the fence etc.*]

SAMSON: If he ever sleeps. I cannot understand the man, going to sleep in the churchyard with all that dead-body.

SALUBI: That is how to make money you know. If you make abracadabra with spirits you can get money from them.

SAMSON: You think Professor has money?

SALUBI: The man too clever. One of these days I will find out where he hides his money. He may even be millionaire.

SAMSON [*wistfully.*]: Sometimes I think, what will I do with all that money if I am a millionaire?

SALUBI: First I will marry ten wives.

SAMSON: Why ten?

SALUBI: I no fit count pass ten.

SAMSON: Just like you to waste money on women.

SALUBI: Why not? What else can a man do with a million pounds?

SAMSON: Me, I will buy all the transport lorries in the country, then make Kotonu the head driver.

SALUBI: Kotonu? Who be Kotonu? He get experience pass me?

SAMSON: You? Don't make me laugh. You are not fit to wipe the cow-dung from his tyres. You I will make my private driver—and if you come near me with a dirty uniform like that, I will have you thrashed like a horse.

SALUBI: Who get dirty uniform? I wash am starch am yesterday. Abi three pence starch no fit stiff am one day?

SAMSON: As for Professor, I will give him special office with air-conditioner, automatic printing press and so on and so forth, so he can forge driving licences for all my drivers. The man is an artist and, as a millionaire, I must support culture.

SALUBI: The day the police catch you . . .

SAMSON: Which kind police? They will form line in front of my house every morning to receive their tip. No one will touch my lorry on the road.

[*He lifts the Professor's chair, dumps it on the big table and climbs on to it, leaps down almost immediately and whips the coverlet off Kotonu who stirs and slowly wakes up later. Wraps the coverlet around his shoulders and climbs back on the table. Takes out the Professor's glasses and wears them low on his nose. Puts on an imposing look and surveys a line in front of him with scorn. Breaks into a satisfied grin.*]

SAMSON: E sa mi.[1]

SALUBI [*down on his knees, salaams.*]: African millionaire!

SAMSON: I can't hear you.

SALUBI: Delicate millionaire!

SAMSON: Wes matter? You no chop this morning? I say I no hear you.

SALUBI: Samson de millionaire!

SAMSON: Ah, my friends, what can I do for you?

SALUBI [*in attitude of prayer.*]: Give us this day our daily bribe. Amen.

SAMSON [*dips in an imaginary purse, he is about to fling to them a fistful of coins when he checks his hand.*]: Now remember, officers first. Superintendents! [*Flings the coins. Salubi scrambles and picks up the money.*] Inspectors! [*Action is repeated.*] Sergeants! [*Again Salubi grabs the coins.*] Now that is what I call a well disciplined force. Next, those with one or two stripes. [*Flings out more money. Salubi retreating to a new position, picks up the largesse.*] Excellent! Excellent! And now, those who are new to the game. [*Same action.*] You may go now. And good hunting friends. [*He and Salubi collapse laughing. Kotonu has sat up watching.*]

SALUBI: Haba, make man talk true, man wey get money get power.

SAMSON: God I go chop life make I tell true. I go chop the life so tey God go jealous me. And if he take jealousy kill me I will go start bus service between heaven and hell.

SALUBI: Which kin' bus for heaven? Sometimes na aeroplane or helicopter den go take travel for Paradise.

SAMSON [*reverting to his role.*]: Come here.

SALUBI: Yessssssah.

SAMSON: Have you had a wash today?

SALUBI: Myself sah?

1. 'Sing my praise.'

SAMSON: Open your mouth . . . go on, open your mouth. Wider! It stinks.

SALUBI: Sah?

SAMSON: It stinks. It stinks so much that I will promote you Captain of my private bodyguard. When the police bring their riot squad with tear-gas and all that nonsense, you will open your mouth and breathe on them. That is what is known as counter-blast.

SALUBI: Yesssssssah.

SAMSON: But you must take care not to breathe in my direction. A compost heap has its own uses, as long as the wind is blowing in the other direction. There have been times when you actually dared to breathe in my face.

SALUBI: Me sah? To breathe into millionaire face. My very self sah?

SAMSON: Your very self ma? Do you accuse me of lying?

SALUBI: I sorry too much sah.

SAMSON: And your driving is becoming a menace. You drivers are all the same. When you get on an endless stretch of road your buttocks open wide and you begin to fart on passengers in the first-class compartment. Is that right?

SALUBI: Yesssssssssah. I mean no sah. At all at all sah.

SAMSON: Now I want you to take the car—the long one—and drive along the Marina at two o'clock. All the fine fine girls just coming from offices, the young and tender faces fresh from school—give them lift to my house. Old bones like me must put fresh tonic in his blood.

[*Busy with laughter, they do not see the Professor approach. Salubi is the first to see him, he stands petrified for some moments, then begins to stutter.*]

SALUBI: Samson . . . Professor . . . !

SAMSON: What about him?

[*Salubi, with trembling finger, points in his direction, but Samson refuses to turn round.*]

You think you have seen a new born fool do you? What would Professor be doing here at this time of the day?

[*As Professor gets to the door, Salubi dives under the table. Samson, too late, turns round and stares petrified.*

Professor is a tall figure in Victorian outfit—tails, top-hat etc., all thread-bare and shiny at the lapels from much ironing. He carries four

enormous bundles of newspaper and a fifth of paper odds and ends
impaled on a metal rod stuck in a wooden rest. A chair-stick hangs
from one elbow, and the other arm clutches a road-sign bearing a
squiggle and the one word, 'BEND'.]

PROF. [*he enters in a high state of excitement, muttering to himself.*]:
Almost a miracle . . . dawn provides the greatest miracles but
this . . . in this dawn has exceeded its promise. In the strangest
of places . . . God God God but there is a mystery in everything.
A new discovery every hour—I am used to that, but that I
should be led to where this was hidden, sprouted in secret for
heaven knows how long . . . for there was no doubt about it,
this word was growing, it was growing from earth until I
plucked it. . . .
[*He has reached the place where his table normally is. Puzzled,*
he looks round, but does not see Samson perched above him.]
But is this my station? I could have sworn . . .
[*Suddenly suspicious, he clutches the road-sign possessively.*]
If this is a trick I swear they shan't take it from me. If my
eyes were deluded and my body led here by spells I shall not
surrender the fruit of my vigil. No one can take it from me!
[*He looks up at last, sees Samson, scrutinizes him carefully.*]
You sir, are not one of my habituals, or I would know you.

SAMSON: N-n-n-no.

PROF.: So, you admit it, and it is no use pretending you are.

SAMSON: No . . . I mean . . .
[*Looking down suddenly, Professor sees Salubi's rear protruding from*
under the table. He strikes a defensive position, brandishes the
chair-stick and jabs him again and again.]

PROF.: Come out of there. I can see you. How many of you are
there? Come out come out. You may be the devil's own army
but my arm is powered with the unbroken Word!

SAMSON: P-p-please sir, I think you have made a mistake.

PROF.: I have?

SAMSON: Perhaps you missed your way.

PROF.: You think I did? Indeed anything is possible when I pursue
the Word. But . . . and mind you tell the truth . . . you are
not here to take the Word from me?

SAMSON: Oh no . . . not at all. You must have missed your way
that's all.

PROF.: Then I must hurry. [*Turns to go, stops.*] But first, can you
    tell me where I am?

SAMSON: Oh yes. In the wrong place.

PROF.: Ah. I thought so. Strange that I should find myself here.
    I was drawn perhaps by some sympathy of spirit. Do you
    happen to follow the path yourself?

SAMSON: What path? I mean . . . no . . . aren't you in a hurry?
    Good-bye.

PROF. [*surveys his height with new wonder.*]: Yes, you seem a knowing
    man, cutting yourself from common touch with earth. But that is
    a path away from all true communion . . . the Word is not
    to be found in denial.

SAMSON: I agree . . . please go now, we are rather busy.

PROF.: May I ask who you are? I am, I confess, a little dazed by my
    error, but I have vague recollection of your face . . .

SAMSON: Not in the least. I am sure we have never met before.

PROF.: You live here?

SAMSON: Yes . . . er . . . I own the place. In fact, I am a
    millionaire.

PROF.: You are what?

SAMSON [*gaining courage.*]: Yes, that's right. A millionaire.

PROF.: I am so confused, but I have sight and vision only for the
    Word and it may chance, sometimes, that I miss my way
    among worldly humans. [*Going.*]

SAMSON: That is what I have been trying to tell you. Good-bye.

PROF. [*shaking his head sadly.*]: Such dangers beset us who seek after
    the Word. [*He sees Kotonu sitting up, stops.*] But I do know *you*.
    You are the coast-to-coast driver who gave up the road.

SAMSON: Did he? I mean who? Oh him. Why, I employed him
    only this morning. He must have changed his mind.

PROF.: Aha, did I not say that I was drawn here on a wave of
    sympathy? I knew I could not miss my way without reason.
    [*Samson signals Kotonu frantically to get Professor out.*]

KOTONU: If you like Professor, I will come home with you.

PROF.: But your employer . . . ?

SAMSON: . . . has no objection at all. Take him. In fact I no longer
    need him. He dreams too much. Go on, you are sacked.
    Good-bye to both of you. Good-bye . . . good-bye.

PROF.: Come then, I have a new wonder to show you . . . a

madness where a motor-car throws itself against a tree—
Gbram! And showers of crystal flying on broken souls.

SAMSON [*suddenly alarmed.*]: Wait! What was that about an
accident?

PROF.: Are you that ignorant of the true path to the Word. It is
never an accident.

SAMSON: Well call it what you will. But you are not taking him
to see that sort of rubbish.

PROF. [*bristling.*]: How dare you? Do you take me for a common
gawper after misery?

SALUBI [*from beneath.*]: Samson are you mad? For God's sake let
them go.

PROF. [*to Kotonu.*]: This millionaire—did he purchase your soul too?

KOTONU: Pay no attention Professor, let's go.

SAMSON [*almost plaintive.*]: Kotonu don't go with him.
[*Professor approaches him.*]

SALUBI: Now he is going to find us out you stupid tout.

PROF.: My bed is among the dead, and when the road raises a
victory cry to break my sleep I hurry to a disgruntled swarm
of souls full of spite for their rejected bodies. It is a market of
stale meat, noisy with flies and quarrelsome with old women.
The place I speak of is not far from here, if you wish to come...
you shall be shown this truth of my endeavours—

SAMSON: No thank you very much. I don't willingly seek out
unpleasant sights.

PROF.: You are afraid? There are dangers in the Quest I know, but
the Word may be found companion not to life, but Death.
Three souls you know, fled up that tree. You would think, to
see it that the motor-car had tried to clamber after them. Oh
there was such an angry buzz but the matter was beyond repair.
They died, all three of them crucified on rigid branches. I
found this word growing where their blood had spread and
sunk along plough scouring of the wheel. Now tell me you
who sit above it all, do you think my sleep was broken over
nothing, over a meaningless event?

SALUBI: Don't answer him Samson. Just let him go.

SAMSON: But there is no need to take Kotonu to see it.

SALUBI: Let him go before it is too late.

KOTONU: Let's go Professor. [*He ushers Professor towards the door,*

turns back to Samson.] It is only a business trip. Stop fidgeting.
[*They go.*]

PROF.: But you must not think I accept all such manifestations as
truth. It may be a blind. I know this is not the Word, but every
discovery is a sign-post . . . eventually the revelation will stand
naked, unashamed . . . the subterfuge will be over, my cause
vindicated. . . .

[*His voice trails off in the distance. Samson and Salubi remain
motionless until they can no longer hear him.*]

SALUBI [*crawls out and dusts himself.*]: All I can say is, you have the
luck of a hunter's dog. I mean, if ever a thief more than deserved
to be caught red-handed. . . .

SAMSON: But what did Kotonu mean by that?

SALUBI: What?

SAMSON: He said he was going on a business trip. This is a funny
way to talk about a thing like that.

SALUBI: But he was going on a business trip.

SAMSON: What business trip?

SALUBI: Get out. You are his mate aren't you? Do you want to
pretend you don't know?

SAMSON: What don't I know?

SALUBI: Well where do you think I get this uniform?

SAMSON: Stole it of course. It's just like you to rob a dead man.
Common shop-lifter. When Sergeant Burma was alive you
wouldn't dare.

SALUBI: I am glad you can joke about it. Because I bought it from
your mate.

SAMSON: From Kotonu? Are you gone mad?

SALUBI: Why don't you open your eyes and see who is now
operating behind that tailboard?

SAMSON: And who will I find? Your father's decomposing corpse?

SALUBI: If he's there then your friend must have put him there for
sale?

SAMSON: You are a liar!

SALUBI: You wait. When he returns you will see for yourself.

SAMSON: Don't talk rubbish. That was Sergeant Burma's department.

SALUBI: Sergeant Burma is dead.

SAMSON: And when did Kotonu become his business partner?

SALUBI: Not partner friend, successor. Kotonu has taken over.

SAMSON [*wildly.*]: Liar! You're just a dirty back-biter.

SALUBI: I am saying nothing. You'll see for yourself.

SAMSON: When? When? How could it happen and I not know about it?

SALUBI: Where do you hide your eyes? Look, better get down before you continue to deceive yourself. If Professor stumbles in here again he won't be so blind this time.

SAMSON [*getting down slowly.*]: Oh God. Oh God. I don't believe it. But what is Kotonu trying to do? Is he pretending he doesn't care?

SALUBI: Look, just put this back before the old man returns. He can't make the same mistake twice.

[*They re-arrange the table.*]

SAMSON: He won't come back. A mistake like that always scares him. He thinks it proves that he has gone deeply wrong somewhere. You'll see. When he comes in the afternoon we will hear all about it.

SALUBI: I still think you are a lucky man. Any moment I expected him to knock you off the table with that word business.

SAMSON: But Kotonu is not like that. What is he trying to do? This isn't necessary at all. I only said take back your licence, not start keeping shop for the mortuary.

SALUBI: Well you wanted him back on the road didn't you? So now he's back full blast. General trader and—perhaps occasional supplier too.

SAMSON: So you're taking your evil mouth curse him are you? It's your head will supply that kind of goods you chronic accident of a driver!

[*Sits down dejected.*]

SALUBI: You are not yet thankful for your escape. You've gone and sat in Professor's chair again.

SAMSON: Right now I don't care. Kotonu has gone with him and I bet he comes back worse than ever.

SALUBI [*going.*]: Why you no surrender self? The man say'e no want drive again but you continue worry am as if you na in wife. Haba! Abi when den born am dem tie steering wheel for in neck?[1]

SAMSON: This is all Professor's doing. And it was on him I was

1. 'Was he born with a steering wheel tied to his neck?'

pinning my hopes, I was thinking he might be able to reform this runaway mate of mine. Now he goes and shows him yet another crash.

SALUBI: He's mad. Why you dey worry your head for dat kind person? Abi you tink say Kotonu no sabbe de man dey craze. [*The window of the church is thrown open suddenly, revealing the lectern, a bronze eagle on whose outstretched wings rests a huge tome. Shortly afterwards music from the organ billows out towards the shack. Samson listens for some time.*]

SAMSON: He's not as good as the first man—that's what Professor says.

SALUBI: Why he dey come play dat ting every morning self? Nobody dey inside church.

SAMSON: Rehearsal stupid. You think people just sit down in front of the organ and play just like that? Ah, when Professor was Professor, he would go up after the service and correct the organist where he went wrong. And even during the singing if he heard a wrong note he would shake his head and look round the church making tch-tch-tch-tch-tch. Every time the organist saw that, he knew he was in serious trouble.

SALUBI: Why'e no kuku play the ting inself?

SAMSON: Where were you born that you don't know about Professor?

SALUBI: I only know there was the matter of church funds? Did he go to prison?

SAMSON: You think they just put somebody in prison like that? Professor his very self? Of course you don't know your history. When Professor entered church, everybody turned round and the eyes of the congregation followed him to his pew—and he had his own private pew let me tell you, and if a stranger went and sat in it, the church warden wasted no time driving him out.

SALUBI: Dat one no to church, na high society.

SAMSON: You no sabbe de ting wey man dey call class so shurrup your mout. Professor enh, he get class. He get style. That suit he wears now, that was the very way he used to dress to evening service. I tell you, the whole neighbourhood used to come and watch him, they would gather in this very bar and watch him through the windows, him and his hundred handkerchiefs spread out on the pew in front of him. . . . [*Samson has begun to act*

Professor, spreading out a few greasecloths and rags on a bench and kneeling behind them. He is a meticulous fop in demeanour. Suddenly he rises, makes a formal bow.] That bow, it means that the preacher has just mentioned the name of Jesus Christ. And let me tell you enh, the preacher directed his sermon to Professor for approval. [*He sits, listening attentively. Suddenly he frowns, takes a notebook from his books and writes in it.*] That means a point of controversy, to be hotly debated after church. [*Dabs his brows gently and gravely lays the handkerchief aside.*] He never used a handkerchief twice. Never.

SALUBI: What about the day they said he fought with the bishop?

SAMSON: Which kind of fighting?

SALUBI: Didn't he slap the bishop?

SAMSON: I don't think you understand anything I've been telling you. You think Professor could ever descend to such bushman taxi-driver stuff? My friend, they did have a fight but it was a duel of gentlemen. Look, I'll tell you what happened. Just because the bishop thought he had B.A., B.D. . . .

SALUBI: How much?

SAMSON: B.D. Bachelor of Divinity stupid. But B.D. or no B.D. the man just couldn't knack oratory like the Professor. In fact everybody always said that Professor ought to preach the sermons but a joke is a joke, I mean, the man is not ordained. So we had to be satisfied with him reading the lesson and I'm telling you, three-quarters of the congregation only came to hear his voice. And the bishop was jealous. When the bishop came on his monthly visit and preached the sermon after Professor's lesson, it was a knock-out pure and simple. Before bishop open in mout' half de church done go sleep. And the ones who stayed awake only watched Professor taking notes. [*Whips out his notebook and stabs it with furious notes.*] That means, serious grammatical error. Bishop done trow bomb!

SALUBI: En-hen. If na you be bishop and somebody dey do dat kin' ting you no go vex?

SAMSON: Wait small you no hear de proper fight yet. That was the day the wall of Jericho [*he points.*] fell down. The bishop thought he would teach Professor a lesson. So during sermon, he began to use Jesus Christ every other sentence. At first Professor tried to keep it up. [*He rises, bowing and sitting and bowing and sitting, more and more rapidly without however losing his elegance and general fastidiousness, discarding one handkerchief after the other.*] I was there. So was Kotonu. The usual crowd was here too but we all got so excited that we ran from here and climbed the wall to see better. We wanted to see which of them would win, whether Professor would get cramp for in neck or the bishop would run out of grammar. [*The organ music carries on the conflict in tone and pace.*] The congregation was very silent, they knew what was happening and they knew this was the final duel between their bishop and their lay-reader. . . . [*Samson makes a sudden sharp bow, and remains there for some moments. When he speaks he still retains the position.*] That was how Professor solved it. He made one more bow and he stuck there. The bishop sermonized his head off, the church shook with reverberations from passionate grammar but na so Professor bend in head—'e no move one inch. [*Samson sits, shaking his head in remembered admiration.*]

SALUBI: But how wall come fall down?

SAMSON: That was out fault. We were riding the wall like a victory horse—everybody. Grown-up customers and all the riff-raff, turning somersaults in and out of the churchyard. Suddenly— Gbram!

SALUBI: With you on top?

SAMSON: You no fit tell me from rubble I tell you. The whole church rushed out but there was no need. Nobody was injured. You can imagine, everybody running out just when the bishop was shaking the pulpit and blasting humanity to hell. That is why the wall was not re-built, the bishop forbade it. Sheer spitefulness I call that.

SALUBI: What time he tief the church funds then?

SAMSON: He didn't steal anything.

SALUBI [*shrugs.*]: One of these days I will find out where he hides the money.

SAMSON: You try. Professor will cockroach you like an old newspaper.

SALUBI: You tink I fear all dat in nonsense?

SAMSON [*wistfully.*]: The parish was really hot soup in those days. Politics no get dramatic pass am.[1]

1. 'Politics are not half as dramatic.'

SALUBI: Me a dey go find work. De whole morning done vanish for your cinema show.

SAMSON: Where you dey run go self? Siddon here make we talk.

SALUBI: Not me. If I find lorry wey want experienced tout I go come call you.

SAMSON: Who beg you? Commot my friend.

SALUBI: Okay. Siddon here dey make cinema. [*Goes.*]

SAMSON [*ambles restlessly round the room.*]: A fine shape I am in when I actually want that stink-bug to stay and keep me company. Ogiri mouth.[1] [*He grows more and more dejected.*] If he gets a job before Kotonu puts us back on the road the man will become simply intolerable. All the fault of that Kotonu. What use am I, a tout without his driver. I should have known it would come sooner or later. He's never acted like a normal person. When other drivers go out of the way to kill a dog, Kotonu nearly somersaults the lorry trying to avoid a flea-racked mongrel. Why, I ask him, why? Don't you know a dog is Ogun's meat? Take warning Kotonu. Before it's too late take warning and kill us a dog.

[*As his grumbling gets in stride, Kotonu returns with an armful of motor parts, an old shoe, a cap etc. Goes into the mammy-waggon stall through hidden entrance upstage. He can be heard occasionally but he tries to move silently. Occasionally he lifts up the top-half tarpaulin covering and pushes out an object, trying to remain unobserved by Samson. Half-way through Samson's moaning, one of the lay-abouts strums his guitar, begins to sing*]:

> Ona orun jin o eeeee
> Ona orun jin dereba rora
> E e dereba rora
> E e dereba rora
> Ona orun jin o eeeee
> Eleda mi ma ma buru
> Esin baba Bandele je l'odan
> Won o gbefun o
> Eleda mi ma ma buru
> Esin baba Bandele je l'odan
> Won o gbefun o

---

1. 'Skunk mouth.'

[*The others hanging by the fence join in idly. Samson turns angrily on the leader.*]

SAMSON: Get out get out. Is that the kind of song to be singing at this time of the morning? Why don't you go and look for work?

[*As if accustomed to this kind of outburst, the man waves Samson off, goes out. Samson turns, sees Kotonu who has finished in the stall and is now stretched full-length on the bench.*]

I didn't see you come back.

KOTONU: You were talking to yourself when I came.

SAMSON: Did you hear what I said? I hope you did because it's all true so I hope you heard every word of it. Where is Professor?

KOTONU [*following his time-table.*]: Wandering over empty streets picking up his dirty bits of printed matter.

SAMSON: He is not likely to come back is he?

KOTONU: No. That business here has unsettled him. He is still trying to work out a meaning—you're lucky he didn't suspect you.

SAMSON: Didn't you bring anything back from the wreck?

KOTONU: What do you mean?

SAMSON: Don't think I don't know. You have been taking over Sergeant Burma's business.

KOTONU: Who told you?

SAMSON: Never mind. But I never thought it was like you somehow. After all, what excuse have you? You haven't been to war. You cannot pretend to be an out-and-out cannibal like Sergeant Burma.

KOTONU: A man gets tired of feeling too much.

[*Outside, the gang resume their song, singing the lewd verse now.*]

> Bebe yi ga e-e-e
> Bebe yi ga sisi je nda mi'ra
> E e sisi je nda mi'ra
> E e sisi je nda mi'ra
> Bebe yi ga, o po o
> Omi tide pe mi l'okobo Mo yo
> Sibesibe me le f'asape laya o
> Won ndi bebe leko o won ndi bebe
> Eko mo roye o, ah mama
> Eko lawo ya o egungun d'enia

[*Interspersed with salutations called out to passing friends and abusive comments on favourite targets.*]

KOTONU: Where is Zorro who never returned from the North without a basket of guinea-fowl eggs? Where is Akanni the Lizard? I have not seen any other tout who would stand on the lorry's roof and play the samba at sixty miles an hour. Where is Sigidi Ope? Where is Sapele Joe who took on six policemen at the crossing and knocked them all into the river?

SAMSON: Overshot the pontoon, went down with his lorry.

KOTONU: And Saidu-Say? Indian Charlie who taught us driving? Well, tried to teach you anyway and wore out his soul in the attempt. Where is Humphrey Bogart? Cimarron Kid? Have you known any other driver take an oil-tanker from Port Harcourt to Kaduna non-stop since Muftau died? Where is Sergeant Burma who treated his tanker like a child's toy?

SAMSON: Just the same . . .

KOTONU: Sergeant Burma was never moved by these accidents. He told me himself how once he was stripping down a crash and found that the driver was an old comrade from the front. He took him to the mortuary but first he stopped to remove all the tyres.

SAMSON: He wasn't human.

KOTONU: But he was. He was. A man must protect himself against the indifference of comrades who desert him. Not to mention the hundred travellers whom you never really see until their faces are wiped clean by silence.

SAMSON: I see them. I am in the back with them and I see them. I talk to them and I abuse their grandfathers. But I don't carry on like you do.

KOTONU: You know, Professor is a bit like Sergeant Burma. He was moving round those corpses as if they didn't exist. All he cared about was re-planting that sign-post. To see him you would think he was Adam re-planting the Tree of Life.

SAMSON: All right thank you. I don't want to hear any more.

[*Kotonu slides back into his favourite position, lying by the wall of the store or sitting up against it. Most of the time he is half-asleep, indifferent to what goes on around him. Enter Chief-in-Town, a politician.*]

CHIEF-IN-TOWN: Captain!

SAMSON [*without turning round.*]: They've all gone.

CHIEF: Which motor-park?

SAMSON: Who knows? Anywhere they find a picking.

CHIEF: How long ago did they leave? I said I might need them this morning.

SAMSON: No idea.

CHIEF: You are new around here. Are you . . . one of the boys?

SAMSON: I won't thug for you if that is what you mean.

CHIEF: You will, you will . . . just give yourself a few more days sitting doing nothing. What about your friend?

SAMSON: He used to be my driver and I his tout. Now he doesn't want any part of the road—except what is left of the sacrifice.

CHIEF: Sacrifice? What sacrifice?

SAMSON: Never mind. He doesn't thug either, and that is all you really want to know.

[*Enter Say Tokyo Kid with a leap over the fence.*]

SAY T.: Chief-in-Town!

CHIEF: The Captain!

SAY T.: Chief-in-Town.

CHIEF: Say Tokyo Kid!

SAY T.: No dirty timber, thas me Chief.

CHIEF: How is the timber world?

SAY T.: Life is full of borers Chief. I feel them in my tummy. Chief-in-Town! I was already on ma way to the moror park when your car passed me. I shoured but you didn't hear nuthin.

CHIEF: I need ten men.

SAY T.: Today?

CHIEF: This moment. Didn't you get my message?

SAY T.: No.

CHIEF: I sent my driver. He said he gave it to an old man in a black tuxedo.

SAY T.: That would be Professor. He don't like us doing this kinra job. Well what's cooking Chief? Campaign.

CHIEF: No. Just a party meeting.

SAY T.: Oh. Are we for the general party or . . .

CHIEF: You know me, Personal Bodyguard.

SAY T.: Chief-in-Town!

CHIEF: How soon can you round them up?

SAY T.: Ten minutes, fifteen minutes—no more.

CHIEF: I want the toughest you can find. This meeting is going to be hot.

SAY T.: You know you can count on me Chief. What about . . . ?

CHIEF: Stuff?

SAY T.: Yeah Chief. You got the old Chacha-Mu-Chacha?

[*Chief-in-Town takes out a small packet. Say Tokyo snatches it greedily.*]

SAY T. [*examines it, sniffs it.*]: Stuff Chief. Real stuff.

CHIEF: I will send the Land-Rover to the motor park.

SAY T.: No Chief. Send it here. I'll send round the word.

CHIEF: Don't fail me. Fifteen minutes.

SAY T.: Chief-in-Town!

[*Chief-in-Town goes. Say Tokyo quickly rolls himself a stick of hemp, sits in a corner and starts to inhale.*

Samson breaks from a corner where he has been poking the spider with a stick.]

SAMSON: You know, you remind me of a spider.

KOTONU: Why?

SAMSON: Yes, that's it. You are living just like a spider. This is your brother in this corner.

KOTONU: What are you getting at now?

SAMSON [*peering.*]: Facially, it even resembles you.

KOTONU: But I haven't got so many legs.

SAMSON: Who told you? Four rear tyres, two front and two spare. That is eight altogether. But you prefer to lie there and vegetate.

KOTONU [*irritably.*]: I knew it would be something like that. Why won't you give up?

SAMSON: Anyway, when you get tired of being a trader in dead lorries Chief-in-Town can take you up as a thug.

KOTONU: It isn't such a bad idea. At least I will see a man's face before I bash it in. Driving doesn't guarantee you that.

[*Say Tokyo Kid, his eyes fixed and glazed, achieves the 'state'. He seizes the big drum and goes out to the fence. Beats out the summons for his gang and returns to the shack while the echoes carry on. He sets about rolling more of the sticks for his gang who roll in one by one. Samson moves beside Kotonu, watching. They sit around the table, dragging on the hemp.*

Through the door a uniformed policeman, Particulars Joe, thrusts his]

[*head through the door and sniffs the air, turns outside to look up and down the road and slides into the room. Barks suddenly.*]

PARTICULARS JOE: Wey your particulars?

A THUG: Particulars Joe!

PARTICULARS JOE: I say gimme your particulars.

[*Say Tokyo reaches out a stick of weed to him which he accepts behind his back. Darts back to the door and sits apart sniffing the weed. He gives a quick nod of appreciation to Say Tokyo who graciously waves it aside. One of his thugs picks up drum and taps out a slow rhythm. Say Tokyo, his eye shining madly, leaps up. Lights up Joe's cigarette.*

Say Tokyo slowly flexes his arm muscles, looking from one arm to the other, luxuriating in the feel of his strength.]

PARTICULARS JOE: Say Tokyo Kid!

SAY T.: I'm all right boy.

PARTICULARS JOE: No dirty timber.

SAY T.: No borer in re ol bole.

SAMSON: Oh what wouldn't I give for Professor to enter now.

SAY T. [*spits.*]: That's what would happen if your Professor came in. I don give a damn for that crazy guy and he know it. He's an awright guy but he sure act crazy sometimes and I'm telling you, one of these days, he's gonna go too far.

A THUG: The Captain!

SAY T.: I'm Say Tokyo Kid and I don't fear no son of man.

SAMSON: Yes you can talk now. But you run here fast enough to guzzle his wine.

SAY T.: So what? So long his guy keeps bringing that swell froth on every gourd, I'm gonna come here to pay ma respects. But a don' go for no ceremony abour' it. A don't mind his crazy talk, but all the rest of it, man, it ain't for Say Tokyo Kid.

PARTICULARS JOE [*somewhat dizzily.*]: Say Tokyo.

SAY T.: Thas me officer.

[*Particulars Joe gets groggier and groggier as the scene progresses, swaying more and more until by the end of the dance he is clutching his stomach and slithers to the ground.*]

PARTICULARS JOE: Gedu!

SAY T.: Thas me boy.

PARTICULARS JOE: No dirty timber.

SAY T.: Thas me kid.

PARTICULARS JOE: Igi dongboro lehin were!

SAY T.: Yio ba baba e.

PARTICULARS JOE: Gbegi ma gbe'yawo!

SAY T.: Yio ba 'ponri iya a'laiya e.

PARTICULARS JOE: Olomokuiya. [*Say Tokyo grins, both hands held in an insulting gesture.*][1]

SAY T.: I mean, a man has gotta have his pride. I don't carry no timber that ain't one hundred per cent. fit. I'm a guy of principles. Carrying timber ain't the same as carrying passengers I tell you. You carry any kind of guy. You take any kind of load. You carrying rubbish. You carrying lepers. The women tell you to stop because they's feeling the call of nature. If you don't stop they pee in your lorry. And whether you stop or not their chirren mess the place all over. The whole of the lorry is stinking from rotting food and all kinda refuse. That's a passenger lorry.

SALUBI: Say Tokyo Kid!

SAY T.: Thas me boy. No time for nonsense!

SAMSON: I don't know. I like to deal with people. Just think, carrying a dead load like that from one end of the world to another ...

SAY T.: Dead! You think a guy of timber is dead load. What you talking kid? You reckon you can handle a timber lorry like you drive your passenger truck. You wanna sit down and feel that dead load trying to take the steering from your hand. You kidding? There is a hundred spirits in every guy of timber trying to do you down cause you've trapped them in, see? There is a spirit in hell for every guy of timber. [*Feels around his neck and brings out a talisman on a string.*]

You reckon a guy just goes and cuts down a guy of timber. You gorra do it proper man or you won't live to cut another log. Dead men tell no tales kid. Until that guy is sawn up and turned to a bench or table, the spirit guy is still struggling inside

---

1. 'Nothing like a sound club on the back of a looney!
'May it land on your father.
'Wedded, not to a wife but to timber.
'May it hit the fountainhead of your great grandmother.
'Ah, what sufferings for such as give birth.'

it, and I don't fool around with him see, cause if your home was cut down you sure gonna be real crazy with the guy who's done it.

KOTONU: Yeah, I suppose so.

SAMSON: You don't believe that rubbish do you?

SAY T.: You call it rubbish! Well you tell me. Why ain't I cut and bruised like all those guys? Cause timber don't turn against her own son see? I'm a son of timber. And I only drive timber see?

THUG: Son of timber!

SAY T.: That me kid. A guy is gorra have his principles. I'm a right guy. I mean you just look arrit this way. If you gonna be killed by a car, you don't wanna be killed by a Volkswagen. You wanra Limousine, a Ponriac or something like that. Well thas my principle. Suppose you was to come and find me in the ditch one day with one of them timber guys on ma back. Now ain't it gonna be a disgrace if the guy was some kinda cheap, wretched firewood full of ants and borers. So when I carry a guy of timber, its gorra be the biggest. One or two. If it's one, its gorra fill the whole lorry, no room even for the wedge. And high class timber kid. High class. Golden walnut. Obeche. Ironwood. Black Afara. Iroko. Ebony. Camwood. And the heartwood's gorra be sound. [Thumps his chest.] It's gorra have a solid beat like that. Like mahogany.

THUG: No dirty timber!

SAY T.: Timber is ma line. You show me the wood and I'll tell you whar kinda insects gonna attack it, and I'll tell you how you take the skin off. And I'll tell you whar kinda spirit is gonna be chasing you when you cut it down. If you ain't gorra strong head kid, you can't drive no guy of timber.

SAMSON: Just the same it doesn't much matter what you are carrying when it rolls over you.

SAY T.: You kidding? Just you speak for yourself man. And when that guy of timber gits real angry and plays me rough, I just don't wan no passenger piss running on ma head. You know, just last week I pass an accident on the road. There was a dead dame and you know what her pretty head was smeared with? Yam porrage. See whar I mean? A swell dame is gonna die on the road just so the next passenger kin smear her head in yam

porrage? No sirree. I ain't going with no one unless with ma
own guy of timber.

[*The drummer beats louder and raises a heavy, drowsy voice.*]

> Eni r'oro ke juba
> Ohun oju ri
> K'o ba de'le a mo'ra
> Ohun oju ri
> Eni r'oro ke juba
> Ohun oju ri
> Ko ba de'le a ru'bo
> Ohun oju ri
> B'e de dele d'ojumo
> Ohun oju ri
> Oruwo re a pitan
> Ohun oju ri
> Eni r'esu ke yago
> Ohun oju ri
> Eni s'agberef'elegun
> Ohun oju ri

[*The slow song and drugged movements pick up tempo,
interpolated with war-whoops and yells until the sound of the truck
is heard and they stamp out to a violent beat and somersaulting
war-dance, hoisting up Particulars Joe and bearing him out.*]

SAMSON [*shouting after them.*]: I hope you all get beaten up!

[*Almost immediately, from the church side of the shack comes
violent knocking.*]

Now what other lunatics are those?

[*Three men are outside, within the shadow cast by the shack. Two
are drivers, the third is obviously a car owner, well dressed in a rich
agbada. They take turns to speak.*]

1ST MAN: Open up. Come on now, open up the shop. We've
waited just about enough. It's a whole week since Sergeant
Burma died, what are you waiting for?

2ND MAN: Is business to stand still while you laze around sleeping
and drinking tombo? Even old wrecks go on wheels, let's see
the tyres.

3RD MAN: I could use a hub with mine. Come on open up the shop.

1ST MAN: And I want that cap all drivers favour. A six-inch visor
in tinted plastic. Goes over the eye and cheats the sun.

2ND MAN: He must have plenty. Where is the man? Kotonu! Don't you know the morning is half the day?

1ST MAN: Professor chose you, we're not complaining. But man you've got to give us service.

2ND MAN: Kotonu! [*Bangs again on the wall.*] Makes a man wish Sergeant Burma were alive.

3RD MAN: He would never waste a day. If he wasn't there his wife deputized.

1ST MAN: If she wasn't there you helped yourself. Accounts to be settled on the twenty-punctual.

2ND MAN: Month-ending na debt-ending. Sergeant Burma never hear excuse.

3RD MAN: If you no settle here you go settle am for heaven.

ALL: No he never let us down. Sergeant Burma never let us down.

SAMSON: Shoo shoo, you no dey sleep for house?

1ST MAN: Abi dis one craze. Wis kin sleep for this time?

2ND MAN: Tell am make 'e come open shop.

3RD MAN: You tink say weself we no sabbe sleep?

SAMSON: 'E no well. No worry am.

1ST MAN: 'E no well 'e no well, na dat one we go chop? Call am make e comot onetime.

2ND MAN: This Kotonu na failure. Wetin 'e think 'e be?

3RD MAN: Where is Professor? We will have to tell the old man.

1ST MAN: But he doesn't come till evening when the church shadow is on the shack.

2ND MAN: Well he's somewhere on the road, let's go try and dig him out.

3RD MAN: Oh but this is nonsense. Burma never let us down.

ALL: No he never let us down.

1ST MAN: Spare plugs, fuses, petrol cover.

2ND MAN: Windscreen wiper twin carburettor.

3RD MAN: Tyre chassis hub or tie-rod.

1ST MAN: Propeller pistons rings or battery

2ND MAN: Rugs car radio brakes silencer

ALL: Where there is crish-crash call Sergeant Burma

1ST MAN: Every seam of second-hand clothing

2ND MAN: Trousers sandals ties assorted

3RD MAN: Handbags lipstick cigarette holder

1ST MAN: Toys for children, springs and crankshaft

2ND MAN: Hoods umbrellas, poor Sergeant Burma

ALL: No he never let us down, no he never quit his post.

1ST MAN: Let's go. We'll get Professor to chase this one.

2ND MAN: Call himself a petty-trader?

3RD MAN: He's giving a bad name to Bosikona.

1ST MAN: Him! Trying to step in Burma's boots.

2ND MAN: If Burma's a soldier, he's a boy scout.

3RD MAN: His days are numbered. Let's get Professor. [*Going.*]

1ST MAN: Oh Sergeant Burma how we miss you.

ALL: No he never let us down. Burma never let us down. [*Offstage by now.*]

[*Enter Salubi, dog-tired. He carries a bowl of soup and a mound of eba wrapped in leaves.*]

SALUBI: No luck. And my legs are dead.

SAMSON: You should leave them in your trousers and starch them with your clothes.

SALUBI: It is no joking matter.

SAMSON: I wish you would take a bath. I could smell your approach five minutes before you come in.

SALUBI: Good for you. And I hope you get your Kotonu back on the road soon so I can have some peace.

SAMSON: And I hope you get your Yessah Yessah job soon so we can breathe some fresh air.

SALUBI: You are just like a haggling market woman. Why don't you go and get your fresh air from the motor park. Before you two came I used to have a clear three hours here by myself, three hours of peace before the others start to drift here and bite their finger-nails.

SAMSON: And pick lice off their bodies—don't leave out your own speciality.

[*Salubi opens his mouth to reply, gives up and sits down to his meal. He has just stirred the soup with his finger when Samson pounces on him.*]

SAMSON: What is that? You haven't got stockfish in there have you?

SALUBI: Stockfish? Oh you mean this panla? Certainly!

SAMSON: The whole world is surely determined to ruin me. Get it out of here quickly.

SALUBI: What are you talking about? Do you know any self-respecting driver who will eat eba without panla?

SAMSON [*clamps his hand over Salubi's mouth and throws an apprehensive glance at Kotonu.*]: Shut up for heaven's sake! Don't I have enough trouble without you coming to add to it with your rubbishy tastes?

SALUBI: Eh, wait a minute.

SAMSON [*helping him to remove the foodstuffs.*]: Just get it out of here.

SALUBI: What is all this? You haven't any right to drive me out of here. Professor doesn't mind me at all.

SAMSON: That is what you think. But he particularly objects to stockfish. He says the smell disturbs his spirits. Now go out before he comes and catches you here.

SALUBI: I don't believe that lie.

SAMSON: You are lucky Kotonu is asleep. The Professor put him in charge against that sort of thing. If he wakes up he will report you and the Professor will deal with you.

SALUBI [*scampering.*]: Don't think you can frighten me with that. I don't care one panla for your Professor. He can't do me anything.

SAMSON: Good. Very good. I'll tell him when he comes. I'll tell him about this morning. And he'll send the word to get you in the dead of night.

SALUBI: Tell him if you like. One of these days the police will catch up with him. And they'll put him where he belongs— in the lunatic asylum of the prison. Don't think you can scare me with that word business.

SAMSON: Just go out. I will deliver your message. [*Ushering him out.*]

SALUBI: Deliver it. I don't care. Or do you think I don't know about the church funds? Tell him the day the police catch him I will come and testify against him. The man is a menace. Pulling up road-signs and talking all that mumbo-jumbo.

SAMSON: Yes, yes, I'll tell him. But don't ever bring stockfish in here again.

SALUBI: A bit of stockfish won't do his brain any harm—you tell him that.

[*Samson drives him out. Looks anxiously towards Kotonu and appears satisfied that he hasn't overheard. Begins to pace up and down. Stops, tip-toes past Kotonu and tries to see into the stall through a gap in the wood.*]

KOTONU: I didn't lock it. Just remove the board.

[*Samson jumps, walks away angrily.*]

SAMSON: Who do you think is interested in your morbid merchandise?

KOTONU: I never said you were.

SAMSON: Just the same, you astonish me. There are many sides to you which I have never suspected. I mean, to think that we grew up together.

KOTONU: I wish you would stop walking up and down. I am trying to sleep.

SAMSON: Shouldn't you open up shop. Somebody might want a dripping cushion from the last crash.

KOTONU: I haven't begun selling yet. Need a few more days to work myself up to it.

SAMSON: Who do you think you are fooling? Didn't you sell Salubi his uniform?

KOTONU: I didn't sell him anything. He stole it. I saw him take it so I said he was welcome to keep it.

SAMSON: He didn't buy it?

KOTONU: I gave it to him.

SAMSON: That man not only stinks like Lagos lagoon, he lies like a Lagos girl.

KOTONU: Leave him alone. Why do you keep on at him?

SAMSON: I'll tell you why. He is waiting to take your licence.

KOTONU: Well why doesn't he say so?

SAMSON: Oh he won't say a thing you can count on that. But he keeps hanging around so he can buy it cheap off you. Then Professor will perform his artistry on it.

KOTONU: When he comes tell him he can have it.

SAMSON: I'd sooner give it to a dog. In fact give it to me now. I no longer trust you with it.

KOTONU: Take it. It is hanging up over there.

[*Samson retrieves the licence, puts it in his pocket.*]

SAMSON: At least I will see that we get a decent price for it—and not from any smelly monkey in uniform either. Nine years we have been together and now all you want to do is be a shop-keeper.

KOTONU: And sleep.

SAMSON: Yes sleep. Stay in one spot like a spider. And what about

me? How am I to live without the running board of a passenger
lorry?

KOTONU: There are so many drivers looking for a good
conductor. One of them will take you.

SAMSON: Yes. One of them will take me. Nine years we have
worked together, and now you want me to go and join any
driver who happens along.

KOTONU: Suppose I had got killed in an accident? It could have
been us at the bridge.

SAMSON: But it wasn't. The other lorry overtook us—that's divine
providence for you.

KOTONU: One mile. Only one more mile and we would have
been first at the bridge.

SAMSON [angry.]: Why do you keep on about it? They overtook
us—that's their luck. It was anybody's chance.

[He walks about the room. Stops to look at the spider.]

SAMSON: Your brother is having a dinner. Hm. Just the wings left
of that fly.

KOTONU: The road and the spider lie gloating, then the fly buzzes
along like a happy fool . . .

SAMSON [very hurriedly.]: All right all right.

KOTONU: But why they and not us? Their names weren't carved
on the rotten wood.

SAMSON [walking rapidly away from the corner.]: All right I've heard
you. I can understand. I am not deaf.

KOTONU: What's the matter? I was only trying to understand.

SAMSON: I don't want to know. Just don't give up driving
that's all I am trying to tell you. [Kotonu shrugs, relapses.] I
mean, just look at it like a reasonable man. What else are you
good for? Nothing.

[Professor enters from the side of the church. With dignified caution
he looks round to make sure he is not observed. Looks through the open
window as if he is peeping through a narrow chink. Tests the walls
with his walking stick. Pokes crevices in the wall for signs of
weakening. Shakes his head sadly, crosses the road to the shack.]

SAMSON: Such a sinful waste of talent. There isn't any driver in
the whole of Africa who commands the steering wheel like
you.

KOTONU: Oh let a man sleep can't you?

[*Samson sees Professor, rushes to relieve him of his bundles and sets them on the table. Professor gives him a very condescending nod, lays aside his stick very carefully.*
Methodically he stacks the bundles on one side of the table, removes pen, pencil, rubber and some paper from his pockets and sets them out before him. Samson watches this daily ritual in rapt fascination. From his waistcoat the Professor now pulls out a pocket-watch by the chain, examines the time and winds it.]

SAMSON: How is the Word today Professor?

PROF.: Trapped. Fast in demonic bondage. I looked at the walls. They have not begun to give. But I can wait. Continue the search with patience. Avoid mirages—had one this morning. If it had happened on a hot afternoon with the sun heavy on the tar, I could understand. That's the hour of mirages. But a mirage in the morning! No matter. I am prepared now—they shan't fool me again.

[*He extracts a newspaper from a bundle and begins to study it, using a hand lens. Samson tip-toes back to Kotonu.*]

SAMSON: Why don't we ask him what he thinks about it?

[*Kotonu pretends to have fallen asleep.*]

Answer. I know you're not asleep.

KOTONU: Yes, yes, ask him anything.

SAMSON [*goes over, timidly.*]: Please sir ... sir ... Professor ... sir ... [*Professor looks up.*] I ... we ... my friend and I, we wonder if you would favour us with your opinion on a very delicate matter.

PROF.: You are consulting me?

SAMSON: Yes Sir, we would value your opinion very much.

PROF. [*with emphasis.*]: This is a consultation.

SAMSON: Oh I am sorry, very sorry sir. I was a little forgetful. [*He fishes out a threepence and places it on the table. But Professor continues to look straight ahead of him. Nervously Samson adds a penny. Then another. He is about to add a third but he decides to protest.*] But Professor, we are both out of a job.

PROF. [*looks at him, then at the money. Shrugs, puts the coins in his pocket.*]: All right then, but only for you. If you let anyone know I will give you the full bill. My kindness would be plagued by beggars if I gave them a chance.

SAMSON [*gratefully*.]: Oh I won't breathe a word I swear. You really are a kind person.

PROF. [*affixes his monocle and stares hard at Samson*.]: Hm. I would say your problem is straightforward. You are in some kind of difficulty.

SAMSON: You have stated it exactly sir.

PROF.: In fact, one might almost say that you are about to pass through a crisis of decisions.

SAMSON: Ah, I don't know that one Professor.

PROF.: How could you? You are illiterate. It is lucky for you that I watch over you, over all of you.

SAMSON: Yes sir, Er, about our problem sir . . .

PROF.: Life is difficult for the faithless. But do not despair.

SAMSON: Yes Professor. Now about our difficulty sir. As you know sir, my friend used to be a driver.

PROF.: He has a new job—with a millionaire.

SAMSON: Who? Oh he . . . er . . . he resigned . . . no he was sacked. He told me himself, he says he was sacked when he accompanied you somewhere.

PROF.: You accuse me perhaps of . . . sabotage?

SAMSON: Me sir? Not in the least, the thought never crossed my mind. Please Professor just forget that whole business, forget it altogether. It is just that he never wanted to drive anyway, and that's his trouble.

PROF.: Increase his salary.

SAMSON: No sir, it isn't that. He simply doesn't want to drive at all. I mean Professor, I have been his apprentice for the past nine years. And now he wants to give up. He doesn't want to touch another steering wheel—except as spare part of course.

PROF.: He'll lose his pension.

SAMSON: There is no pension in the job.

PROF.: What! No pension? What is your Trade Union doing about it?

SAMSON: Professor, what I mean is, how can a man cut off part of himself like that. Just look at him. He is not complete without a motor lorry.

PROF.: He is not? [*Turns to stare at Kotonu.*] What sort of an animal is he?

SAMSON: Animal? I mean to say, Professor! Ask anybody here. Everybody knows Kotonu. From Lagos to Monrovia they know him. And they know Samson his mate, his apprentice, his conductor and passenger collector. Look Professor, the road won't be the same without him.

PROF.: He was a road mender too?

SAMSON: Sir? But I told you he is a driver.

PROF. [*takes out his watch and looks at it.*]: Hm.

SAMSON: Is it working now Professor?

PROF.: No. But it still tells the time.

KOTONU [*sitting up.*]: Isn't Murano here?

SAMSON [*agitatedly.*]: You see Professor. Now Murano has become his evensong.

PROF. [*looks up at the church window.*]: It is not yet the hour of sacrament.

SAMSON [*turns angrily to Kotonu.*]: That is all you want to do now. Sit here dropping saliva until Murano turns up.

KOTONU: What's wrong with that. I say I want to retire.

SAMSON: People retire at sixty—like Professor here.

PROF. [*without looking up.*]: A small correction—I am not yet sixty. Fifty-nine pounds seven shillings and twenty-one pence— that is my real age.

KOTONU: And build up the business.

SAMSON: Yes. By giving away uniforms to anyone who can steal one. You fancy yourself a business man don't you?

KOTONU: Why not? Sergeant Burma didn't do badly. If he could do it so can I.

SAMSON: Look Professor, help me to talk to him. It is just what our people say—the man with a head is looking for a cap and the man with a cap lacks the head. When you think how much a licence costs in this place.

KOTONU: I'm not complaining.

SAMSON: Why should you? I paid for your licence. But I don't complain because it was a good investment. Was.

KOTONU: Yes, was. Until this. [*From the store he pulls out a full Ogun mask, held in shape with sticks.*]

SAMSON: I don't know why you still retain that!

KOTONU: It has to stay with me. [*Bows deeply.*]
My humble quota to the harvest of the road.
[*Drops it suddenly.*] God, God, if only I had never taken your money for my driving test.

SAMSON: It would only have grown mould where I buried it.
You see Professor, the magic of a motor engine simply
refused to reveal itself to me. Kotonu was the clever one.
From the word go he could drive better than Indian Charlie.
Oh, Indian Charlie was our master. God rest his soul in peace
but that man nearly murdered me. Fai fai fai! Every day forty
slaps at least. So I knew that driving was not meant for people
like me. I gave my savings to Kotonu for his test.

KOTONU: I should never have taken it.

SAMSON: It would only have rotted underground. I couldn't use
it for anything else but my licence fee. That's why I buried it in
the churchyard.

PROF.: You buried it where!

SAMSON: In the churchyard. I put it in a cigarette tin and buried
it near a gravestone. And swore there and then that if I
uprooted it for any other purpose all the spirits in that
burial-ground should follow me home and haunt me for three
days and nights.

PROF.: Very risky. Very risky. Conjuration is no light matter you
know. Never fool around with spirits.

SAMSON: Oh I know that. But it came to the same thing really
because I used it for Kotonu and he took me on as his partner.

PROF.: You know the Word?

SAMSON: What is that Professor?

PROF.: Oh the conceit of insects! The butterfly thinks the flapping
of his wings fathered the whirlwind that followed. The
burrowing beetle feels he powered the arm of the eruption.
Do you claim to have communed with spirits in the last
respository of damned souls?

SAMSON: I only said I kept my money there.

PROF.: So the dead are now your bank managers?

SAMSON: No sir, I . . .

PROF.: No harm in it, no harm in it. Do they give overdrafts though?

SAMSON: Well I only kept the money in a cigarette tin.

PROF.: But you couldn't have known the Word could you? A
gravestone turns slow and gentle on the hinge; angels trapped
by day in illusions of concrete rise in night's parole; the dead
earth opens at your feet—my friend, confronted with the
Resurrection, would you know the Word?

SAMSON: Would I what what Professor?

PROF.: Daylight marble lies! Oh mocking God! To think that even worms were given the Word—else why do they hold our flesh in such contempt?

SAMSON: Do you mean for instance, if Kotonu died now and I met him at night?

PROF.: Would you know the Word?

SAMSON: Well I don't know which word. But I might try Our Father which art in Heaven and take to my heels.

PROF.: And your friend. Does he know the Word?

SAMSON: Kotonu.

KOTONU: Hm.

SAMSON: The Professor is talking to you. He says what would you say in the cemetery.

PROF.: You reduce it all to nonsense burying your faith in cigarette tins. You should invest it. My friend, the Word is a living word not a grave-robber's prayer of appeasement.

SAMSON [highly indignant.]: I am not a grave-robber. I tell you it was my own money. I kept it there in a cigarette tin. It was there for two years before I even touched it.

[He walks over distractedly to the corner, looks at the web.]

Oh, he's finished.

KOTONU: He is never finished, he's only resting.

SAMSON: I don't mean the Professor. Your dining brother.

KOTONU: I wonder which driver that was. Or may be a passenger.

SAMSON [furiously.]: Oh yes just go on. Now I have started you off you won't let us rest. Why don't you just admit you are tired?

KOTONU: But I've said so already.

[Salubi rushes in. Stops, then goes straight for the Professor.]

SALUBI: Professor, I need a licence.

PROF.: It is past my hour of consultation.

SALUBI: Oh, an oversight. Forgive me sir. [Places a shilling on the desk.]

PROF. [picks up the shilling and affixes his monocle.]: At a glance, I would say that you need some sort of official document.

SALUBI: Oh yes sir. A driving licence. Such a chance Professor— I knew it would come if I persevered.

PROF.: I would also deduce that your need is somewhat urgent.

SALUBI: Desperate sir. I must get a licence now now. This job is first class. If I don't get it I will commit suicide.

PROF.: God rot your coward bones! Do you think not enough people die here that you must come and threaten me with death? You spurious spew. You instrument of mortgage. You unlicensed appendage of the steering wheel—[*throws the shilling out of door.*] I refuse to touch your case.

SALUBI [*prostrating flat on his belly.*]: Oga I beg you sir. I sorry too much. I will never do so again sir.

PROF. [*in mounting rage.*]: Get out. Get out! And don't let me see you in here again. Do you think I keep pews at the waking for any false contractor to death. Suicide! May the elusive Word crack your bones in a hundred splinters!

SALUBI [*cowers, terror-stricken.*]: Professor I beg you, not that. Anything but that.

PROF.: May your tongue of deception be rotted in pestilence from the enigma of the Inviolate Word.

SAMSON: Professor sir, Professor . . .

SALUBI: Professor, I beg you in the name of your father, no put that your conjuration on top me head. Kotonu . . . help me beg him . . .

SAMSON: Sir, please sir, he won't do so again. I will vouch for him—he won't do so again.

PROF.: Get out of my sight, and the Word follow you as you leave my threshold.

[*He sits, plunges himself straight into his usual occupation with the papers.*]

SALUBI: Kotonu, won't you people put in a word for me? I swear I won't do so again. Never say die sir. Never say die—that is my motto from now on. I will paint it on every lorry I see— Never say die! Samson, help me now. Tell Professor to take in curse commot for my head. Enh. Samson call me I beg you, call me make Professor hear me answer to my motto.

SAMSON: Salubi.

SALUBI: Never say die!

SAMSON: Salubi Salubirity.

SALUB : Never say die.

SAMSON: Salubi omo agbepo.[1]

SALUBI [*hesitates a fraction but Samson is unyielding.*]: Never say die.

SAMSON: You mout' stink like night-soil lorry.

1. 'Son of the night scavenger.'

SALUBI: Never say die.

SAMSON: Your body and lice day like David and Jonathan.

SALUBI: Never say die.

SAMSON: Ole ngboro fear no foe rob in own grandmamma.[1]

SALUBI: Never say die.

SAMSON: Iwin ogodo.[2] Ten like you and soap-factories close down.

SALUBI: Never say die.

SAMSON: Professor sir, I think he is truly repentant. Kotonu and I, we beg you to forgive him.
[*Receiving no response, he turns his back, takes some money from a deep pocket and returns to Professor. Half-way he stops, goes to Salubi and rifles his pocket for more money, all of which he places very apologetically on the table.*]

PROF. [*without bothering to look.*]: And double the usual consultation fee.

SALUBI [*leaps up like a man reprieved from death.*]: Yes sir, anything sir. I am so very thankful I swear I will never do so again.
[*Puts the money on the table and prostrates himself.*]
Ah I thank you Professor. I thank you very much. It's my ignorance sir, don't be vexing with me like that. After all a father doesn't to vex with his children like that.

PROF.: Photograph?

SALUBI [*rapidly producing two snapshots.*]: Here sir. Everything is ready.

PROF.: Are you an escaped convict? This photo looks villanous.

SALUBI: Me sir? But I have never go to prison in all my life.

PROF.: A gaol-bird. I know one when I see it. This photo confirms it.

SALUBI: Oga I swear ...

PROF.: Come back tomorrow morning. You have all the smell of a prison yard about you.

SAMSON: I told you you should wash.

SALUBI: Please sir, Professor, don't disappoint me. Is a matter of life and death. Enh! I mean to say ...
[*He stops short, horrified at what Professor's reaction would be.*]

PROF. [*gives him a long cold stare.*]: Get him outside before I change my mind.

1. 'Robber abroad, fearless one, will rob his own grandmother.'
2. 'Imp of the swamp.'

[*The man retreats, goes over to one of the benches and tucks himself unobtrusively in a corner.*]

PROF.: Outside. Outside.

[*Salubi runs out.*]

SAMSON [*follows him and looks out. Salubi is crouching near the door.*]: I thought so. Dead scared like that but he can't even go away. And why?

KOTONU [*sitting up.*]: Why? But you heard the man, he wants his licence.

SAMSON: He knows Professor will take his own time. No it's because Murano will soon arrive. That is how you will become if you give up driving. You are lucky Murano doesn't know how you all depend on him.

KOTONU: He is late today.

PROF. [*looks at the church window.*]: He'll come at the communion hour. When that shadow covers me in grace of darkness he will come.

KOTONU: Yes, he always seems to time it well.

PROF.: They cannot cast me out. I will live in the shadow of the fort. I will question the very walls for the hidden Word.

KOTONU: If I may ask, Professor, where did you find Murano?

PROF.: Neglected in the back of a hearse. And dying. Moaned like a dog whose legs have been broken by a motor car. I took him—somewhere—looked after him till he was well again.

KOTONU: And you set him to tap palm wine for you?

PROF. [*rises, goes over to Kotonu.*]: I think you are an astute man, or simply desperate. You grope towards Murano, the one person in this world in whom the Word reposes.

SAMSON: Much use that is to him. He cannot use his tongue.

PROF.: Deep. Silent but deep. Oh my friend, beware the pity of those that have no tongue for they have been proclaimed sole guardians of the Word. They have slept beyond the portals of secrets. They have pierced the guard of eternity and unearthed the Word, a golden nugget on the tongue. And so their tongue hangs heavy and they are forever silenced. Do you mean you do not see that Murano has one leg longer than the other?

SAMSON: Murano? But his legs are the same.

PROF.: Blind!

KOTONU: Oh I admit he limps. Anyway he seems okay to me.

PROF.: When a man has one leg in each world, his legs are never the same. The big toe of Murano's foot—the left one of course—rests on the slumbering chrysalis of the Word. When that crust cracks my friends—you and I, that is the moment we await. That is the moment of our rehabilitation. When that crust cracks . . . [*Growing rapidly emotional, he stops suddenly, sniffs once or twice, wipes his misted glasses, returns briskly to his table.*]

SAMSON [*goes over to Kotonu.*]: I have often thought of following that Murano you know. He sets out about five o'clock in the morning, goes in that direction. And he doesn't come back until five in the afternoon. That's a long time to tap a little wine. Have you ever considered where he goes?

KOTONU: Why should I?

SAMSON: One of these days I will follow him some of the way . . .

PROF. [*sharply.*]: You are tired of life perhaps?

SAMSON: I didn't say anything.

PROF.: Those who are not equipped for strange sights—fools like you—go mad or blind when their curiosity is pursued. First find the Word. It is not enough to follow Murano at dawn and spy on him like a vulgar housewife. Find the Word.

SAMSON [*disinterested.*]: Where does one find it Professor?

PROF.: Where? Where ascent is broken and a winged secret plummets back to earth. Ask Murano.

SAMSON: But he cannot talk.

PROF. [*cunningly.*]: You see. They know what they are doing. [*Enter two of the lay-abouts, with broken heads. One collapses on a bench and the other rushes through to the water-pot, drinks like a camel, pours the rest over his head and slides down beside the pot. Professor looks at them with anger then returns to his work with a ferocious concentration.*]

SAMSON [*timidly.*]: Professor, if you could just find one word to persuade Kotonu not to give up driving, I would be satisfied with that.

PROF. [*hits the table suddenly.*]: That's it! I knew there was something I had forgotten. A solution, a compensation, a redress, a balance of inequalities . . . bring me your friend's driving licence.

SAMSON [*reaching for it.*]: You think it might be in the licence Professor?

PROF.: What?

SAMSON: The Word.

PROF.: Do you think I spend every living moment looking for that? What do you think I am—a madman? [*Puts on a pair of glasses and examines the licence carefully with the additional aid of the hand lens. Places Salubi's photograph over Kotonu's. Sighs. Sadly.*] It is a sign of my failing powers when I am glad for alterations this easy to hand. Not so long ago I would have spurned such clumsy craftsmanship, built a new document from old electric bills and those government circulars in which food-sellers wrap their food.

[*He turns his pen on the documents.*]

SAMSON [*alarmed.*]: What are you thinking of doing Professor?

PROF.: Nearly a year since I celebrated my hundredth forgery. It is difficult always to forge from scratch, and I am getting old. Once I could do three licences in a week and not feel the strain. Now if I manage one, I feel the life has gone from me. This needs only a little adjustment. A neat transfer, not a basic forgery.

SAMSON: But Professor, what about us? Our livelihood! I asked you to convince him to return to the road but you want to cut him out altogether. What will we live on?

PROF.: He will find the Word.

SAMSON: The Word? Will that fill his belly or mine?

PROF.: Samson. Lion-hearted Samson with an ass's head, can you not see that your friend will never drive again?

SAMSON: How do you know? It is only a phase and he will get over it.

PROF. [*pierces him with a sudden prolonged earnestness*]: Tell me my friend, were you ever a millionaire?

SAMSON: What . . . who er me . . . I don't understand Professor.

PROF.: I had a strange experience this morning. Missed my way and was received into the palace of millionaire. Your friend guided me out or I might still be lost and wandering. In return I took him to the latest offering of the Word. I have accepted him—and you—like the others. Where do you come from? When do you take leave of me? [*He shrugs.*] But there, as the blood and the waste clung to his feet, I knew him. And I tell you, before my eyes, he was touched.

SAMSON: I could have told you that. He is self-indulgent with
feeling.

PROF.: No no, not that. He was touched [*Looks round at Kotonu
and then taps his head.*]—here. I've known madmen on both
sides of the grave, but he . . . [*Shakes his head, pitying.*] Don't
expect him to drive again.

SAMSON: He will. He must. He knows no other life but driving,
he can use his hands for no other purpose than to turn the
heavy wheel, and to throw that wretched gear which I never
mastered.

PROF.: And you I suppose think you cannot breathe unless you are
swinging on the tailboard and the exhaust pipe is puffing
poison in your face?

SAMSON [*amazed.*]: You understand it Professor sir. I mean, for
a man of books, you really do. But please help him understand
it. We were pupils together, and I know he was conceived
in the back of a lorry.

KOTONU: Samson! I was only born in a lorry.

SAMSON: Oh what do you know? Believe me Professor, his father
used to tell me some things which would shock you sir. Even
if your are a man of the world it would still shock you. He
used to talk to me as if I was a grown man.

PROF.: He had a father?

SAMSON: Oh yes. He was a truck-pusher, they called him Kokol'ori.
He was the first of the truck-pushers and the randiest between
Obalende and Agege. You know Professor, those who came
after him ended up with big transport business, but not his
father. He began with one truck and he ended up with that same
truck. The only change was that he covered the wooden wheels
with rubber.

PROF.: Ah, another man ruined by kindness!

SAMSON: Kind? Kotonu's father kind? He was too fond of women
that's all. A truck-pusher now, who are his greatest customers?

PROF. [*indignantly.*]: I have never dabbled in that trade.

SAMSON: Women traders sir. The market women. They are the
backbone of Omolanke transport business. But Kokol'ori
would not take a penny from them. Instead, he made
honeymoon with them. Anywhere. In the back of the stalls,
under Carter Bridge . . . in the truck itself. Once he was locked

up in a cell. Where others would have broken out and escaped,
he broke into an adjoining cell where a woman was detained
and spent the night with her. Oh he used to tell me all his
adventures. In fact I used to be the go-between for all his
doings. He was sensitive that way, he would never use his own
son, so Kotonu doesn't really know much about his affairs.
[*Enter three more of the touts, supporting one another. They flop
down like a defeated army.*]

PROF. [*staring at the gang with terrifying venom.*]: Mortify his flesh.
Sentence him to mortify his flesh.

KOTONU: Oh it's too late now. He's dead.

SAMSON: Kotonu and I grew up together helping him to push the
truck. [*Confidentially to the Professor.*] You know Kotonu was
really conceived in a push-truck. Kokol'ori told me himself.
He said he parked the truck on a slight rise in the ground and
when he began to make honeymoon on top of Kotonu's mother,
the truck started to roll downhill. Perhaps that was why he was
so fond of him. Of all his sons Kotonu was the only one he
would acknowledge.

[*Professor, increasingly scandalized, looks relieved at last.*]

PROF.: Well, at least he was legitimate.

SAMSON: Oh yes. The push-truck had a licence. And a genuine
licence too, not like one of yours.

KOTONU: He left me the truck.

SAMSON: He had little else to leave. Just the truck.

KOTONU: He died before I became a driver. If he had been alive
he would have slept with six women, to celebrate my becoming
a driver. But he died before that, of a lorry in his back. It
beat his spine against a load of stockfish. It was what he carried
mostly—stockfish. That day the truck was piled high with it.
[*The group begins to dirge softly.*]

SAMSON: We were both there. Pulling the truck in front while
he pushed behind. The bales of stockfish nearly reached the
sky. If Carter Bridge had been joined above the road, the load
of dried fish would have touched it. We were thrown forward . . .

KOTONU: Buried in stockfish. It was all I remembered for a long
time, the smell of stockfish. Torn bodies on the road all smell
of stockfish have you noticed?
[*The dirge wells up gradually.*]

SAMSON [*whispering.*]: Professor, Professor . . .

PROF. [*turns hurriedly to studying his papers.*]: I'm busy.

SAMSON: But what are you going to do about it sir? If he doesn't drive the boss will take the lorry from us.

PROF.: Let me concentrate will you! Take your lives away from me or I will drive you out.

[*The dirge continues.*]

> Iri se l'oganjo orun ni ki lo ti je
> Iri se l'oganjo orun ni ki lo s'orun
> Iri erun ta si mi l'ese iku gb'omi tan
> Iri erun ta si mi l'aiya otutu eru mu mi
> Iku se ni o, akoni l'aiye lo
> E ba mi kedun, Kokolori o . . .

SAMSON: But Professor sir . . .

PROF. [*shouting above the dirge.*]: Leave me. Leave me. You intrude your persons on me. I offer you shelter, nothing more. Leave me or lose yourself in obscurity like all who come here. Who gave you leave to demand this preference? Get out of my sight.

SAMSON [*almost tearfully.*]: But you must help me. He is going to become like the others. In a month he will lose the touch and he will have to drift back here for a pick me-up.

PROF.: Oh you think you are special enh? Different from the rest of them. You think there is something degrading in taking shelter under my wings? [*Turns on the singers with sudden fierceness.*] And stop that disgusting wail you rejects of the road. [*The singing stops at once. They cower before his rage which mounts as he speaks.*]

Vermin. Judases you god-forsaken judases you sell your bodies and you have just done again have you not? You think you are reckless and brave but how can a stupid ox or a runaway train talk of courage. I offer you a purpose but you take unmeaning risks which means I, I must wait and hope that you return alive to fulfil the course I have drawn for you, so you sell again and again for the lure of money.

THUG: But Professor we need the loot.

PROF.: Shut up! Shut your mercenary mouth!

[*The thug gives up. Abruptly Professor takes up his work.*]

SAMSON [*with much hesitation.*]: You shouldn't waste your time on those boma boys Professor . . .

PROF. [*putting down his work, stares him calmly in the eye.*]: What do
   you want? [*Samson fidgets, losing courage.*] Well?

SAMSON: It's nothing Professor, nothing.

PROF.: What sound is that?

   [*An increasing rumble of metallic wheels on stone. The lay-abouts,
   recognizing the meaning, become newly sobered, take off their caps
   in respect. Kotonu has lept up, staring in the direction of the noise.*]

PROF. [*more insistently.*]: What is that sound?

SAMSON: They are bringing them in Professor. The accident on the
   bridge.

PROF.: And must they so noise their presence about? Waste!
   Waste! I never knew them. How can they tell me anything?

SAMSON: They are coming in for mass burial.

   [*The black side of a lorry moves slowly past, blotting out the
   interior of the shack with its shadow, moves towards the church in
   which lights are now seen through the open window. Only this light
   now permeates the shack.*]

PROF.: Oh I could preach them such a sermon for the occasion. I
   could awaken pain with such memories . . .

SAMSON: Oh yes you could Professor. We still remember the
   days . . .

   [*The organ leading, the choir begin a funeral hymn.*]

PROF. [*shakes his head sadly.*]: The choir began off key. By the last
   verse the dead will be glad they are dead.

   [*The thugs begin to file out towards the church.*]

   You are going over to them?

THUG: Only to wait outside and pay our last respects sir.

PROF. [*hesitates, while they wait uncertainly. Then his manner changes,
   becoming urgent.*]: Oh yes you must. Get out. [*To Samson.*] You
   too, go if you wish. And your friend.

SAMSON: I've seen enough. You forget we were there. Right behind
   them as they went over.

PROF.: Ah yes. You were so near . . . perhaps in that is contained
   a promise. But I feel cheated just the same. Such a prodigal
   hearse, and not one of you within it.

SAMSON [*horrified.*]: What are you saying Professor?

PROF.: Not one of you . . . cheats, you godless cheats, not one of
   you!

SAMSON: Do you hear him Kotonu?

KOTONU [*rising.*]: Since when did you get bothered by what Professor says? Let's go.

SAMSON: Where? The funeral?

PROF.: Leave. I want some moments' quiet. Go and join the lament for the chosen.

KOTONU: Come on.

[*They leave. Professor is alone for a few moments. Enter Murano from the opposite side, very uncertainly, his tapper's 'cradle' hung over his shoulders.*]

PROF. [*without turning.*]: I thought it might happen, that is why I let them go. Hearing the sound of the organ and the singing you would wonder if the sun had played tricks on your sight. But [*turns to him*] as you can see, it is not yet dusk. This is not our evening communion only a requiem for departed souls. I even came this morning [*he chuckles*] I must take no chances. Morning is the time for funerals, and who knows, even they may have stumbled on that wisdom. So I . . . missed my way here—to keep watch. [*His manner changes suddenly, becoming abrupt.*] But you must return quickly, before you are seen. All faces are the same in twilight or by night. The Word needs no vulgar light of day to be manifest. Go now.

[*Footsteps are heard coming towards the door. Professor gestures desperately.*]

PROF.: Hide! Hide!

[*Murano hides just on the other side of the store. Enter Salubi, remains just inside the door scanning the room.*]

SALUBI: That's strange. [*Professor raises his head.*] I swear I saw someone sneak inside. It could be a thief.

PROF.: And you think I might need the protection of another thief?

SALUBI: No sir . . . I . . . what I mean is that I saw when the others went to the funeral so I thought someone might be coming to rob the store, knowing the place to be deserted.

PROF.: It isn't—as you see.

SALUBI [*hastily withdrawing.*]: I made a mistake . . . so sorry to disturb you at all sir, very sorry indeed. . . . [*He sees part of Murano sticking out.*] Hah!

PROF.: Are you still there?

[*Salubi makes a sign to him to be silent, pulls a knife and tip-toes backwards out of the room. Professor waits, listening hard, signs to Murano to go out the same way as Salubi. Murano moves a few steps but another sound arrests his escape—Salubi arriving to trap him from behind. Murano stays on the other side of the store. Enter Salubi, knife at the ready.*

Murano tip-toes round the store and comes up behind Salubi. Salubi listens, then lifts the tarpaulin suddenly and sweeps the knife in a wide curve into the space. Murano throws the cradle loop over his head and twists it. The knife drops and Salubi, his back still turned to his assailant, struggles to tear the rope from his neck. Desperate with fear, he flails towards Professor, moaning for help.]

PROF. [*looking dispassionately at the scene.*]: Perhaps . . . if you promised not to look in his face . . . [*Salubi nods frantically, choking*] . . . so that you could not recognize him at an identification parade . . . [*again Salubi nods, more weakly.*] Now walk towards me, and look back only if you want to die. [*He signs to Murano to release him. Salubi staggers down to the Professor, chafing his neck. Murano swiftly disappears.*]

PROF. [*bending down to his work.*]: And now take your carrion from my sight.

PART TWO

[About an hour later]

PROF.: And you brought no revelation for me? You found no broken words where the bridge swallowed them?

SAMSON: How could we think of such a thing Professor?

PROF.: A man must be alert in each event. But the store then? Surely you brought new spare parts for the store?

SAMSON: Sir . . .

PROF.: You neglect my needs and you neglect the Quest. Even total strangers have begun to notice. Three men sought me out on the road. They complained of your tardiness in re-opening the shop.

SAMSON: Oh these foolish men . . .

PROF.: Understand, that shop sustains our souls and feeds our bodies. We lose customers every day.

SAMSON: It is no use Professor. You don't know what we've been through. The man is in no condition to start trading in that kind of stuff.

PROF. [*bangs the table*].: But you bring back nothing at all. Nothing. How do you expect me to make out your statement for the police?

SAMSON: Ah but you always manage Professor.

PROF.: On nothing? You exaggerate your notion of expressiveness in your friend's face. Call him here. [*Kotonu comes forward. Professor glares angrily at him.*] It is only a degree of coarseness, that's all. [*Rummages among the papers.*] I need a statement form. Here is one . . . now you tell me, you who return empty-handed and empty-minded, what do I write! Well? What happened at the bridge? You say the lorry overtook you—good. [*Writes.*] Lorry was travelling at excessive speed. You see, I can make up a police statement that would dignify the archives of any traffic division but tell me—have I spent all these years in dutiful search only to wind up my last moments in meaningless statements. What did you see friend, what did you see? Show me the smear of blood on your brain.

KOTONU: There was this lorry . . .

PROF.: Before the event friend, before the event. Were you accessory before the fact?

KOTONU: Even before the bridge, I saw what was yet to happen.

PROF. [*puts down the pen. Softly—.*]: You swear to that?

KOTONU: It was a full load and it took some moments overtaking us, heavy it was.

PROF. [*writing furiously.*]: It dragged alongside and after an eternity it pulled to the front swaying from side to side, pregnant with stillborns. Underline—with stillborns.

SAMSON: Sensible men turn from what they may not see. Don't you agree Professor?

PROF.: Get one of those herbalists to inoculate him then. Not those Ministry of Health people you understand? Use the herbalists. What's the Ministry's needle after all except for sewing the Word together or the broken flesh. But mostly the tattered Word. Twelve lashes everyday on his bare back and plenty of ground peppers pasted into the tracks that's the only effective inoculation.

KOTONU: I swear it was what I saw. The lorry was filled with people but there was not one face among them . . .

[*The Professor continues scribbling fast.*]

SAMSON: Because they had rags on their faces. It was only a kola nut lorry from the North and the rear half was filled with people. The truck was top-heavy as always. And they had cloth on their faces to keep out the dust.

KOTONU: Oh yes the dust. The wraith of dust which pursued them.

SAMSON: There you are, you admit it—the dust. How could you see anything for dust? Only vague shapes . . .

KOTONU: But it cleared I tell you. Before my eyes it cleared and I saw I was mistaken. It was an open truck and it carried nothing but stacks and stacks of beheaded fish, and oh God the smell of stockfish! But we caught up with them finally . . . at the broken bridge, and you shouted—

SAMSON: Look out Kotonu! [*A violent screech of brakes.*]

KOTONU: It's all right. I've seen it.

[*They walk forward, skirt an area carefully and peer down a hole in the ground.*]

KOTONU: I didn't know that a hearse could be this size. The gates would never open wide enough to take it, not in our burial-ground.

SAMSON: Don't go too near the edge. The planks are rotten.

KOTONU: This is a huge hole they've made. And the side is completely gone.

SAMSON: For God's sake be careful!

KOTONU: You are wrong. This hole was never dug for me.

SAMSON: Does this wretched bridge look choosy to you? Just be careful that's all.

KOTONU: I tell you the hole was never dug for me. It isn't one mile since they overtook us remember?

SAMSON: Get off the rotten edge!

KOTONU: [coming away.] You fret too much.

SAMSON: Mourners stay well behind the heap of loose sands.

KOTONU: And the breast-beater threatens to follow her husband into the grave only when the strong arms of her brothers restrain her—oh I know that cant.

SAMSON [laughing.]: Be comforted they plead, and she is. Comforted. As the reverend preacher said to his congregation, Comfort ye my people. And the half-illiterate interpreter said, Comfort ye—this Comfort; my people—is my people. This Comfort is my people.

TOGETHER: Comforti yi, enia mi ni.[1] [They laugh, a distinct edge of hysteria.]

PROF.: But there is this other joke of the fisherman, slapping a loaded net against the sandbank. [Looks round him.] When the road is dry it runs into the river. But the river? When the river is parched what choice but this? Still it is a pleasant trickle—reddening somewhat—between barren thighs of an ever patient rock. The rock is a woman you understand, so is the road. They know how to lie and wait.

SAMSON [anxiously.]: Kotonu . . .

PROF. [writing.]: Below that bridge, a black rise of buttocks, two unyielding thighs and that red trickle like a woman washing her monthly pain in a thin river. So many lives rush in and out between her legs, and most of it a waste.

SAMSON: The passengers are coming out.

PROF.: Belched from the bowels of some gluttonous god . . . God they looked so messed about.

1. 'My people.'

SAMSON: Kotonu, they are coming out.

KOTONU [*fiercely.*]: Rubbish! They are dead!

SAMSON: No. I mean our own passengers. [*Turns and runs back towards the lorry frame.*] Get back will you. Go on, get in, it's nothing. We were just testing the bridge that's all. Don't start delaying us you hear.

KOTONU: No no let them. It's much safer they all cross on foot. Get them across and I'll try and edge the lorry past the gap.

SAMSON: No, first let me test the planks. I'll jump on them and see.

KOTONU: And weaken them some more? No no, we can manage.

SAMSON: You are sure there is enough room?

KOTONU: You have begun to doubt me?

SAMSON [*turns round.*]: All right all right, come down all of you. What is all that rubbish? No waste of time you hear? Lef' your load, I say lef' your dirty bundle. Lef am. All right I sorry I no know say na your picken. Make you all walka this side. If una wan look make you go look for other side. You foolish people, wetin you stop dey look now? Black man too useless, unless una get rubbish for look you no dey satisfy. Hurry up, no waste of time. [*He runs forward suddenly.*] God punish you, you wretched woman, why you dey carry your picken look that kind thing? You tink na cowboy cinema? Commot my friend . . . a-ah, these people too foolish. Na de kind ting person dey show small picken? If'e begin dream bad dream and shout for night you go rush go native doctor. Foolish woman! Na another man calamity you fit take look cinema.

[*As he herds them across the bridge, the drivers begin dirging softly.*]

KOTONU: We should have got there first.

SAMSON [*despondently.*]: Kill us a dog Kotonu, kill us a dog. Kill us a dog before the hungry god lies in wait and makes a substitute of me. That was a thin shave. A sensible man would see it as a timely warning, but him? I doubt it. Not for all the wealth of a traffic policeman. Dog's intestines look messy to me he says—who asked him to like it? Ogun likes it that's all that matters. It's his special meat. Just run over the damned dog and leave it there, I don't ask you to stop and scoop it up for your next dinner. Serve Ogun his tit-bit so the road won't look at us one day and say Ho ho you two boys you look juicy

to me. But what's the use? The one who won't give Ogun
willingly will yield heavier meat by Ogun's designing.
[*The lay-abouts stop dirging, remain standing awkwardly in their
usual place, looking uncertainly towards Samson.*]

SAMSON: Anything wrong?

THUG. We ... er ... you see Say Tokyo Kid is not here or he
would do it. So perhaps you would just say something.

SAMSON: Oh, all right. [*He composes himself as do the others, head
bowed.*] May we never walk when the road waits, famished.
[*Too late Professor covers up his ears, shaking his head angrily.
The others relax into their seats.*]

PROF. [*intensely.*]: It is lucky for you that you brought a god on to
my doorstep. I would have seared your blasphemous tongue
this instant with the righteous vengeance of the Word.

SAMSON [*almost in a general appeal.*]: But what have I done now?
[*Professor resumes his work, still much impassioned.*]
[*to Kotonu.*] Do you know what he was talking about?
What god on his doorstep?

KOTONU [*leaps up, agitated.*]: He said that? A god on his doorstep—
did he say that?

SAMSON: You heard him.

KOTONU: I must find out. Professor ...

PROF.: Re-open the shop.

KOTONU: But Professor.

PROF.: The shop my friend the shop! The shop must be re-opened
at once. I don't permit shuttered windows in my household.
[*Pointing to the church.*] They are the ones who bar up their
windows. I have nothing to hide. Have you?

KOTONU: But I must know Professor. What did you find on your
doorstep?

PROF.: I forbid you to foist your troubles on me. Open up the
shop!

KOTONU: I came to you for help. How much longer must I wait?

PROF.: Open the shop. Like you all I also wait but you do not hear
me complain.
[*Kotonu hesitates, goes to the store and disappears behind the
tarpaulin cover, begins to re-arrange the junk.*]

SAMSON [*pleads very sincerely.*]: Don't make him do it Professor sir.
Give the store to someone else.

PROF.: I make no one do anything. But are you telling me
  Sergeant Burma was a better man? Your friend appears, if
  I may say so, to have the edge on Burma. Well, hasn't he? Or
  do you say he is inferior clay?

SAMSON: They are different people.

PROF.: I didn't open this house for different people. And he isn't.
  Sooner or later you prove it. Like flies you prove it. Like
  Ramadan you prove it. Like mosquito larvae on the day of
  the sanitary inspector you prove it. I have not worn my feet
  along the roads for nothing. Anyway you cannot neglect the
  material necessities of life. How does he intend to live since he
  won't drive?

SAMSON: We have savings.

PROF. [his eyes light up.]: You have savings?

SAMSON [with sudden caution.]: Well, a little. Not much you know.
  I have to do the saving for both of us.

PROF. [affixes the monocle and stares him out.]: How much have you
  saved?

SAMSON: Nothing much Professor, only . . .

PROF.: I must know the truth.
  [Samson, squirming, eventually gives in. Turns his back on Professor,
  and from the deep recesses of his baggy trousers, brings out a pouch.
  Hurriedly he extracts a note from it and hides it, places the rest on
  the table.]
  Any paper? Paper Paper. Where is the Government I.O.U.,
  the thing which promises to pay on demand.

SAMSON: Where would I get such a thing sir?

PROF. [opens the bag at the mouth and peers into the contents.]:
  What you ought to form is a syndicate.

SAMSON: I don't quite understand.

PROF.: You never do. Where is that scum? Go find him.
  [Samson goes. As he turns his back. Professor tries to extract a coin
  from the bag but Samson looks back just then. Professor is left with
  no choice but to carry out his action after a natural hesitation,
  explaining quite calmly.]
  For initial expenses you know.

SAMSON [pokes his head around the corner.]: Wake up. Professor
  wants you.

SALUBI [jumps up and runs to Professor.]: Is it ready sir?

PROF. [*hands him a coin.*]: Go and buy my usual. Only the puffed
  kind you understand. And groundnuts. Crisp ones, not soggy.
  Hurry up!

SALUBI.: Will it be all right about the licence sir?

PROF.: Get going!

  [*Salubi runs out.*]

SAMSON: With all due respects Professor sir, I don't quite see how
  that will come under initial expenses.

PROF.: We had to get rid of him. Or you can have him spying on
  us if you like.

SAMSON: But Professor, he was already outside.

PROF.: That is why it was necessary to call him in.

  [*Samson scratches his head, puzzles it a bit, gives up.*]
  Now what are your assets? A driving licence, and your small
  savings. Right? Now that creature who went out just now will
  pay well for his licence. I suggest half his first salary, payable
  in one-monthly instalments.

SAMSON: But we are not selling it.

PROF.: I'll make out the I.O.U. [*He pats the bundle of assorted papers.*]
  See that? Not even death can boast such a tower of I.O.Us.

SAMSON: We are not giving up the road!

PROF.: I propose we set up a syndicate, calculate the assets, decide
  on a policy. As a special concession I will permit you to come
  in as equal partners with me. I hold half the partnership, you
  and your friend can have the other half. Fifty-fifty all the way.

SAMSON: Excuse me Professor, this . . . assets as you call our
  money, do you happen to have any yourself?

PROF. [*pats his paper bundles.*]: Almost too much of it. I offer you
  sanctuary in my tower of words.

SAMSON [*wide-eyed.*]: You mean there is money hidden in that?
  And everyone thinking you were penniless all this time!

PROF.: Money? What money?

SAMSON [*trying to peep into one end of a bundle.*]: You might even
  be a millionaire and we never knew it. I always thought you
  weren't as mad as people thought.

PROF. [*whips out his stick, threatening.*]: Take your snail slime
  secreted eyes off the living testament before I poke them off.
  Do you think I would foul up eternal beads of cowries with
  minted commerce? How dare you! It is true I have not found

the Word but tempt me and I shall unleash its elemental truths on your head.

SAMSON [*recoils, but bravely.*]: Well you always mislead a man. I thought your assets were in there.

PROF.: And so they are fool. Somewhere in that granary is that elusive kernel, the Word, the Key, the moment of my rehabilitation. From what cesspit was this object dragged that you set it against the select harvest of a faithful gleaner? Get it off!

[*Sweeps the pouch off the table with the stick, the coins roll out, scattering all over the floor.*]

SAMSON [*chasing and gathering them.*]: You are a very confusing person Professor. I can't follow you at all. Of course if you mean I.O.Us. it makes some sense especially government I.O.Us. Only, will they stand up in a court of law? The ink has faded on most of them. I mean, look at it yourself.

PROF.: When I form a syndicate, I come in on my own terms.

[*Samson hesitates and approaches the table.*]

SAMSON: But if I may make a humble suggestion sir, Professor is not a cockroach is he?

PROF.: What are you talking about?

SAMSON: I mean, is Professor a cockroach? Or a termite? Because, otherwise, how will that kind of asset fill his belly?

[*Professor goes back to studying the papers, underlining a phrase, ringing a word here and there. Samson shakes his head and proceeds to search for the remaining money.*]

KOTONU [*picks up a coin which has rolled to his feet.*]: There is one here Samson.

SAMSON [*runs to take it.*]: Ah thank you, thank you.

[*Kotonu returns to the stall.*]

Wait. Let me take off your shoes.

KOTONU: What for?

SAMSON: A driver must have sensitive soles on his feet. Unlike his buttocks. His buttocks would be hard. Heavy-duty tyres. But not the feet you see. Because he does not walk so much, and he has to be able to judge the pressure on the pedals exactly right. I have such thick soles you see so I always revved the engine too much or too little. Then it was Fai! Fai! Fai! You think say I get petrol for waste? Take your foot commot for

ancelerator! Small small! I say small small—you tink say dis one
na football game. Fai fai fai! You dey press brake—Gi-am!—
as if na stud you wan' give centre back.[1] I say do am soft soft!
Fai fai fai! All a waste of time. Every time I started the lorry
it went like a railway—gbaga gbaga—like clinic for hiccup.
Other times it would shoot off like sputnik—fiiiiom! That was
when I got it worst of all—Fai fai fai fai! You wey no fit walka
na fly you wan' fly?[2] Ah, sometimes I wonder why I didn't
go deaf. [*He stands for a while, trying to remember what Kotonu's
slippers are doing in his hands.*] Where did I get these ... Oh yes,
you walk about the floor in your bare feet. If you step on a
coin let me know. I know I wouldn't feel a thing.
[*Kotonu goes back to his work. Samson continues to search. Enter
Salubi with guguru wrapped in paper. Like one who is accustomed to
this, he cups his hands in anticipation.*]

PROF. [*as he takes the parcel.*]: Is it good? Soft? Crisp?

SALUBI: The best sir. I buy it from the usual woman.

PROF. [*examining the wrapping of the parcel.*]: That Tapa creature is
a genius. She never lets me down. [*Without looking into the
parcel, he empties the contents in Salubi's hands, who bows
gratefully, joins the thugs and they talk in whispers. Professor
smoothes out the paper itself and proceeds to read it, turns to the
hand-lens, makes notes and underlines sections.*] Economic. Almost
stingy. But there are the cabalistic signs. The trouble is to find
the key. Find the key and it leads to the Word ... very strange
... very strange ... a rash of these signs arrived lately ... that
woman of Tapa knows something, or else she is an unconscious
medium. Oh God, Oh God, the enormity of unknown burdens,
of hidden wisdoms ... say the Word in our time O Lord,
utter the hidden Word. [*With sudden explosiveness.*] But what do
these mean? These signs were made by no human hands. What
in the power of hell do they mean!

SAMSON [*coming closer and looking over Professor's shoulder.*]: I think
they are pools Professor.

PROF.: I beg your pardon.

SAMSON: Football pools sir. Pools. Don't you ever play pools?

PROF.: I have little time for games.

1. 'You apply the brakes as if you are tackling a centre back.'
2. 'You can't walk but you want to fly?'

SAMSON: No no sir. It is no game. You can make your fortune on
  it quite easily.

PROF. [*studies him with new interest.*]: You are a strange creature my
  friend. You cannot read, and I presume you cannot write, but
  you can unriddle signs of the Scheme that baffle even me, whose
  whole life is devoted to the study of the enigmatic Word?
  Do you actually make this modest claim for yourself?

SAMSON [*wearily.*]: Professor, I am claiming nothing. Look.
  Somebody has filled it up and thrown it away. You see it?
  It's all filled up—at least it looks like it. A cross here, or as the
  Tax Collector would say—Mr. Samson, his Mark. And then
  a lot of O here and there. That is how to fill a football coupon.

PROF.: Is that so?

SAMSON: Oh yes sir. Now here . . . this is where you write your
  name. You write it for me. Just put Samson there.

PROF.: You are a brave man. You would dare this in your name?

SAMSON: Please sir, just write my name. I will spell it for you—
  Sa-mu-son. [*The Professor writes, shrugging.*] Have you written
  the address?

PROF.: You have an address too?

SAMSON: The police always wrote—No fixed address. You may
  do the same. No, no, write . . . Samson, Apprentice Driver
  to Kotonu, LE 2539, NO DANGER NO DELAY—
  Everybody knows No Danger No Delay. No, I forget,
  somebody else is driving No Danger now. So perhaps you'd
  better write, hm, let's see . . . [*Professor throws down the pen
  and pushes the form aside but Samson does not notice.*] . . . yes all
  right, write Care of Accident Supply Store, Professor's Bar.
  You never know in this world. I will post it. After all, it is an
  asset—to use your own word now. A friend of mine—he was
  a messenger—sent in one of these. He won thirteen thousand.
  Now he owns half the houses in Apapa and they have made him
  a Senator. You never know you see. If I won something I will
  put it on a new lorry, put Kotonu to drive it. Mind you, I am
  not looking for thirteen thousand or anything like that. Ten
  thousand will do me—one must not be too greedy. Even five
  thousand is no child's purse-money . . . Just think, look at it on
  the newspaper—Samson the Champion Agbero wins five
  thousand.

KOTONU: I think I am standing on a penny.

SAMSON [*rushing there.*]: What did I say? If it was I, I could have that penny buried in my feet and I would not feel it. [*Picks it up.*] And a penny it is you know. I mean, it could have been a shilling, but his feet told him it was a penny. That is really how to press your accelerator.

KOTONU: Do you think something may have happened to Murano?

PROF.: What can happen to Murano? A shadow in the valley of the shadow of! Are you so conceited that you spare your concern for him?

[*A short silence. Samson sidles up to the Professor.*]

SAMSON: Professor.

PROF.: En-hm.

SAMSON: May I ask you something? A little personal?

PROF.: Why not? Even God submits himself to a weekly interrogation.

SAMSON: Thank you sir. Now, it is only as a matter of interest. You mustn't be offended sir, because I really want to know. I mean . . . is it true . . . that is, what I want to find out is . . .

PROF.: In short, you want to know whether people are right when they say I am mad.

SAMSON: No sir, certainly not. What I wanted to know is . . . well, you used to read the lesson in English in that church and we all used to enjoy your performance. In fact I don't mind telling you that you inspired many of us to start attending private classes. I was on that wall—and Kotonu too—the day it crashed to the ground. But what has puzzled me is this, because you see I can't stand it when people—I don't want to mention names—when they make nasty remarks about it—I mean, did you have a source of private income. What I mean is Professor, what really happened about the er . . . you know . . . this matter of church funds?

PROF.: Sins and wages and sin—[*Stops. Turns and faces the church.*] If you could see through that sealed church window you will see the lectern bearing the Word on bronze. I stood often behind the bronze wings of the eagle; on the broad span of the eagle's outstretched wings rested the Word—oh what a blasphemy it all was but I did not know it. Oh yes, I stood then on the other side of that window—then it was always open, not barred and bolted as it now is, from fear—[*Samson blinks hard, rubs his eyes.*]—through that window, my sight led straight on to this spot. In my youth, let me tell you, in my youth we went out and waged a holy war on every sore as this. We pulled down every drinking shack and set fire to it, drove out the poisoners of men's brains.

SAMSON [*spiritedly.*]: And they didn't fight back? You try that here and see what happens to you.

PROF.: Oh the Word is a terrible fire and we burned them by the ear. Only that was not the Word you see, oh no, it was not. And so for every dwelling that fell ten more rose in its place until they grew so bold that one grew here, setting its laughter against the very throat of the organ pipes. Every evening, until I thought, until one day I thought, I have never really known what lies beyond that window. And one night, the wall fell down, I heard the laughter of children and the wall fell down in an uproar of flesh and dust. And I left the Word hanging in the coloured light of sainted windows. . . . [*Almost humbly.*] As you will notice, I have made certain alterations. That corner was not there before. I have scraped the walls. Installed an electric light. Red neon. It is, I think, likely that I left the church coffers much depleted . . . but I remember little of this. Have you heard anything?

SAMSON: Oh no.

PROF.: Like your friend, I wished to retire into business. My pension would have sufficed but since I was sacked for blasphemy I was due for none. I forget now how much it was, it is so difficult to remember details. Do you know this is the only house of rest from which you can see into the altar? But still, the business of the church funds addles my thoughts.

SAMSON: Well you must have a clear conscience or you would have run away.

PROF. [*mildly.*]: Run away? But I must be near the eagle, for his brazen image bore on its back the first illusion of the Word. Nevertheless they cast me from gace. And of all the windows of that church, only that is kept shut. [*Confidentially.*] You see, they know I am always watching, watching and waiting, waiting for the careless moment, so they keep jealous guard over the Word.

SAMSON [*looking.*]: But Professor, all the windows are open. Even the ones up the tower.

PROF. [*cautioning with a wagging finger.*]: Be careful. They weave a strong spell over human eyes.

SAMSON: Oh no. I can see all right. The window is wide open. I was here this morning when the organist opened it for practice.

PROF.: Have you sold your soul for money? You lie like a prophet.

SAMSON: But it is the truth Professor.

PROF.: Truth? Truth? Truth my friend, is scum risen on the froth of wine.

SAMSON: All right all right, have it your own way.

[*Continues to cast glances at the window.*]

PROF.: Do let me know if you hear anything ... about the matter of the church funds.

SAMSON: I would forget about it if I were you. They would have done something by now if they wanted to.

PROF.: The dust in the belfry never quite settles. It only awaits the next clangour of the bell. Come closer ... closer ... [*Samson with obvious reluctance, obeys. Professor draws down his head sharply, whispers piercingly in his ear.*] Be like a bat. Keep your ears stuck to the vestry door. If I lose the station all is lost. I must watch what they do. I must see what goes on at the altar, at the pulpit. And you watch with me ... see that no changes are made without my permission.

SAMSON [*struggling to get free.*]: Yes sir, yes sir ...

PROF.: Up the aisle with them and into the chancel. Don't let their cassock deter you, the eagle sides with me. We will do battle, but first we must find the Word ...

SAMSON: Oh yes sir, of course Professor.

PROF.: For the day will come, oh yes it will. Even atonement wilts before the Word ...

[*Samson breaks free with desperate strength, flees upstage only to be met by the explosive fall of the tailboard. Right on the sound the light changes, leaving only the store area in light. Falling grotesquely after the board, is the mask. A moment later, Kotonu emerges from behind the mass of junk and clothing. Immediately, the mask-followers fill the stage searching for their mask-bearer. Kotonu stands dazed but Samson quickly raises the board and pushes the mask under it. It is a Drivers' festival and they are*]

*all armed with whips and thick fibre stalks. Two carry a dog
tied to a stake and brandish matchets. Dashing everywhere with the
steady leader-and-refrain chant they break off sporadically for brief
mutual whipping contests, dashing off again in pursuit.*]

SAMSON [*as soon as they disappear.*]: Help me lift him on board.

KOTONU: You saw it. Nothing could have saved him.

SAMSON: Come on come on.

KOTONU: It's all your fault. You said we should come.

SAMSON: That is neither here nor there. Let's hide him before they
return.

KOTONU: But it wasn't my fault. Nothing could have saved him.

SAMSON: For heaven's sake man help me carry him up.

KOTONU: You know my reflexes are good Samson, but the way
he ran across . . .

SAMSON: They'll be back this way again.

KOTONU: But what was he running from? It was almost as if
he was determined to die. Like those wilful dogs getting in the
way of the wheels.

SAMSON: I am not the police Kotonu. Neither are those people.
They talk with matchets. Across the throats—matchets!

KOTONU: Did you ask me here to be their butcher? You saw him,
the way he fled across. Just tell me, was I to be part of this?

SAMSON [*manhandles the figure into the lorry and replaces the tailboard.*]:
Now get in and START THE ENGINE!

KOTONU: It's probably stalled.

SAMSON: What kind of talk is that? Have you gone mad? You
haven't even tried man.

KOTONU: But it wasn't my fault.

SAMSON [*peers into the distance.*]: They are coming again. Kotonu,
for the last time!

KOTONU: Let me look underneath the mask.

SAMSON: Have you gone mad . . . too late anyway, they've filled
the road. But run at least. Come on let's run!

KOTONU: But who is he? Why did he run across?

SAMSON: You're hopeless. [*Hurriedly he pulls down the tarpaulin.*] But
at least don't give us away. Look as if we are part of the festival.
If there is danger one of us will have to get inside the mask.
Do you understand?

[*Dumbly, Kotonu nods. The maskers come in again, performing the dance*

of the whips, darting off again and back, looking for the missing god.
One of them dashes suddenly to the lorry and lifts up the tarpaulin.
With desperate speed Samson snatches a whip from the nearest
person and gives him a cut across the legs. The man readily accepts
the invitation, and a contest follows.]

SAMSON [*shouts above the din.*]: Now Kotonu, now! [*Kotonu*
hesitates, visibly frightened.] Kotonu! Strip the mask and get
under it! Kotonu it's the only way.
[*As if suddenly wakened, Kotonu starts, climbs into the lorry.*
The whip-dance grows fast and furious. Samson manoeuvres himself
near the tailboard from time to time.] Hurry Kotonu! For heaven's
sake hurry!
[*There is a sudden violent movement against the canvas and Samson,*
scared, rushes there. Almost at the same time, the masquerade comes
through in violent throes, a figure in torment. There is a loud yell
from the dancers and the whipping and chanting becomes more
violent, aiding the god's seeming possession.]

KOTONU [*tearing at the clothes, demented.*]: It's all wet inside, I've
got his blood all over me. [*They dance and whip one another*
around the masquerade, leaving a clear space for his frenzy.] It's
getting dark Samson I can't see. His blood has got in my
eyes. I can't see Samson. [*Samson, wildly irresolute, battles on*
with his latest challenger.] Samson where are you? My eyes are
all clammed up I tell you. Samson! Samson! Samson!
[*His struggles become truly frantic, full of violent contortions. Gradually*
he grows weaker and weaker, collapsing slowly on the ground until
he is completely inert. The dancers flog one another off the scene.
A slow black-out, and a half-minute pause.
They are all back to normal. Enter Particulars Joe.]

PARTIC. JOE: Did he come in here?

SAMSON [*turns away with undisguised boredom.*]: No, he went the
other way.

PARTIC. JOE: Are you sure?

SAMSON: Am I sure about what?

PARTIC. JOE: That he went the other way. I could have sworn I
saw him come in here.

SAMSON: Nobody came in here.

PARTIC. JOE: Are you sure you know who I mean? Sort of tall
but a little on the short side. Tribal marks, but beginning to

wear off . . . in fact, unless you looked closely you might think
he had no tribal marks at all. Rather light in complexion, mind
you it's a bit dark in here, so you could easily think him a
somewhat darkish fellow. He was wearing a huge agbada but
then, he could have shed it while I was chasing him.

SAMSON: Who are you chasing today?

PARTIC. JOE [*coming in fully.*]: Well, it is the usual trouble you
know. A hit-and-run-driver.

KOTONU: Is the victim dead?

PARTIC. JOE: I had no time to find out.

KOTONU: You were so determined to catch him you left the body!

PARTIC. JOE: Oh no, the suspect himself took care of that. You see,
he collided against a goat.

SAMSON: Ho ho ho, you really are full of surprises. So it's a goat today.

KOTONU: And you are chasing the man for colliding with a goat?

PARTIC. JOE: Well you see, he stopped . . .

SAMSON: You said just now he did not stop.

PARTIC. JOE: Oh he didn't stop. That is, he stopped you see. He
picked up the goat and then ran off with it. Just think of that.
The next thing you know they'll all be running off with
mortuary claims. [*Looking at Kotonu.*] You wouldn't know
anything about that sort of thing would you?

PROF. [*without looking up from his work, after a nervous silence.*]:
Why don't you sit down a while officer. You must be tired
from all this running around, and Murano will soon be here.
[*Looks towards the church window.*] They ought to light up before
long. [*Brings out the watch.*] The organist is rinsing his dirty
face in cold water. The pastor is fixing his borrowed collar-stud.
And the communicants are beating their husbands.

PARTIC. JOE: Well I really ought to go after this suspect . . .

PROF.: Later later, he won't get away. Do sit down.

PARTIC. JOE: That is very kind of you sir, very kind of you. I
could do with a rest to tell the truth.

SAMSON: God! All this pretence. He knows very well why he
comes here. Somehow he always chases his suspects here at this
time of the day.

PROF.: Tolerance. Tolerance my friend. There will be enough for
everyone. Enough to breed unawareness which you all seek in
your futile ways.

SAMSON: Well I don't mind the others, but him . . . hey just a
minute.
[*Particulars, about to sit down, sees a coin in a floor crack and is
transferring it into his pocket. Samson runs across and snatches it.*]
That happens to be mine.

PARTIC. JOE [*blandly.*]: That's O.K. Natural mistake on my part.
Money has been left for me in more unlikely places believe me.

SAMSON: Well at least wait until I am back on the road before you
collect tolls.
[*Particulars folds his arms and waits.*]

PROF.: How is the criminal world my friend?

PARTIC. JOE: More lucrative every day Professor.

PROF.: Not for the criminal I trust.

PARTIC. JOE: Oh no sir. That would only corrupt them.
[*A brief silence, Samson has gone to look at the spiders, he keeps
poking the web gently with a stick.*]

PARTIC. JOE: I haven't seen your hand on the roads lately
Professor.

PROF.: I am slowing down. I have to cut down on distractions.
I need all my strength for uncovering the Word. Forgery saps
my powers.

PARTIC. JOE: Do let us know when you retire. It will be a great
load off our minds. We spend more time separating your own
handiwork than we do in detecting the general forgery. We
would be so sorry to make a mistake.

PROF.: I would be too. And yet it might not be such a bad idea.

PARTIC. JOE: I beg your pardon sir.

PROF.: I spend much time considering it. Too many people come
to me for help. They depend on me and I find I am reluctant
to let them down. That worm over there for instance, he is
awaiting a document. These two tormented devils are my
patients. Other people's sorrows sap my energy and these days,
it is not so easy to be deaf. A spell in prison might help me.
Conserve my scattered energies.

PARTIC. JOE: You will be disillusioned Professor. Prison is the least
solitary community in the world.

PROF.: I will insist on being difficult. Then the warders will punish
me with solitary confinement.

PARTIC. JOE: The food is terrible.

PROF.: Just bread and water. That would not be asking much, plain bread and water.

PARTIC. JOE: Well, y-y-yes it might work. Taken that way it might work.

PROF.: I know it will.

PARTIC. JOE [*after much hemming.*]: Professor, I ... er ... hate to appear to be self-seeking, but after all sir, you are a man of the world and you will understand my position I trust. I mean Professor, I have been, you will admit, very co-operative and loyal ...

PROF.: Stop worrying your head officer. I promise you no other person will have the credit of arresting me.

PARTIC. JOE [*vastly relieved.*]: Thank you sir, thank you very much. That is something to look forward to.

[*Samson spits on the ground, turns his back on him.*]

PROF.: Charity my friend, charity. [*To Particulars.*] I will let you know when it is time. When a man retires he must be able to retire somewhere. I look forward to contemplation in solitude.

SALUBI [*leaping up suddenly.*]: Murano!

PROF: Sit down you fool. Murano makes no sound.

[*Enter Say Tokyo Kid.*]

SAY T. [*looks round a little worriedly.*]: I ain't late am I?

SALUBI: Say Tokyo! Say Tokyo Kid!

SAY T.: Salubi Salubirity! Say man, everybody garrered round the goorold place. How's business kid?

SALUBI: Say Tokyo Charranooga Shoe-Shine Boy!

SAY T.: Thas me. I'm allright boy. [*Sees the officer and recoils. Makes to pull an imaginary gun from his belt.*] Whas that guy doing around here?

SAMSON: Say Tokyo!

SAY T.: I say boy it sure is good to be back among friendly faces. Goorold Samson the Champion Tout! And Kotonu the demon driver himself, coast-to-coast Dakar to Yola Koton Kafiri to Kontagora No Danger No Delay Here Today Gone Tomorrow. How's business kid?

SAMSON: Moving moving on greased wheels thank heavens.

[*Say Tokyo looks at his men with prolonged contempt and they slink further and further into the corner.*]

SAY T.: You see rem? If Ah'd been butchered and chopped in a

thousand pieces they wouldn't have been able to tell what
happened to me. Tell me Samson, ain't they already making
dirge for Say Tokyo Kid? They sure goor a that sorta thing.

SAMSON: What happened Tokyo? They all looked as if you
were . . . well, outnumbered.

THUG: We never got to the fight. The road played us foul. A tree
had fallen across the road and our driver didn't see it in time.

SAY T.: Yeah sure. And none of you cares to finrout what become
of your Cap'n.

THUG: Well we looked. You had disappeared.

SAY T.: You think a man disappears in the middle of the road
without cause? There was no river, it wasn't on a bridge so
you couldn't say I had been washed away.

THUG: But Say Tokyo, you simply vanished.

SAY T.: Because ah was off in pursuit of the murderers you damned
cowards. That tree didn't fall by itself. It was knocked across
the road. I was sirring in front so ah saw the gang just before
we turned the corner and hit the tree.

THUG: Well we were in no shape for chasing anyone.

SAY T.: They weren't in no shape for standing up against we
either. They thought they killed us when the truck
sommersaulted. Man they just turn tail and fled. And you were
so full of self-pity you didn't even wait to finrout. I could have
been chopped to pieces in that bush and no one would
remember ah existed.

THUG: Well, we didn't know.

SAY T.: God, don't you know yer Cap'n? You think I can just
disappear like that?

SALUBI: Say Tokyo Kid!

SAY T.: That's me. You know I drive nothing but timber. Are you
so godless that you think a little timber across the road would
finish me?

PARTIC. JOB [*who has been making notes.*]: Has this accident been
reported? Or any other accident. Has anyone anything to
declare? You know the regulations.

SAY T.: That ain't ma business.

PARTIC. JOB: Give me the particulars.

SAY T.: If you wanre pareculars you go in that bush and dig inside
the sommersaulted truck. I ain't re driver.

PARTIC. JOE: I take it No Casualty?

SAY T.: There may be one if you don't quit asking me questions.

PARTIC. JOE [*moving towards Professor.*]: Sir, if I may use a little portion of your assembly time . . . since our beloved Murano is not yet here sir . . .

PROF.: What for officer?

PARTIC. JOE: On investigation sir. Unreported accident Suspicion of foul play and accessories before and after the fact.

PROF.: Be careful. [*Spoken mildly, and he turns and resumes his work.*]

PARTIC. JOE [*saluting smartly.*]: Very kind of you sir. We shall of course look forward to returning the compliment. [*Whips round sharply to Kotonu in dramatic-interrogator pose.*] Where were you the day of the Drivers' Festival? On the Feast of Ogun the dog-eater. Where?

KOTONU: Where?

PARTIC. JOE: Answer me—where? And I hereby warn you that anything you say or do will be taken and used in evidence et cetera et cetera. Speak up where were you?

SAMSON: Come to that where were you yourself?

PARTIC. JOE: I don't fancy dogs.

SAY T.: A spy! I always reckoned I couldn't trust that guy.

PARTIC. JOE: On investigation. Duty before friendship. Were you at the Festival of Drivers? Account for your movements.

PROF. [*not looking up.*]: Was that the day of the miracle officer?

PARTIC. JOE: It was the day a god was abducted Professor.

PROF.: Abducted?

SAY T. [*rising.*]: My wife's brother was there.

PARTIC. JOE: Eye-witnesses only I said. No housewives' gossips et cetera.

THE GANG: That's good enough . . .
   He's an eye-witness . . .
   I saw him there . . .
   His wife's brother is acceptable . . .
   You police are all the same . . .
   Taking bribes is all you know . . .

SAY T.: Now you look here officer, you trying to insult ma family?

PARTIC. JOE: All right all right, you're an eye-witness. Speak on. [*Nods and mumbles of approval.*]

SAY T.: It was after all, our own festival, so I don't reckon it's any
of your business what happened to the guest of honour that
day. [*Cheers.*] 's far as we git the marrer, Ogun came among us
in possession before their very ...

GANG: We saw it. We all saw it.

SAY T.: Before our own very eyes. And surrenly, he vanished.
Surrenly he vanished. Ain't gor nuthin' more to say. And
you also can now close up that notebook of yours and—
suddenly—vanish!
[*Prolonged cheers.*]

PARTIC. JOE: Well that may be good enough for you but it isn't
good enough for ...

KOTONU: If I may say something ...

GANG: Shurrup ...
Case closed ...
To hell with policeman ...
Ogun break all dem head. ...

KOTONU [*going down to the Professor.*]: Professor, I never even saw
his face ...
[*Particulars trails him, notebook at the ready. Professor pays no
attention.*]
We drove down all night. We dared not wait Professor, the
sacrificial knives of those men were right at our backs. ...
We parked the lorry outside here with the dead man in it.
We were waiting for you to come, we couldn't think what to
do. Well, by morning the body was gone. ...

PARTIC. JOE [*scribbling furiously.*]: What body? What body?

KOTONU: Only the mask was left Professor. The body was gone.

PARTIC. JOE: Tangible evidence, the mask. Where is it?
[*The Gang tries singing to counter their voices. The pace of action
is rapid.*]

SAMSON [*at the top of his lungs.*]: Where the hell is that Murano?

PARTIC. JOE: I beg to apply for a search warrant. Compliment to
be returned at the very earliest opportunity.
[*Professor waves him on. He turns and dives into the store.*]

SAMSON: That's private property. [*Tries to bar his way.*]

PARTIC. JOE: In the name of the law!
[*Reaches a hand into the store towards the mask. Say Tokyo pulls
his cap down his face and Samson quickly substitutes a military*]

uniform so that the policeman's hand grabs this. The mask is then
taken out and thrown from one person to the other until it is hidden
under the Professor's chair. Particulars frees his eyes, clutching the
uniform triumphantly.]

Concrete evidence of tangible evidence—what's this!

SAMSON [*his hands across his chest, dolefully.*]: Poor Sergeant
Burma.

THE GANG [*with equal solemnity.*]: Poor Sergeant Burma.
[*Samson takes the uniform, puts it on.*]

PARTIC. JOE: I say, that's Sergeant Burma's uniform. I'd know it
anywhere.

SAY T.: You mean you knew old Sergeant Burma?

PARTIC. JOE: Knew him? We were at the front together. Lifelong
friends me and Burma. Told him to come into the police
force, but oh no, he preferred his wretched motor transport.

SAMSON: Only fools drive oil tankers. They are clumsy monsters.

PARTIC. JOE [*reminiscing, sentimental.*]: He loved them. Oloibiri to
Lagos. Port Harcourt to Kano. And he always said, God bless
the oil companies for bringing out my genius. And he drove
his tanker like a tank. Of course he was huge himself, like his
truck.

SAMSON: Till the tanker did for him.

PARTIC. JOE: There was little wrong with the end of Sergeant
Burma. He went up in a pyre that would have honoured
Sango himself. Such a big man. He had to crouch in the
driver's cabin.

SAMSON: And a voice like a referee's whistle . . . [*mimicking.*] You
see this monster . . . that is nothing. I drive bigger tanks in
Burma campaign. I drive supply caravans, and I turn-turn this
picken with one hand. Na picken 'e be. Na small picken. You
wan' try? You tink say na every Tom Dick and Harry fit drive
tanker? My friend, me na veteran driver.

PARTIC. JOE: Every year on Remembrance Day, over in that
church, he put that on. And I had mine plus a Long Service
ribbon. It is peaceful to fight a war which one does not
understand, to kill human beings who never seduced your wife
or poisoned your water. Sapele to Burma—that was a long
way for a quarrel.

SAMSON [*gives a quick act of polish to the medals. Sticks out his chest.*

Assumes full military bearing.]: You think I get these medals for
nothing? They wan' give me the King George Cross self, but
you know how things be for blackman. My major recommend
me for the decoration but dey begin ask how den go give black
man dat kind honour? Another time the general send cablegram
wit' in own hand. 'E say, gi'am Victoria Cross. I say make you
gi'am blackman or no blackman—gi'am. Dey for give me dat
one but when the governor for home hear wetin dey wan' do,
'e cable back say if den give me dat kind superior medal, I go
return my country begin do political agitator. Haba! Justice
no dey for white man world.

PARTIC. JOE: Sergeant Burma survived four years of fighting and
one year as a prisoner of war. . . .

SAMSON: Den beat me so tey my backside dey like dat Zeppelin
balloon. If you put pin for am 'e go burs'.

PARTIC. JOE: On Remembrance day all the big shots were
present and our Professor here read the lesson in his sonorous
tones while the bishop preached a moving sermon, and
Sergeant Burma sang five notes behind the congregation who
sang three notes behind the choir who sang two notes behind
the organ. . . .
[*Strains of a 'remembrance' hymn, the four sections ending in that
order, one after the other, Sergeant Burma last of all, singing
'Africa' style and a prolonged A-a-men to boot. During which . . .*]
Burma, Burma, congregation done finish long time.

SAMSON [*in the same falsetto, jabbing Particulars savagely with the
elbow.*]: Lef' me! I say make you lef' me. Wetin be my
concern for dat one? I no care whether the Governor and
in aide-de-camp finish de same hymn since yesterday. Na
dey go fight for Burma? I tink say dis Remembrance Day
na for we own countryman wey die for combat. [*Turning
round the other way.*] Shurrup yourself. I say make you
shurrup yourself. Na so we dey sing am for army camp and
if you no like am make you commot for church go talk Latin
for Catholic church.

PARTIC. JOE: We were made much of in those days. To have
served in Burma was to have passed your London Matric.
Sergeant Burma looked forward to retirement and his choice
of business came as a matter of course . . . and Professor

offered him the business corner of the drivers' haven . . . the
Accident Corner.

SAMSON: Wetin enh? Wetin? You tink say myself I no go die
some day? When person die, 'e done die and dat one done
finish. I beg, if you see moto accident make you tell me. We
sabbee good business . . . sell spare part and second-hand
clothes. Wetin? You tink say I get dat kind sentimentation?
Me wey I done see dead body to tey I no fit chop meat unless
den cook am to nonsense?[1] Go siddon my friend. Business na
business. If you see accident make you tell me I go run go
there before those useless men steal all the spare part finish.

PARTIC. JOE: Sergeant Burma looked forward to retiring and
doing the spare part business full-time. But of course his brakes
failed going down a hill. . . .
[*The group begins to dirge, softly as if singing to themselves. A short
silence. Samson's face begins to show horror and he gasps as he
realizes what he has been doing.*]

SAMSON [*tearing off the clothes.*]: God forgive me! Oh God,
forgive me. Just see, I have been fooling around pretending to
be a dead man. Oh God I was only playing I hope you realize.
I was only playing.

PARTIC. JOE: Such a fire . . . such a fire. . . . Nothing but black
twigs left of the veteran of the Burma campaign . . . I went
to break the news to his wife. You know what she said?

SAMSON: No no, talk of something else I beg you.

PARTIC. JOE: She said, I always told him not to gather dead men's
wallets. And she was coming here to set fire to the whole store.

PROF.: Set fire to my store!

PARTIC. JOE: That's what I told her. Maybe the goods belong to
your husband I said, but the idea was Professor's.

PROF.: A spiritual ownership—more important than the material.

SAMSON: I wish she'd burnt the whole place.

PARTIC. JOE: She wasn't going to burn his money though. Oh
Sergeant Burma was a rich man. He searched the pockets
before the police or the ambulance came. Looting was after all
the custom in the front. You killed your enemy and you robbed
him. He couldn't break the habit.

1. 'I who have seen so many corpses that I cannot eat meat unless it is
overdone?'

SAMSON: But this is not war.

PROF.: Liar. Even these rags [*waving a newspaper*] understand its nature. Like a battlefield they always say. Like a battlefield.

SAMSON: Oh well, they all caught up with him. People don't do that sort of thing and get away with it.

PARTIC. JOE: Are you getting superstitious in your old age Samson?

SAMSON [*desperately to Kotonu.*]: You should never have touched the stuff.

KOTONU: Why not? Much more peaceful to trade in death than to witness it.

PARTIC. JOE [*recollecting.*]: Hoi hoi hoi! You bloody dealer in death—Where were you on the day of the Drivers' Festival?

SAMSON: Speak to the Professor. He handles everything for us.

SAY T. [*derisively.*]: That's gorrim. Well whar you wairing for? Ain't you gonna interrogate the Professor?

[*They push and egg him on, forming a semi-circle behind him.*]

PARTIC. JOE: Sir . . . at the suggestion of these hangers-on of yours . . . thinking sir, that as a man who wanders on the roads quite a bit and picks up significant events which would escape the ordinary eye, we were wondering sir, if you may chance to have er . . . discovered something which . . . er . . . might be able to assist the police in their investigations. . . . Sir.

PROF.: May an ignorant man ask what god you pretend to worship?

PARTIC. JOE: Same as the other sir, the road.

SAMSON [*whispering.*]: Professor, don't forget I paid my consultation fee. . . .

PARTIC. JOE: Any assistance sir . . . the compliment will be repaid, that's an official guarantee.

PROF.: It is true I am a gleaner, I dare not be swayed by marvels. Stick to the air and to open earth, wet my feet in morning dew, gleaning loose words from the road. Remain with the open eye of earth until the shadow of the usurping word touches my place of exile. But I broke my habit. I succumbed to the flaunting of a single word, forgot that exercise of spirit which demands that I make daily pilgrimage in search of leavings. I deserted my course, and—rightly—I lost my way. That was the vengeance of the Word. [*His manner changes*

gradually, becomes more deliberate, emphatic, like someone giving a lecture. And they listen, attentive, as if to a customary lesson in their daily routine.] But don't we all change from minute to minute? If we didn't we wouldn't hope to die. Well, same as the road. My favourite paths are those trickles among green fastnesses, on which whole forests are broken up—between the falling dew and the evening mists the nature of those paths changes right beneath my feet. But I am set in my ways—I should have followed my daily route. [*Turns in his chair, half-facing them.*] I pick my words only among rejects. [*He pats the bundles.*] You must have observed it. But I have no new finds to show you today because today was my day of error. I wandered on my favourite roads as usual, but I had not the courage to pick them up where they lay, stray and neglected. That word which I plucked early in the day was full-bellied, it was a robust growth, well-nourished, stout and pithy. And in my foolish excitement I uprooted it and bore it off, a trophy from the war. For my blindness I missed my way. I suppose I should ask your forgiveness for claiming pacts with words which grow above my station. My task is to keep company with the fallen, and this word rose in pride above spiked bushes. We must all stick together. Only the fallen have need of restitution. [*He turns round to his table, waves them off.*] Call out the hymn. Any song will do but to restore my self-confidence make it a song of praise. But mind you don't disturb me. I feel like working.
[*Falls straight on his papers as the group sings his favourite praise-song.*]
Professor anjonnu t'awa
Professor anjonnu t'awa
Baba wa l'oke baba
Baba wa l'odo baba
Eni ba ma a gbe mi san'le, ko da'wo duro
Mo leni lehin, ejo ragbada l'ori awo
A y'awo pada, ejo ragbada l'ori awo
Ota o lef'ori omo baba gun'yan je
A b'oro soro a b'elerigbo b'okele
Baba wa l'oke baba
Baba wa l'odo baba. . . .

[*As they sing, Professor gives short, cynical laughs. Then he turns round suddenly, vicious contempt in his voice, and they stop.*]

PROF.: If you think I do this from the kindness of my heart you are fools. But you are no fools, so you must be liars. It is true I demand little from you, just your presence at evening communion, and the knowledge you afford me that your deaths will have no meaning. Well look at you, battered in pieces and I ask no explanation. I let you serve two masters, three, four, five, a hundred if you wish. But understand that I would live as hopefully among cattle, among hogs, among rams if it were Ramadan, I would live as hopefully if you were ant-heaps destined to be crushed underfoot. But I suppose you my friend, would dare to call this also, accident?

KOTONU: Professor, I haven't said anything.

PROF.: Not you. Your friend. But I thank you all who hasten the redeeming of the Word. You are important I promise you. Everyone here is important. Your lives whittle down the last obstacle to the hidden Word.

PARTIC. JOE [*turning back sheets in his notebook.*]: In that case sir, perhaps we will be of mutual assistance to each other. Our investigations indicate that the man who was possessed at the Festival of Drivers was a palm wine tapper by trade. The coincidence involved will be of great interest to my bosses, but I am, as you know sir, a humble man and very approachable.

SAY T.: Hey, wairaminute wairaminute . . .

SAMSON: Kotonu, did you hear that?

PARTIC. JOE: Professor sir, have you anything to say?

PROF.: Remember my warning. Be careful I said. Be careful. If my enemies trouble me I shall counter with a resurrection. Capital R. I shall set up shop in full opposition—I have the advantage.

PARTIC. JOE: Is that your last word Professor?

PROF.: That is my message. [*Brings out his watch.*] And now Murano should arrive. But remember my warning.
[*Footsteps approaching.*]

KOTONU: Somebody is coming.
[*Say Tokyo spins round, imaginary pistol at the draw.*]

SAY T.: You just stay right there and don't move.
Enter Murano, bearing a large, outsize gourd. White froth topped.

*Say T. gives a huge leap in the air, tosses the 'gun' in the air.
Catches and fires several shots in all directions. General relaxation
and hum of contentment.*]

PROF. [*looks at his watch.*]: On time as usual my boy. Welcome.
[*Murano sets down the gourd beside him, prostrates. Goes inside to
fetch a variety of bowls and calabash cups. There is a very elegant
glass for Professor which he polishes carefully. Professor examines
the finished job through his monocle, Murano spills a libation to earth.
Then they sit with their eyes on the Prof. awaiting a signal. A few
moments, and lights appear through the stained glass windows.*]

PROF.: Hearken! [*First softly, gradually building up, the sound of organ
music.*] Observe the saintly progress of the evening
communicants! [*Organ music continues.*] Note, [*pointing to the
glass window*] I hold nothing against the rainbow, considering it
to be good. I hold nothing against lights, against colour,
finding in it mists and fragments of the Imminent grace on
earth. But I said ... I mean, I only sought to make my
meaning clear, and I could not escape the source of my own
sense of wonder ... God! He called it blasphemy.

[*Murano pours palm wine for everybody.*]

What if they were children? Is truth ever to be hidden from
children? Yes, what though there was the spirit of wine upon
me. It was Sunday, Palm Sunday and each child bore a cross of
the tender frond, yellow and green against their innocence. What
I said, I did not deny. ....

[*He begins to chuckle in spite of himself the moment he holds out the
glass.*]

You should have seen his face, oh you should have seen his
glory face! He was such a busybody that bishop, and it was his
just reward for sneaking up on me during Sunday School. ....
What are you doing teacher he said? I turned, and there
behind me stood the figure of judgement. Why, explaining the
lesson of the rainbow to my pupils. And how, he asked, did
I hear you explain it just now? So I told him, very gently. ....
Child, I said, my dear child, God painted the sign of the rainbow,
a promise that the world shall not perish from floods. Just as he
also carved the symbol of the palm, a covenant that the world
shall not perish from thirst.

[*Loud laughter, dying off gradually to a silence which is again*

gradually filled by organ music. Professor listens for some moments,
then turns to the band.]
Wipe out that sound, God forgive them.
[*Murano refills his glass, squats on the floor beside him. The band*
begins playing, drowning the organ music almost at once. When
a cup is emptied, the owner summons Murano, who refills it. The
singing runs freely, uninhibited. Say Tokyo Kid is obviously
recounting his adventures, especially to Salubi. Professor resumes his
studies.]

SAY T.: [*his voice suddenly above the din.*]: Say whas wrong wir that kid?
He sure acting funny.
[*It cuts across the noise, they mostly turn to look at Murano who*
has seen the mask and lifted it out, his face working with an
effort of the mind. Kotonu has come to the table, his eyes fixed on
the mute, the silence reaches the Professor and he looks at
them.]

PROF.: Why, my dear coast-to-coast driver, what is the matter?

KOTONU: Nothing Professor nothing.

PROF.: Is the child interested in that costume? You must
remember he's a child and bright things attract him. Murano
has no mind. He neither speaks nor hears nor remembers, and
one leg is shorter than the other.
[*Murano, at the sound of the Professor's voice has almost begun to*
be afraid. About to throw aside the mask.]

KOTONU: Professor, I asked you once . . .

PROF.: If Murano was the god-apparent?

SAMSON: And for God's sake, Professor, give a straight answer
for a change.

PROF.: Murano could not reveal much, returning instinctively
to his old trade, tapping wine from trees; beyond that, he had
retained no further link to what he was or where he had been.
That, that especially where he had been. And waiting, waiting
till his tongue be released, [*desperately*] in patience and in
confidence, for he is not like you others whose faces are equally
blank but share no purpose with the Word. So, surely Murano,
crawling out of the darkness, from the last suck of the throat of
death, and Murano with the spirit of a god in him, for it came
to the same thing, that I held a god captive, that his hands held
out the day's communion! And should I not hope, with him,

to cheat, to anticipate the final confrontation, learning its
nature baring its skulking face, why may I not understand . . .
[*He stops, looks around him.*] So, why don't you ask him you
runaway driver, why don't you ask him to try it on, see if it
fits. . . .
[*He pulls up Murano, takes him into the store, pulls the canvas
behind him.*]
Let us forget the mute one.
[*He waves to the group and they resume playing, uncertainly, afraid.
Very slowly, a small measure of gaiety returns. But they all remain
nervous, expectant.*]

SAY T.: Come on, service me the stuff. [*He gives one of his men the
cup.*] And hurry up cause lak a said, we'r gerring out of this
joint soon. I don' reckon on staying long in re same place
as that Professor guy.
[*His attention is fixed constantly on the store.*]

THUG: Cap'n. . . .

SAY T.: Shurrup wharre hell you mean? I tell you I found their
hideout. We goinra pay them a surprise visit tonight whether
you lak it or you don't.
[*Samson finds himself doing a running battle with a fly. He loses
eventually, the fly succeeds in landing in his wine. Samson leaps up
angrily, scoops out the froth with the fly in it, and carefully takes the
fly between two fingers. After a moment's thought he takes the fly
to the spider's web, throws it in, and stays to watch the spider seize
it, a satisfied grin spreading over his face.*]

SAMSON [*obviously slightly drunk.*]: Got him? A-ah, he understands
the game all right. Easy as chucking an unwilling passenger
into a lorry. I may not be an expert driver . . . in fact I must
confess, I am no driver at all, got thick soles and the gear
always goes in the wrong place. But one thing no one will
deny . . . Salubi!

SALUBI: Wetin?

SAMSON: Say Tokyo.

SAY T. [*absently.*]: Whas cooking kid?

SAMSON: Just tell me you two. What do they call me?

SALUBI: Samson Baba Agbero.

SAMSON: Yeah boy.

SAY T.: King of Touts.

SAMSON: Na me dat. As you see me like this, I am a quiet,
peace-loving man, but when we get to motor park, I don't
know my brother again.

SALUBI: King of Touts! Champion of motor park!

SAMSON: I'm all right. Murano. Service me man. God bless you,
man devil or whatever you are, God bless you. Murano?
Where's he gone? 'E fun awon enia wonyi . . . ni oti.[1] Yah!
Go and ask of me. From Dorma-Ahenkro to Abidjan.
Ask anyone who is the greatest tout of them all. Samson thas
me, King of Touts.

PARTIC. JOE: Samson Baba!

SAMSON: I'm all right. Ti o l'eru ese! [*Begins to demonstrate his
tactics.*] Sisi! A-ah. Sisi o. Sisi wey fine reach so na only bus
wey fine like we own fit carry am.[2] Wetin now sisi? Oh your
portmanteau, I done put am inside bus. Yes, certainly. We na
quick service, we na senior service. A-ah mama, na you dey
carry all dis load for your head? A-ah. Gentleman no dey for
dis world again . . . Oya mama, we done ready for go
now; na you be de las' for enter . . . Hey, Kotonu, fire am,
make am vu-um . . . oga abi[3] you no hear? We done ready for
go—no delay us at all at all. Come o, come now. Service na
first class, everything provided. If you wan' pee we go stop,
No delay! Wetin you dey talk? I say no delay? Which kin'
policeman? Abi you know dis bus? No Delay . . . no policeman
go delay us for road. This bus get six corner and we done put
bribe for each corner. No nonsense no palaver. Ah, olopa, my
good friend corporal, make you come join we bus now . . .
look in neck, 'e done fat pon-pon-pon e done chop bribe so
tey in neck dey swell like pig belle[4] . . . oh corporal come on
sir, come on for we bus sir . . . a-ah long time no see.
Welcome o, how family sah, ah-ah, na you dey look so-so thin
like sugar-cane so? Abi den dey give you too much work.
Ah, o ma se o,[5] na so policeman life be . . . hn, onijibiti,[6] 'e

1. 'Soak these people in wine.'
2. 'Sweetheart, when a girl is as pretty as you, only transports like ours will
match her.'
3. 'Mister.'
4. 'Look at his neck plump and greasy, he has taken so many bribes that his
neck is swollen like a pig's belly.'
5. 'how sad.'   6. 'bloody crook.'

done chop bribe in face dey shine like tomato. Ah, misisi, misisi, na you bus dey wait you here. . . .

[*From inside, the canvas is pushed aside, emerging silently, the egungun. The laughter dies out gradually all eyes on the apparition. One by one the hands splutter and die on the instruments.*]

SALUBI [*trying to sneak out.*]: No one is playing around with my sanity. I'm not staying to witness this.

PROF.: Let no one move!

[*Salubi hurriedly sits.*]

PARTIC. JOE: Professor, you know I am not superstitious. I mean, in my position I can't afford to be. But this . . . I swear sir, I would sooner you forged a hundred insurance policies.

PROF.: I must hope, even now. I cannot yet believe that death's revelation must be total, or not at all.

SAY T.: I reckon this has gone too far. I ain't scared like all these people so I'm telling you, you're fooling around where you ain't got no business. . . . I'm Say Tokyo Kid and I don't give you one damn!

PROF. [*explosively.*]: Do you cringe because you are confronted by the final gate to the Word? My friends, Murano is dumb and this creature suffers from gutturals like a love-crazed frog and yet you let the one sustain your spirits and the other fill you dead with awe. [*Shouting at the band.*] Play you croakers, play! Or have the blessings of Murano's daily pilgrimage dried already in the hollows of your cheeks? Play and burst your flooded throats before I draw the bowstring of the Word and the veiled shaft bores paths of faith across your cowering mind. Do I feed you wine for nothing? Play you foul-mouthed vermin of the road!

[*They obey him slowly, beating out the rhythm of agemo emerging from the bowels of earth.*

He goes round with the gourd, waving aside Samson who offers to help. The egungun continues to dance and the group pick up quickly when Professor approaches them.]

PROF.: I hope you will not think my gratitude excessive, but you make me feel that I was back among my Sunday-School children. It is a painful thing to desert one's calling—ask your friend over there who still cannot tear himself from the road.

Following in the path of Sergeant Burma is no substitute—he
will find that out.

SAY T. [*whispers fiercely to Salubi.*]: I don't want no curse on my
head.

SALUBI: Let's not annoy him. You know how he is.

SAY T.: Annoy him! Do you want to go blind from things you
shouldn't see.

PROF.: We have after all, to decide many things, as for instance,
who next runs our store. The coast-to-coast driver is a little
tired and the regular customers have lost patience.

SAY T. [*hoarsely to Salubi.*]: I ain't afraid. Even if he's master of the
spirits of every timber I ever wrestled with, I can teach him
a lesson.

PROF. [*filling Samson's cup.*]: It is not in my nature to be trusting.
Human beings, even such as you prove so tenacious, and I have
despaired again and again. But I hope you will remember
that we formed a syndicate.

SAMSON: I had forgotten all that business Professor.

PROF.: So I cannot desert you. I only hope, whoever it is, that you
will not balk me, that you will not keep me waiting until I am
beyond benefiting from our settlement. . . . One must cheat
fear, by fore-knowledge.

[*They all keep their eyes on him, with varying reactions, mostly
fear. The egungun continues to dance, Professor to dispense the
drink.*]

I feel powered tonight, but that is usual. But I also feel at
last a true excitement of the mind and spirit. As if that day has
been lowered at last which I have long awaited. Surely I am
not alone. If I am that, then I have wasted evenings of
instruction on you. [*Mildly, almost with tiredness.*] You dregs,
you emptied faces, have I shared my thoughts with you for
nothing?

[*The dance of the masquerade becomes wilder, racked by spasms, the
gradual build-up of possession.*]

SAY T.: Stop it! Stop it! [*Hitting his gang wildly.*] Who you calling
boss anyway? I say stop playing along with this sacrilege.

PROF. [*with a terrifying roar.*]: Play!

SAY T.: This has gone far enough.

PROF.: You make yourself conspicuous. Sit down!

[*The egungun has become thoroughly possessed. Say T. seeing this
leaps at Professor, neatly wrests the gourd from him and smashes it
against the far wall.*

*The figure is suddenly still. For some moments they both stand
motionless, facing each other. Suddenly they lock. With no sound but
hissed breaths they heave and gripe at each other in a tense elastic
control.*

*Salubi watching intently, dips his hand in his pocket and brings out
a clenched fist. Finding a moment when Say Tokyo is well placed,
he slides an object along the bench and Professor, who has not looked
at the combatants at all is attracted by this movement and leaps for
his stick, too late. Say Tokyo grasps the knife as Professor's stick hits
Salubi hard on the wrist, plunges the knife in Professor's back.
Professor jerks upright, his face masked in pain. There is a dead
stillness of several moments. Panicking suddenly, Say Tokyo
attempts to pull the knife from Professor's back. The still mask
appears to come to life suddenly, lifts Say Tokyo in a swift
movement up above his head, the knife out and in Say Tokyo's
hand, smashes him savagely on the bench. Say Tokyo tries to rise,
rolls over onto the ground and clutches the train of the mask to him.
Rising gradually, the driver's dirge.*

*Slowly the mask spins, spins, sinking lower as the Professor
staggers to his table. He begins in an involuntary movement to
gather up his papers. His strength falters. He makes a vague
gesture of the hand, like a benediction.*]

PROF.: Be even like the road itself. Flatten your bellies with the
hunger of an unpropitious day, power your hands with the
knowledge of death. In the heat of the afternoon when the
sheen raises false forests and a watered haven, let the event first
unravel before your eyes. Or in the dust when ghost lorries
pass you by and your shouts your tears fall on deaf panels and
the dust swallows them. Dip in the same basin as the man that
makes his last journey and stir with one finger, wobbling
reflections of two hands, two hands, but one face only. Breathe
like the road. Be the road. Coil yourself in dreams, lay flat in
treachery and deceit and at the moment of a trusting step, rear
your head and strike the traveller in his confidence, swallow
him whole or break him on the earth. Spread a broad sheet for
death with the length and the time of the sun between you

until the one face multiplies and the one shadow is cast by all the doomed. Breathe like the road, be even like the road itself. . . .

[The mask still spinning, has continued to sink slowly until it appears to be nothing beyond a heap of cloth and raffia. Still upright in his chair, Professor's head falls forward. Welling fully from the darkness falling around him, the dirge.]

THE END

GLOSSARY OF PIDGIN WORDS

abi: do you mean to say?; or
am: him; her; it
chop: eat; enjoy
dey: which; who
fit: is able to
haba: ha!
kuku: *used for emphasis like* self
na: it's
na so: just so
picken: child; children;
wes, wis: what?; what kind of?; which?; what's the?
wetin: what
wey: which; who

TRANSLATIONS OF YORUBA SONGS

165. (Drivers' dirge)
    It's a long long road to heaven
    It's a long road to heaven, Driver
    Go easy a-ah go easy driver
    It's a long long road to heaven
    My Creator, be not harsh on me
    Bandele's horse galloped home a winner
    But the race eluded him.

166. (Drivers' dirge cont.)
    This waist-ruff is piled high, high
    This waist-ruff is piled high, the lady
    Has made me wet my pants
    Oh she is cause of my sticky pants
    Some high ruff she's piled on her waist.
    A harlot called me a eunuch, I rejoiced
    In spite of that I will not take

A prostitute to wife
Oh they pile it high in Lagos
They really pile it high
In Lagos it was my eyes were opened,
It took Lagos to break the secret, where
An ancestral spirit turned mortal

173. (Thugs' war-chant)

Who meets Oro and makes no obeisance
What he shall experience!
When he's home he'll need a hot massage
What he shall experience!
When he's home he'll make thanksgivings
What he shall experience!
And if he fails to make home before dawn.
What he shall experience!
His skull shall tell the tales thereof—oh
What he shall experience!
Who meets Esu and fails to give way
What he shall experience!
Who struts arrogant before ancestral spirits
What he shall experience!

191. (Dirge for Kokol'ori)

It fogged suddenly at noonday
The sun asked, what is this wonder?
The dew of drought settled on my feet
Death deprives us of rain
The dew of drought settled on my breast
And the chill of fear took me
Death has sinned against us
A man among men is gone . . . Kokol'ori

220. (Professor's praise-song)

Professor, our being like demon
Professor, our being like demon
The elder above us
The elder below
The hand that thinks to smash me, let it
    pause awhile
I have one behind me, coiled snake on Mysteries
He moults in season, coiled snake on Mysteries

The foe cannot pound the head of a Father's
    son like yam
Who holds discourse with spirits, who dines with
    the Ruler of Forests
He is the elder above us
He is our elder below ...

THE
BACCHAE OF
EURIPIDES

A COMMUNION RITE

Characters

DIONYSOS

Chorus of Slaves
  LEADER
  OLD SLAVE
  HERDSMAN
  OTHERS

Procession of Eleusis
  MASTER OF REVELS
  VESTALS
  PRIESTS
  FLOGGERS

  TIRESIAS
  KADMOS

PENTHEUS
OFFICER
AGAVE

The Bacchantes
  1ST BACCHANTE
  WEEPING BACCHANTE
  OTHERS

The Wedding Scenes
  1. IN-LAWS
    BRIDEGROOM
    BESTMAN
    BRIDE
  2. SEATED FIGURE
    THREE WOMEN

The Slaves, and the Bacchantes should be as mixed a cast as is possible, testifying to their varied origins. Solely because of the 'hollering' style suggested for the Slave Leader's solo in the play it is recommended that this character be fully negroid.

Acknowledgement

A twenty-year rust on my acquaintanceship with classical Greek made it necessary for me to rely heavily on previous translations in this adaptation of *The Bacchae*. Two versions which deserve especial mention in that I have not hesitated to borrow phrases and even lines from them are those by Gilbert Murray, published by Allen & Unwin, London, and Oxford University Press, New York, and by William Arrowsmith, in *Euripides Five: Three Tragedies*, The Complete Greek Tragedies, edited by David Grene and Richard Lattimore, published by University of Chicago Press, © 1959 by the University of Chicago. My publishers and I gratefully acknowledge the publishers concerned for the use I have made of these translations.

I must also mention the debt to my own *Idanre*, a Passion poem of Ogun, elder brother to Dionysos. From this long poem I have also lifted entire lines especially in the praise chants.

Finally, thanks to the National Theatre of Great Britain who commissioned this adaptation of *The Bacchae*.

Wole Soyinka

To one side, a road dips steeply into lower background, lined by the bodies of crucified slaves mostly in the skeletal stage. The procession that comes later along this road appears to rise almost from the bowels of earth. The tomb of Semele, smoking slightly is to one side, behind the shoulder of this rise. Green vines cling to its charred ruins.

In the foreground, the main gate to the palace of Pentheus. Further down and into the wings, a lean-to built against the wall, a threshing-floor. A cloud of chaff, and through it, dim figures of slaves flailing and treading. A smell and sweat of harvest. Ripeness. A spotlight reveals Dionysos just behind the rise, within the tomb of Semele. He is a being of calm rugged strength, of a rugged beauty, not of effeminate prettiness. Relaxed, as becomes divine self-assurance but equally tensed as if for action, an arrow drawn in readiness for flight.

DIONYSOS: Thebes taints me with bastardy. I am turned into an alien, some foreign outgrowth of her habitual tyranny. My followers daily pay forfeit for their faith. Thebes blasphemes against me, makes a scapegoat of a god.

It is time to state my patrimony—even here in Thebes.

I am the gentle, jealous joy. Vengeful and kind. An essence that will not exclude, nor be excluded. If you are Man or Woman, I am Dionysos. Accept.

A seed of Zeus was sown in Semele my mother earth, here on this spot. It has burgeoned through the cragged rocks of far Afghanistan, burst the banks of fertile Tmolus, sprung oases through the red-eyed sands of Arabia, flowered in hill and gorge of dark Ethiopia. It pounds in the blood and breasts of my wild-haired women, long companions on this journey home through Phrygia and the isles of Crete. It beats on the walls of Thebes, bringing vengeance on all who deny my holy origin and call my mother—slut.

[He looks down on the clouds of smoke wrapped round his feet, rising from the tomb. He scuffs the ground with a foot, scattering ashes and sparks.]

Something lives yet, there is smoke among the rubble. Live embers. The phoenix rises and that is life—wings from cooling cinders, tendrils from putrefaction, motion from what was petrified. . . . There are green vines on the slag of ruin. Mine. As on the mountain slopes, clustering and swelling. They flush, they flood the long-parched throats of men and release their joy. This sacrament of earth is life. Dionysos.

[*From the direction of the 'crucifixion slope' comes a new sound, a liturgical drone—lead and refrain—a dull, thin monotone, still at some distance. A Herdsman carrying a jar darts across the stage to the threshers. Dionysos stands still, statuesque.*]

HERDSMAN: I think I hear them coming.

SLAVE LEADER [*eagerly seizes the jug and takes a swig.*]: What did you say?

HERDSMAN: The Masters of Eleusis. They've begun the revels.

[*The slaves gather round and listen. The jug is passed round.*]

LEADER [*spits.*]: Revels!

HERDSMAN: Which of us is the victim this year?

SLAVE: That old man of the king's household. The one who looks after the dogs.

HERDSMAN [*shrugs.*]: He's old enough to die.

LEADER: He had better survive!

HERDSMAN [*fearfully.*]: Sh-sh!

LEADER: I have said it before. If another of us dies under the lash . . .!

[*The jug is passed to him again. He takes a long draught, sighs.*] There is heaven in this juice. It flows through my lips and I say, now I roll the sun upon my tongue and it neither burns nor scorches. And a scent-laden breeze fills the cavern of my mouth, pressing for release. I know that scent. I mean, I knew it once. I live to know it once again.

HERDSMAN: I think I understand you. Forget it friend.

LEADER: A scent of freedom is not easily forgotten. Have you ever slept, dreamt, and woken up with the air still perfumed with the fragrance of grapes?

HERDSMAN: There is no other smell at this time of the year. If you live in the hills that is. It gets oppressive sometimes, to tell the truth. You know, rather cloying.

LEADER: Surrounded by walls one can only dream. But one day . . . one day . . .

HERDSMAN: Not you. No one will ever trust you outside of the city walls. Dissimulation is an art you will never master. You need

THE BACCHAE OF EURIPIDES

237

the sly humility, the downcast eye. Yes Sire, King Pentheus,
no Sir Honourable Eunuch of the Queen's Bedchamber ...

LEADER: Let's speak of better things. Tell me of those hidden
vineyards. They are like my buried longings: I know each
precious acre of the forbidden terrain, inch by inch. And I
know I envy you. The air of Thebes is sterile. Nothing
breathes in it. Nothing—really—lives. Come closer ...
distend your nostrils ... now breathe in, deeply ... smell!

HERDSMAN: Look, if every time I bring you wine you have to ...

LEADER: Do you smell anything? Anything at all? After the hills
and the vines and the wind can you smell me? Do I live?

HERDSMAN: You promised ...

LEADER [*He makes an effort, takes a deep breath.*]: What does it matter
anyway. An open-air slave or a walled-up slave ... we all
fold our arms and thank the gods for a generous harvest.

HERDSMAN: Generous is not the word for it. The vines went mad
so to speak; they were not themselves. Something seemed to
have got under the soil and was feeding them nectar. The
weight that hung on the vines even from the scrubbiest patch,
each cluster ... [*his hands shape them.*] pendulous breasts of the
wives of Kronos, bursting all over with giant nipples.

LEADER: I felt it on my tongue. The sun has left the heavens and
made a home within the grapes of Boetia.

HERDSMAN: You may say that. It was a joy to tread them.
[*The liturgical drone is now very close.*]
They are nearly here. I must go.

LEADER: Wait. [*Takes hold of him.*] Suppose the old man dies?

HERDSMAN: We all have to die sometime.

LEADER: Flogged to death? In the name of some unspeakable rites?

HERDSMAN: Someone must cleanse the new year of the rot of the
old or, the world will die. Have you ever known famine?
Real famine?

LEADER: Why us? Why always us?

HERDSMAN: Why not?

LEADER: Because the rites bring us nothing! Let those who profit
bear the burden of the old year dying.

HERDSMAN: Careful. [*Points to the row of crosses.*] The palace does not
need the yearly Feast of Eleusis to deal with rebellious slaves.
[*He takes the jug and turns to go.*]

LEADER: Look, tell them on the hills, tell your fellows up there . . .

HERDSMAN [*instantly rigid.*]: What?

LEADER [*hesitates, sighs.*]: Nothing. Tell them—we also are waiting.

[*The Herdsman goes off the same way as he entered. Led by a solemn figure who is the Master of Revels, a procession emerges and proceeds over the rise.*

First, the Master of Revels, next black-robed priests intoning a liturgy, punctuated by hand-bells. After them comes a group of vestals in white. The first pair carry fresh branches, the middle section garlands and flowers, the last pair carry bowls. The vestals are followed by an Old Man, completely white-bearded, dressed in what might approximate to sackcloth-and-ashes, who carries a bunch of used twigs. Behind him are four stalwart figures in red, armed with strong, supple lashes. At every three or four paces the priests ring their bell, upon which the two maidens in front of the Old Man turn and sprinkle him with what might be ashes or chaff, while the four men lay into him from all sides with their whips. A straggle of crowd follows. This sedate procession passes through and around Dionysos without seeing him and proceeds downstage towards the gates of the palace. The slaves have stopped work and are watching. A small ceremony of 'cleansing' is performed on the palace gate. The priests take branches from a bundle borne by the two leading girls, symbolically scour the gates with them, then pile the used twigs on the bunch already borne by the Old Man. He is sprinkled and flogged as before.

At the sight of the Old Man, there is distinct surprise and agitation among the slaves.

Suddenly the Old Man appears to wilt, collapse. A further stroke of the lash brings him to his knees. The intoning continues without stopping, and the lashes. As he falls prone, a bright flash reveals Dionysos on the tomb of Semele. All action ceases. The music of Dionysos.]

DIONYSOS [*smiling.*]: Sing Death of the Old Year, and—welcome the new—god.

[*A prolonged, confused silence. In the threshing-hut the slaves forcefully restrain their Leader who seems bent on giving immediate vocal acknowledgement to the god.*]

SLAVE: You'll get us killed. We'll be wiped out to a man.

ANOTHER: Remember the helots. Don't be rash.

[*Dionysos comes down among the procession. The priests retreat in terror as he turns towards the vestals.*]

DIONYSOS: And the vestals of Eleusis?

VESTALS [*hesitant and fearful.*]: We ... welcome the new ... god.

DIONYSOS: Oh, but joyfully, joyfully! Welcome the new god. joyfully. Sing death of the old year passing.

VESTALS [*liturgical, lifeless.*]: Welcome the new god. Joyfully. Sing death ...

[*They stop, look at one another foolishly. One or two begin to titter and Dionysos bellows with laughter. The vestals regain some relaxation.*]

DIONYSOS: And now try again. Together, with joy.

VESTALS [*courageously.*]: We ...

[*A vestal detaches herself from the group, her eyes riveted on the face of Dionysos. She scoops up a garland as she passes the flower-bearers and comes up to the stranger. He bows his head and she garlands him.*]

THE VESTAL: Welcome the new ...

[*Keels over in a faint and is caught by Dionysos. Carrying her he moves towards the priests.*]

DIONYSOS: And now the priests of Eleusis?

PRIEST: We welcome ...

ANOTHER: ... a miracle, a miracle.

[*They hurriedly edge their way out and flee in the direction from which they made their entry. The floggers also retreat a little way, watchful.*]

LEADER [*breaking loose after the priests' retreat.*]: Welcome the new god! Thrice welcome the new order! [*hands cupped to his mouth, he yodels.*] Evohe-e-e-e! Evohe-e-e-e!

[*The sound is taken up by echoes from the hills. It roves round and round and envelops the scene. All heads turn outwards in different directions, listening. A mixture of excitement and unease as the sound continues, transformed beyond the plain echo to an eerie response from vast distances.*

From the same responsive source, intermingled strains of the music of Dionysos. It swells inwards to the attentive listeners. The vestal in the arms of Dionysos stirs, responding. She lowers herself to the ground slowly, moves into a dance to the music. As the dance takes her close to the Slave Leader he moves away with her; the dance

soon embraces all the vestals and slaves.
Dionysos, smiling, slips off as they become engrossed in the dance.
The music stops, the enchantment is cut off. The fainting vestal
looks round her in growing panic.]

VESTAL: Don't leave us!

[*She runs out in pursuit, the other vestals following.*]

LEADER: Let's follow.

[*The slaves hang back. The euphoria has melted rapidly.*]

SLAVE: I think we've gone too far already.

LEADER: You hesitant fools! Don't you understand?
Don't you *know*? We are no longer alone—
Slaves, helots, the near and distant dispossessed!
This master race, this much vaunted dragon spawn
Have met their match. Nature has joined forces with us.
Let them reckon now, not with mere men, not with
The scapegoat bogey of a slave uprising
But with a new remorseless order, forces
Unpredictable as molten fire in mountain wombs.
To doubt, to hesitate is to prove undeserving.

SLAVE: There is such a fault as rashness.

LEADER: When the present is intolerable, the unknown harbours
no risks.

ANOTHER: I don't know ... why make ourselves conspicuous.
Let the free citizens of Thebes declare for this stranger or
against him.

LEADER: Whose interest will direct their choice? Ours?

SLAVE: No, but ...

[*The slaves look away from one another, uncomfortable but afraid.*
After an awkward silence, the Leader sighs in defeat.]

LEADER: Let us go as far as the gates then. We should know at
least how the Thebans receive him. In our own interest.

[*They follow him out, guiltily.*]

[*The Old Man is left alone with the floggers. As he begins to pick*
himself up painfully, they rush forward to help him up. He brushes
them off angrily.]

TIRESIAS: Take your hands off!

[*He rises, tries to dust himself and winces.*]

1ST MAN: Were you hurt?

TIRESIAS: Animals!

1ST MAN: Oh. We ... didn't mean to.

TIRESIAS: You never do.

2ND MAN: Who was he?

1ST MAN: Yes who was he? Where did he spring from?

TIRESIAS [snorts.]: Who was he? Where did he spring from? Fools! Blind, stupid, bloody brutes! Can you see how you've covered me in weals? Can't you bastards ever tell the difference between ritual and reality.

1ST MAN: *I* was particularly careful. I pulled my blows.

TIRESIAS: Symbolic flogging, that is what I keep trying to drum into your thick heads.

4TH MAN: I could have sworn I only tapped you gently from time to time.

3RD MAN: It's all that incantation. It soaks in your brain and you can't feel yourself anymore.

TIRESIAS: I suppose you would have carried on like you do year after year. Flogged the last breath out of my body.

3RD MAN [among shocked protests.]: How could you think such a thing? You are not a slave. I mean, we do have some control.

TIRESIAS: Yah, you showed it. Anyway what are you standing there for?

1ST MAN: Well ... we ... I mean, we don't quite know what to do.

3RD MAN: I mean, it's a bit of a departure isn't it? Never known anything like this happen before. Well damn it, who was he?

4TH MAN: And the vestals, gone with him.

TIRESIAS: Go after them. You've been cheated of your blood this time so your throats are a little parched. Go up in the mountains and you'll find other juices to quench your thirst.

1ST MAN [irritated.]: You will speak in riddles!

TIRESIAS: The feast has shifted to the mountains—is that simple enough?

1ST MAN [wearily.]: Just tell us what we are now expected to do when we get there?

TIRESIAS: Whatever you wish. Just take your violent presences away from me!

3RD MAN: Well, that's plain enough.

1ST MAN: You know who he was.

TIRESIAS [*draws himself up.*]: Since when has it been the custom for common no-brain wrestlers to cross-examine the seer of Thebes.

1ST MAN: Let's go. [*They exit.*]

TIRESIAS: Swine! [*He feels his body tenderly, then shouts.*] Wait! Which of you kept my staff?

DIONYSOS [*re-enters.*]: Borrow my thyrsus.

TIRESIAS: Thank you. Dionysos I presume?

DIONYSOS: You see too well Tiresias.

TIRESIAS: As if the gentlest emanations from the divine *maestro* would not penetrate the thickest cataract.

DIONYSOS: Yet there is one here who has no defect in his eyes but will not see.

TIRESIAS: I know. Handle him gently Dionysos, if only for his grandfather's sake.

DIONYSOS: Kadmos was pious. Consecrating this ground in memory of my mother at least kept her alive in the heart of Thebes . . . but that is Kadmos. Let every man's actions save or damn him. We shall see what Pentheus chooses to do.

TIRESIAS [*shrugs.*]: I knew that would be the answer. Anyway, thank you for stepping in just now. You were just in time.

DIONYSOS: Were you really in trouble?

TIRESIAS: I was. One can never tell how far the brutes will go. Mind you, I took the precaution of wearing your fawn-skin under my gown. You see how the sack-cloth has been flogged to ribbons. I had to collapse to remind them they were getting carried away again.

DIONYSOS: But what made the high priest of Thebes elect to play flagellant?

TIRESIAS: The city must be cleansed. Filth, pollution, cruelties, secret abominations—a whole year's accumulation.

DIONYSOS: Why you? Are you short of lunatics, criminals, or slaves?

TIRESIAS: A mere favour to Kadmos whom I love like a brother. Kadmos is Thebes. He has yielded all power to Pentheus but I know he still rejoices or weeps with Thebes. And Thebes— well, let's just say the situation is touch and go. If one more slave had been killed at the cleansing rites, or sacrificed to that insatiable altar of nation-building . . .

DIONYSOS: Quite a politician eh Tiresias?

TIRESIAS: A priest is not much use without a following, and that's soon washed away in what social currents he fails to sense or foresee. As priest and sage and prophet and I know not how else I am regarded in Thebes, I must see for the blind young man who is king and even sometimes—act for him.

DIONYSOS: And if you have been flogged to pieces at the end, like an effigy?

TIRESIAS: Then I shall pass into the universal energy of renewal ... like some heroes or gods I could name.

DIONYSOS: Go on.

TIRESIAS: Isn't that it? Is that not why Dionysos?

DIONYSOS: Is that not what?

TIRESIAS: Why you all seem to get torn to pieces at some point or the other?

DIONYSOS: Don't change the subject. Go on about you.

TIRESIAS: I've said it all. What more do you want me to say?

DIONYSOS [He moves close to Tiresias, tugs gently at his beard.]: Poor Tiresias, poor neither-nor, eternally tantalized psychic intermediary, poor agent of the gods through whom everything passes but nothing touches, what happened to you in the midst of the crowd, dressed and powdered by the hands of ecstatic women, flagellated by sap-swollen birches? What sensations coursed your withered veins as the whips drew blood, as the skin of the birches broke against yours and its fragrant sap mingled with your blood. You poor starved votary at the altar of soul, what deep hunger unassuaged by a thousand lifelong surrogates drove you to this extreme self-sacrifice. Don't lie to a god Tiresias.

TIRESIAS: I never lie. I told you the truth.

DIONYSOS: Yes, but only a half-truth, like your prophesies. Tell me the rest.

TIRESIAS [cornered. Finally.]: Yes, there was hunger. Thirst. In this job one lives half a life, neither priest nor man. Neither man nor woman. I have longed to know what flesh is made of. What suffering is. Feel the taste of blood instead of merely foreseeing it. Taste the ecstasy of rejuvenation after long organizing its ritual. When the slaves began to rumble I saw myself again playing that futile role, pouring my warnings on deaf ears. An uprising would come, bloodshed, and I would watch, untouched, merely vindicated as before—as prophet. I approach death and dissolution, without having felt life . . . its force. . . .

DIONYSOS: And just now?

TIRESIAS: You forget. That goes by role. Ecstasy is too elusive a quarry for such tricks. Even if I did shed a few drops of blood.

DIONYSOS [lays his hands gently on the Old Man's shoulders.]: Thebes shall have its full sacrifice. And Tiresias will know ecstasy.

TIRESIAS: Something did begin. Perhaps those lashes did begin something. I feel . . . a small crack in the dead crust of the soul. Listen! Can you hear women's voices? Strange, just then I almost felt my veins race.

DIONYSOS [drawing back.]: Dance for me Tiresias. Dance for Dionysos.

TIRESIAS: That's like asking the elephant to fly. I've never danced in all my life.

[The music of Dionysos is heard. Tiresias stands entranced for some moments, then moves naturally into the rhythm, continues to dance, rapt.

Dionysos watches for a while, then slips off. Enter Kadmos, stands amazed and watches. Tiresias senses his presence after a while and stops, clutching his thyrsus defensively.]

TIRESIAS: It's someone else. Who is it?

KADMOS: Your good friend, Kadmos of the royal house. How goes it with you Tiresias? Are you well?

TIRESIAS: You must be blind to need ask such a question.

KADMOS: Well I confess I do not believe my eyes.

TIRESIAS: Oh Kadmos Kadmos, how I wish you were still king of Thebes.

KADMOS: That's not like you to wish undone what is already done. What's biting you?

TIRESIAS: Your grandson, the foolish, blind, headstrong, suicide-bent king.

KADMOS: Not suicide-bent I hope. His faults I readily admit. But what's he done now?

TIRESIAS: Nothing yet. It's what he's going to do. I know how it

will all end. Oh Kadmos, wisdom is what we need in a king
at this moment, a sense of balance and proportion.

KADMOS: You didn't seem a model of proportion when I came
on you a moment ago. What did you think you were
doing?

TIRESIAS: Saving Thebes again, though I fear that is too late. It
is far far easier to save Thebes from the anger of disgruntled
classes than from the vengeance of a spited god. Neither your
piety nor my new-found ecstasy can help him now.

KADMOS: Tiresias, you know I have no head for conundrums ...

TIRESIAS: Yes, your son takes after you there. But at least you
don't go at every riddle with sledgehammer and pitchfork.

KADMOS: Is there yet another danger that threatens Thebes?

TIRESIAS: None that you or I could help. [*Sounds in the distance.*]
Listen to them! Can you hear that? Can you feel the power of
it Kadmos?

KADMOS [*The significance dawns on him.*]: But you are not with
them. You promised me Tiresias. You promised Thebes.

TIRESIAS: What you hear is another sound, a new order. Your
other grandson took my place. The wanderer has come home.
He's here.
[*The Bacchantes enter to shouts of Bromius! Evohe-e! Zagreus!*]
Quickly. Stand aside and be silent. They sound already
possessed.
[*They hide themselves.*]

BACCHANTE: Where?

BACCHANTE: Where?

BACCHANTE: Where?

BACCHANTE: Where?
[*That cry is taken up, repeated fast from mouth to mouth, ending
with a long, impassioned communal cry.*]

BACCHANTES: Bro-o-o-o-o-mius!

BACCHANTE: Bromius ...

BACCHANTE: Bromius ...

BACCHANTE: Bromius ...
[*Again the name is tossed from tongue to tongue, beginning as a deep
audible breath and accompanied by spasmodic, scenting movements.
It swells in volume and breaks suddenly into another passionate
scream by the leader of the Bacchantes.*]

1ST BACCHANTE: Bro-o-o-o-o-mius! Be Manifest!

Be manifest Bromius, your Bacchantes have taken the field.
You've led us. Lead us now.

ANOTHER: We've journeyed together. Through Lydia and Phrygia...

ANOTHER: Over rivers of gold, Bactrian fastness ...

ANOTHER: Through slopes of the clustering vine.

ANOTHER: Companion of forest and towered cities,
Of the steppes of Persia and wastes of Media.

ANOTHER: Through the dance of the sun on Ethiopia's rivers,
Lakes, seas, emerald oases.

ANOTHER: Rooting deep, ripeness and mysteries
Rooting as vine in the most barren of soils.

1ST BACCHANTE: The silvering firs have trembled, we have seen
    rockhills
Shudder, earth awaken, ramparts of heaven cave
Beasts answer from their lairs, sap rise in the trees
And the sevenfold bars on the gates of Thebes
Splinter—at the Maenads' cry of BROMIUS!

BACCHANTES: Evohe-e-e-e-e-e!

[Re-enter the slaves.]

LEADER [in a ringing voice.]: Bacchantes, fellow strangers, to this
land!

[A gradual hush. They turn towards the sound.]

LEADER: Fellow aliens, let me ask you—do you know Bromius?

[The women turn to one another, still in a haze of possession, but
astonished at such a ridiculous question. One or two continue to moan,
completely oblivious to the interruption.]

1ST BACCHANTE: Do we know Bromius?

LEADER: Bromius. Zagreus. Offspring of Zeus as the legend goes.

1ST BACCHANTE [over a general peal of laughter.]: Stranger, do you
know Bromius?

LEADER: A god goes by many names. I have long been a spokesman
for the god.

1ST BACCHANTE: And yet you ask, do we know Bromius. Who
led us down from the mountains of Asia, down holy Tmolus,
through the rugged bandit-infested hills of the Afgans, the
drugged Arabian sands, whose call have we followed through
the great delta? Who opened our eyes to the freedom of sands,
to the liberation of waters? Do we know Bromius?

LEADER: Do you love his worship?

1ST BACCHANTE: Hard are the labours of a god
Hard, but his service is sweet fulfilment.

LEADER [*coming forward*.]: Then make way. [*They part and he comes among them.*]

WEEPING BACCHANTE [the Fainting Vestal]: What is it? What does the slave want with us? I want my god, the son of Zeus.

ANOTHER: Where shall we seek him? Where find him?

LEADER: Fall back a little. Seal up the streets and let no one intrude.
There is a hymn all believers know.
[*Pause. The Bacchante sizes him up, decides for him.*]

1ST BACCHANTE: Let every mouth be silent. Let no ill-omened words profane your tongues.

LEADER: It is the hour we have long awaited.
What is hidden must some day come to light
Now, raise with me the old old hymn to godhead.
[*The Chorus intone beneath the prayer.*]

1ST BACCHANTE: Blessed are they who know the mysteries of god
Blessed all who hallow their life in worship of god
Whom the spirit of god possesses, who are one
With earth, leaves and vine in the holy body of god.
Blessed are the dancers whose hearts are purified
Who tread on the hill in the holy dance of god.
Blessed are they who keep the rites of the Earth-Mother
Who bear the thyrsus, who wield the holy wand of god
Blessed are all who wear the ivy crown of god
Blessed, blessed are they: Dionysos is their god.

CHORUS: Blessed, blessed, thrice blessed are we:
Dionysos is our god.
[*The first chords of music, oriental strings and timbrels.*]

WEEPING BACCHANTE: Bromius, Bromius . . .

LEADER: Blessed are they who bathe in the seminal river
Who merge in harmony with earth's eternal seeding
Blessed they whose hands are cupped to heaven
Their arms shall be funnel for the rain of understanding
Blessed are all whose feet have trodden the dance of grapes
Whose hands have nursed the vine, earth's gentlest binding
Blessed their joys in the common sacrament, whose beings
Open to intuitions in the liberation of the grape

Blessed, thrice blessed the innocence of acceptance
The arms that reach to a welcome of god
Blessed, thrice blessed, the moment of recognition
Of god without as the essence within.

CHORUS: Blessed, blessed, thrice blessed are we:
Dionysos is our god.

LEADER: For he is the living essence of whom, said heaven
The seed is mine, this seminal germ
Earthed in sublimation of the god in flesh
The flesh in god. I bind my seed in hoops of iron
And though all seek him, safe I hold him
Safe in the loins wherefrom he sprang.
Let all revere the gracious earth,
Womb of the infant deity.

WEEPING BACCHANTE: Bromius, Bromius ...

LEADER: Tribute to the holy hills of Ethiopia
Caves of the unborn, and the dark ancestral spirits. Home
Of primal drums round which the dead and living
Dance. I praise the throbbing beat of the hide
The squeal and the wail of flutes ...

MORE BACCHANTES [moaning.]: Oh Bromius, Bromius.

IST BACCHANTE: It is fallen to me at last, fallen
All fallen to me from the raving satyrs
Fallen at last to me to celebrate his name:
Dionysos! Stranger, honey-voiced
Spokesman of my god. Tell us tales of what you know,
Sing to me again of Dionysos.

[Music. It has the strange quality—the nearest familiar example is the
theme-song of Zorba the Greek—with its strange mixture of
nostalgia, violence, and death. The scene which follows needs the
following quality: extracting the emotional colour and temperature
of a European pop scene without degenerating into that tawdry
commercial manipulation of teenage mindlessness. The lines are
chanted not sung, to musical accompaniment. The Slave Leader is
not a gyrating pop drip. His control emanates from the self-contained
force of his person, a progressively deepening spiritual presence. His
style is based on the lilt and energy of the black hot gospellers who
themselves are often first to become physically possessed.
The effect on his crowd is however, the same—physically—as

would be seen in a teenage pop audience. From orgasmic moans the
surrogate climax is achieved. A scream finds its electric response in
others and a rush begins for the person of the preacher. Handfuls of
his clothes are torn, his person is endangered but he never 'loses his
cool'. As his chant approaches climax a sudden human wave engulfs
him and he is completely submerged under screaming, 'possessed'
lungs and bodies.

As with such scenes there is always something of an overall ugliness
about the manifested emotion. But the radiant isolated votive or two,
or even the few faces of intensely energized spiritual rapture that
stand out in the mêlée indicate something of the awesome depths of
this self-release.]

LEADER: Then listen Thebes, nurse of Semele,
Crown your hair with ivy
Turn your fingers green with bryony
Redden your walls with berries,
Decked with boughs of oak and fir
Come dance the dance of god.
Fringe your skins of dappled fawn
With wool from the shuttle and loom
For the looms are abandoned by throngs of women
They run to the mountains and Bromius before
They follow the violent wand of the bringer of life
The violent wand,
Of the gentle, jealous, joy!

BACCHANTES [*like a wail.*]: Bromius, Bromius . . .

LEADER [*progressively radiant.*]: He . . . is . . .
Sweet upon the mountains, such sweetness
As afterbirth, such sweetness as death.
His hand strap wildness, and breed it gentle
He infuses tameness with savagery.
I have seen him on the mountains, in vibrant fawn-skin
I have seen his smile in the red flash of blood
I have seen the raw heart of a mountain-lion
Yet pulsing in his throat.
In the mountains of Eritrea, in the deserts of Libya
In Phrygia whose copper hills ring with cries of
Bromius, Zagreus, Dionysos,
I know he is the awaited, the covenant, promise,

Restorer of fullness to Nature's lean hours.
As milk he flows in the earth, as wine
In the hills. He runs in the nectar of bees, and
In the duct of their sting lurks—Bromius.
Oh let his flames burn gently in you, gently,
Or else—consume you it must—consume you . . .

CHORUS: Bromius . . . Bromius . . .

LEADER: His hair a bush of foxfires in the wind
A streak of lightning his thyrsus.
He runs, he dances,
Kindling the tepid
Spurring the stragglers
And the women are like banks to his river—
A stream of gold from beyond the desert—
They cradle the path of his will.

CHORUS: Come, come Dionysos . . .

LEADER: Oh Thebes, Thebes, flatten your walls.
Raise your puny sights
To where the heights of Kithairon await you.

CHORUS: Yes, yes . . .

LEADER: On the slopes where Dionysos will come
Run free with you in your labour of song
Your dancing drudgery, your chores of dreaming—
In the truth of night descends his secret—
Hold, embrace it.

CHORUS: Yes, yes . . . set me free . . . set me free.

LEADER: The sun touches the vines on the slopes
And *that* is godhead. Dew falls on the grass
And *that* is godhead. The sap awakens—
A birth
A dawn
A spring
Pure dewdrops down the mountain
That is godhead. And you
Nestled in earth's womb are
Green leaves in winter, woodsap in snow
You are the eternal ivy on the wand of life
Emerald pines that defy the winter
Dates of the oases in drought of deserts.

BACCHANTES: Bromius . . . Bromius . . .

LEADER: Seek him in your breasts with love, within
Your hidden veins, in the quiet murmur of your blood
Seek him in the marrow, in wombstone, he is fount
Of life. He makes an anvil of the mountain-peaks
Hammers forth a thunderous will, he farms the slopes
And the vine tempers his will. In plains and valleys
Nest his joyful Bacchae, his mesh of elements
Reconciles a warring universe.

BACCHANTES: Come Bromius, come . . .

LEADER: He is the new life, the new breath, creative flint
Flood earth with his blood, let your shabby streets
Flow with his life, his light, drum him into the heart
Like thunder. He is the storehouse of life
His bull horns empower him
A bud on the autumn bough, he blossoms in you
His green essence fills your womb of earth. . . .

BACCHANTES: Bromius . . . Bromius . . .

LEADER: There is power in his thyrsus, feel!
It pulses. Feel! It quivers and races with sap.
Throat, tongue, breast, calling forth the powers of life
Hold him, embrace him. His dance covers you
His drums envelop you, your skin is one with his drum
Tuning and straining tight. Spindle and shuttle
In your hand—behold—the wand of god
The hearthstone his thyrsus, thrusting from earth
The fire is tamed in new greenery of life,
In fawn-skin and ivy, and the thorn of life comes
Piercing your blood . . . !

[A long scream from a Bacchante snaps the last restraint of the
women. They rush the Leader and engulf him. He disappears under.
From under the mêlée of limbs, the wild, desperate chant of 'Where?
Where? Where?' recommences, diminishing as the mass of flesh
unravels, dispersed in different directions, groping unseeing. Other
slaves drag their Leader to safety. The chant continues faintly off for
some time after they have all disappeared.

Cautiously, the two Old Men emerge. Kadmos is in a high state
of excitement.]

KADMOS: Why are we waiting. Let's go, let's go.

TIRESIAS: Where?

KADMOS: To the mountains where else? Let's go and do him honour.

TIRESIAS: But are you dressed?

[*Kadmos flings off his cloak, revealing the Dionysian fawn-skin under it.*]

KADMOS: Aren't I? [*Takes Tiresias's hand.*] Here, feel that. You won't find finer foreskin except on Dionysos himself.

TIRESIAS: He isn't circumcised?

KADMOS: Who? Who isn't circumcised?

TIRESIAS: Dionysos. What you said about his foreskin.

KADMOS: Did I? Slip of the tongue.

TIRESIAS [*considers it quite seriously.*]: I wonder how many of that you'd need to make a Bacchic smock.

KADMOS: If that was what Dionysos demanded . . . a couple of thousand slaves forcibly circumcised . . . Pentheus could arrange it.

TIRESIAS: Not for Dionysos.

KADMOS: I suppose not. Anyway how come you to think of such things in the first place?

TIRESIAS: You said it, not me.

KADMOS: Alright, alright. I said it was a slip of tongue. Quite natural at my age.

TIRESIAS: It's not natural at your age, that's the point. I found that significant. It's not natural at all.

KADMOS: When you start on significances you lose me.

TIRESIAS: You are a wily one. Fancy hiding your Bacchic togs under a cloak. You shook me when you first came in, all that pretence, as if you were shocked at the sight of me dancing.

KADMOS: Oh that. I was merely tasting my own resolve. Kadmos, Kadmos, it doesn't befit your age and rank—so I kept telling myself. I was on my way to find you. When I saw you dancing by yourself I said, I'll make a display of my doubts before Tiresias, and watch his reactions. He is old enough to be considered wise.

TIRESIAS [*preening.*]: Enough of that old Tiresias bit. Dionysos has knocked years off my back.

KADMOS: It's going round, it's catching Thebes on the rebound. Thebes has fallen out of love with our fossilized past and needs to embrace a new vitality. Come on, I am rearing to go.

TIRESIAS: Have you a crown?

KADMOS: Have I a crown? Ho ho. [*He reaches into a side-pouch and brings an ivy wreath. Sets it on his head at a rakish angle.*] If only you knew how my head has itched all day to put this on. Here, feel it. What do you think? Not too . . . dashing is it?

TIRESIAS: A bit fanciful for your age.

KADMOS: Now now, no more of that age nonsense. A man is as young as he feels and I feel thirty.

TIRESIAS: Well we'll just say you've set a new fashion then. Under divine inspiration.

KADMOS: Hey, have I told you about my daughters? They've got it really bad you know. They are all up in the mountains frisking around in the very madness of spring.

TIRESIAS: Ah yes, look around and see if those other women dropped bits of ivy while they were prancing about.

KADMOS: Yes, plenty around. What do you . . . ah of course. Hold on, I'll soon wreathe you a crown. [*Picks up a good bit of ivy and begins to weave a crown for Tiresias.*] What a relief to find one's innermost doubts banished once for all. What shall I do when I meet him Tiresias? He's my grandson after all, but still one must be careful with gods mustn't one?

TIRESIAS: Will you know him?

KADMOS: Why not? My own flesh and blood.

TIRESIAS: You've never seen him.

KADMOS: Doesn't matter. Flesh will call to flesh. I already sense his nearness.

TIRESIAS: Pentheus doesn't know his own flesh. And when he does he'll think he's duty-bound to cut it out of himself. If you held out the mirror of longing to him, he will utterly fail to recognize his own image or else he'll smash the mirror in anger.

KADMOS: There you go again talking in riddles. Here's your crown. Trad or trendy. [*He holds it poised over Tiresias's head.*]

TIRESIAS: We-e-e-ell, one is madness two is fashion. I don't like to see you mad.

KADMOS: Done. [*He stands some distance away and returns to adjust the angle.*] Perfect. Fawn-skin and ivy crowns. Oh Tiresias, do you think we've aged before our time?

TIRESIAS: You at least have lived, sower of dragon's teeth.

KADMOS: True. But then I wonder. Perhaps I retired too soon. It is wrong to wait for death isn't it? Simply to do nothing except wait for death. That's hardly a befitting end for a man. Suddenly I wonder about the past. From a life which constantly rejuvenated my bones I sat down and became an administrator. An administrator Tiresias! Then an old-age pensioner—on the court list. I who slew the dragon and bred a race of warriors from his teeth.

TIRESIAS: It is good to rest sometimes.

KADMOS: Then will you tell me why suddenly I feel grape-skins under my feet?

TIRESIAS: Oh come on let's go. Give me your hand.

KADMOS: Here, hold on to me. Where shall we go? Where shall we tread this dance of life, tossing our white heads to the drums of Dionysos. Shall I lead the way to the mountains.

TIRESIAS: Lead the way.

KADMOS: I don't understand it. I am restless with a thousand schemes. Why should I keep thinking now I should never have left the throne to Pentheus? I know he will do something wrong. Shall I arrest him for his own good do you think? There are still soldiers loyal to me. We could stage a *coup d'état*.

TIRESIAS: To the mountains Kadmos. The god awaits us.

KADMOS: Ah well, maybe you're right. It is this new surge of life, I can't explain it. I feel I could even solve any of these riddles you are so fond of. I could dance all night without tiring, simply beating earth with my thyrsus. Hey, where is that anyway?

[*He rummages inside his pouch and brings out a blunt-ended telescoped object which he proceeds to pull out into a thyrsus. The following exchange is done music-hall style.*]

Oh, what a shame you can't see to admire this Tiresias. Here, hold it in both hands, one hand at each end—that's it. Now pull out slowly. See how it works? First collapsible thyrsus in Attica, in the whole world maybe. Made it myself. Couldn't trust the palace joiner not to talk. Shows you how nervous I was, going all that length to disguise the obvious.

[*Plants it on the ground meaning to use it as a walking stick. It collapses and he falls. Tiresias helps him up.*]

The damned thing collapsed.

TIRESIAS: You can't expect it to be as strong as the joiner's.

KADMOS: [*straightens it out.*]: Why not? It works doesn't it. Forgot to put a lock on it that's all. [*The thyrsus collapses again.*] Damn!

TIRESIAS: No good? [*As it fails again.*]

KADMOS: I can't walk through the streets with this. Let's go up in my chariot.

TIRESIAS: Walking is better. It shows more honour to the god.

KADMOS: With the shortest thyrsus in Thebes? I'll be a laughing-stock.

TIRESIAS: Let's go. Put it back in your trousers.

KADMOS [*morosely replacing it in the pouch.*]: I should have let the joiner show me how. But it would only make him cocky. [*They both guffaw.*]

TIRESIAS: Give me your hand? When you step into the dance you'll lose all your silly notions. You accept, and that's the real stature of man. You are immersed in the richest essence of all—your inner essence. This is what the dance of Dionysos brings forth from you, this is the meaning of the dance. Follow the motion of my feet and dance Kadmos. We will dance all the way to the hills. One—Two—Back, One—Two—Back.

KADMOS [*obeys him.*]: I am a man, nothing more. I do not scoff at the will of heaven.

TIRESIAS: No, only fools trifle with divinity. People will say, Aren't you ashamed? At your age, dancing, wreathing your head with ivy? . . . Have you caught it? One—Two—Back, One—Two—Back.

KADMOS: I am not ashamed. Damn them, did the god declare that just the young or women must dance? They mean to kill us off before our time.

TIRESIAS: He has broken the barrier of age, the barrier of sex or slave and master. It is the will of Dionysos that no one be excluded from his worship.

KADMOS: Except those who exclude themselves. Like this one who approaches us Tiresias. [*He stops dancing, makes Tiresias stop.*]

TIRESIAS: Who is it?

KADMOS: The man to whom I left the throne. He seems excited and disturbed. Let us keep out of his way for a while.

[*Enter Pentheus, straight, militaristic in bearing and speech. His attendants have to run to keep up with him. Once on stage he strides angrily up and down.*]

PENTHEUS: I shall have order! Let the city know at once
Pentheus is here to give back order and sanity.
To think those reports which came to us abroad are true!
Not padded or strained. Disgustingly true in detail.
If anything reality beggars the report. It's *disgusting*!
I leave the country, I'm away only a moment
Campaigning to secure our national frontiers. And what happens?
Behind me—chaos! The city in uproar. Let everyone
Know I've returned to re-impose order. Order!
And tell it to the women especially, those
Promiscuous bearers of this new disease.
They leave their home, desert their children
Follow the new fashion and join the Bacchae
Flee the hearth to mob the mountains—those contain
Deep shadows of course, secret caves to hide
Lewd games for this new god—Dionysos!
That's the holy spirit newly discovered—
Dionysos! Their ecstasy is flooded down
In brimming bowls of wine—so much for piety!
Soused, with all the senses aroused, they crawl
Into the bushes and there of course a man
Awaits them. All part of the service for this
Mysterious deity. The hypocrisy! All that concerns them is
Getting serviced. We netted a few.
The rest escaped into the mountains. I want them
Hunted down. Chained and caged behind bars of iron.
I want an end to the drunken dancing
The filth, the orgies, the rot and creeping
Poison in the body of state. I want Order and—
I want immediate results. Go!
[*An officer salutes and exits.*]
And this stranger, who is he? A sorcerer?
Hypnotist? Some such kind of faker I'm sure, vomited
From Lydia, or Media, those decadent lands where
They wear their hair long, ribboned, and curled,
Stink of scent and their cheeks are perpetually

Flushed with wine, their eyes full of furtive
Messages. So goes the report on this intruder.
The charlatan spends his days and nights only
In the company of our women. Calls it initiation.
I'll initiate his balls from his thighs once
We have him safely bound. I'll initiate
That head away from his body. I'll end his
Thumping, jumping, hair-tossing snaking game.
He claims Dionysos lives? Some nerve!
A likely story for a brat who got roasted
Right in his mother's womb, blasted by the bolt
Of Zeus. The slut! Slandered Zeus by proclaiming
The bastard's divine paternity. That myth he instantly
Exploded in her womb, a fiery warning against all profanity.
You'd think my own relations would have learnt
From that family history but no, Ino and Autonoe,
My own mother Agave are principals at the obscenities!
I'll teach them myself. I have woven
Iron nets to trap them. I'll bring an end
To the cunning subversion. . . .
[*He sees Tiresias and Kadmos for the first time.*]

No . . . it's not true!

I won't believe it. Tiresias, seer of Thebes
Tricked out in a dappled fawn-skin? No.
And you, my own grandfather, surely not you!
Not playing at bacchant with wand and ivy!
How awful to witness such foolishness in age.
Oh you disgust me, you, playing with infant toys.
I beg you now, shake off that ivy, drop
The wand of shame. Drop it I say!
[*He wheels back on Tiresias.*]
This is your doing Tiresias; I know
You talked him into it, and I know why.
Another god revealed is a new way opened
Into men's pockets, profits from offerings.
Power over private lives—and state affairs—
Don't deny it! I've known your busy priesthood
Manipulations. You try all you can, cleverly
To influence matters which belong to better trained

Heads than yours. It's all read in the entrails
Of fowls and goats of course. A new god!
Soon we'll have state policies revealed
In brimming cups of wine—by heaven!—
If you were not such a mouldering old ruin
You'd soon be rattling chains with others
Caged for smuggling in this lecherous gospel.
I warn you, presume too far on that protection and
I'll convince you Thebes is wide awake.
Thebes shall stop at nothing to preserve her good name
Faced with anarchy and indecency.

KADMOS: Do not blaspheme son. Have some respect
For heaven. Or at least for your elders.
I am still Kadmos, I sowed the dragon's teeth
And brought forth a race of supermen.
You are born of earth yourself—remember that.
Will the son of Ichion now disgrace his house?

TIRESIAS: Oh it's so easy for some to make speeches.
They pick a soft target and the words rush out.
Now listen you. Your tongue runs loose
Makes a plausible sound and might
Almost be taken for sense. But you have none.
Your glibness flows from sheer conceit.
Arrogant, over-confident and a gift—yes—
A gift for phrases, and that makes you a great
Danger to your fellow men. For your mind
Is closed. Dead. Imprisoned in words. A new life
Comes into our midst, so vast, so potent
Soon it will be powerful all over Greece, but
You cannot feel it. Wake up Pentheus, open your heart.
Shall I tell you what to look for in this being?
Think of two principles, two supreme
Principles in life. First, the principle
Of earth, Demeter, goddess of soil or what you will.
This nourishes man, yields him grain. Bread. Womb-like
It earths him as it were, anchors his feet.
Second, the opposite, and complementary principle—
Ether, locked in the grape until released by man.
For after Demeter came the son of Semele

And matched her present with the juice of grapes.
Think of it as more than drug for pain
Though it is that. We wash our souls, our parched and
Aching souls in streams of wine and enter
Sleep and oblivion. Filled with this good gift
Mankind forgets its grief. But wine is more!
It is the sun that comes after winter, the power
That nudges earth awake. Dionysos comes alive in us.
We soar, we fly, we shed the heavy clods of earth
That weigh down the ethereal man
To that first principle. Balance is the key.
Now take this answer for your smear of bastardy
Though Dionysos needs no advocate. Too soon alas
You'll find that he can speak—and act—on his own behalf.
You ridicule the story men commonly repeat, that
This god was sewn into the thigh of Zeus?
Why do men quibble and clutch the literal for the sense?
If I should say to you Pentheus, you sprang from the loins
Of Kadmos here, full-formed, even to the teeth you so
Irreverently snap at me, what would it mean? Is the man
Not fully present in the seed? And the offspring
Of the son of Ichion, are they not even now ensconced
Within that dangling pouch between your thighs?
Offspring whose genesis you now endanger
By a sharp tongue wagging impiously?
It's not for me to say if Zeus had his scrotum
Sewn to one side of his thighs or
In-between like—presumably—yours.
Let's leave mythology aside. Think only of
And come to terms with what we know.

PENTHEUS; And what do we know—apart from your
    casuistry?
TIRESIAS: Our human condition, made of those two principles.
PENTHEUS: I said, apart from your quibbling.
TIRESIAS: Use your eyes Pentheus. I cannot see but I do
    Know. And feel. And so do you, though you will not
    Accept. You see this power made manifest
    Yet you deny it. Think again of human fate—
    What is this but a journey towards death.

Extinction. But visions open up another world, give
Strength and consolation. Through Dionysos we
Transcend that putrefaction of the flesh that begins
From the instant of our drawing breath.
This is a god of prophecy. His worshippers
Like seers, are endowed with mantic powers.
Reason is cluttered by too much matter, details,
Cravings, acquisitions, anxieties. When he invades the mind
Reason is put to sleep. He frees the mind
Expands and fills it with uplifting visions.
Flesh is transcended. What else? Where else?
At war you'll find him, confounding the enemy
With the unnatural courage of his followers.
And at Delphi too, home of Apollo, sanctuary
Of reason. How else does the priestess enter
The oracular state?

PENTHEUS [*angry*.]: That's blasphemy!

TIRESIAS: Slander perhaps, or heresy. A priestess is no god.
You are the blasphemer.

PENTHEUS: I warn you . . .

TIRESIAS: Is it not customary to pour libations
At the altar of Apollo? This is
To pour the body of god itself and through
His intercession win the favour of heaven.

PENTHEUS: You are quibbling again, you are trying
To wriggle out of the smear you laid upon
Apollo's priesthood.

TIRESIAS: What Apollo does not reject cannot harm
His servant. A drop for the altar, the rest
To smooth the passage of prayers down the throat.

PENTHEUS: You go too far Tiresias!

TIRESIAS: Not so far as Dionysos means to go. Oh
Accept him Pentheus. Look up at the rockhills.
Whom do you see bounding
Over the high plateau among the peaks?
Who is the rustle of wind in pine forests, shaking
Winter into life with green branches? It's he.
Dionysos is here
In your state. He is at work

All over the world.
Accept him
Pour wine for him
Put vine leaves in your hair for him
Dance for him.

PENTHEUS: You would love that. Madness and folly
Ever seek company. Licentiousness requires
The stamp of approval from a head of state
To break the last barriers of restraint.
Then power passes into the hands of those
Who prove the most self-abandoned.

TIRESIAS: If only you would lose this notion that power
Is all that matters in the life of man.
Do not mistake for wisdom these fantasies
Of your sick mind. Abandonment? Dionysos, I admit
Will not restrain desire in man or woman.
Yet if a woman is chaste in nature she stays
Uncorrupted in the rites of Dionysos.
Restraint is something people must practise
Themselves. It cannot be imposed. Those
Who have learnt self-discipline—the greatest
Guarantee of human will and freedom—
Will not then lose it for losing themselves
To Dionysos. Answer me, is control not built
Upon self-knowledge?

PENTHEUS: What if it is?

TIRESIAS: Dionysos grants self-knowledge. With that thought
I leave you. There is still time.
Save yourself if you can: look inwards, ask—
Does Pentheus truly know himself?

KADMOS: Son, you are pleased to have men crowd
Around the city gates to welcome you,
And every street rings with the name—
'Pentheus! Pentheus!' A god deserves no less.

TIRESIAS: Come, we have done our duty.
We shall dance you and I, partner each other
An ancient foolish pair perhaps, but—dance we must
Not fight this power. I pity Pentheus
His terrible madness. There is no cure,

No relief from potions. Nor from preaching.

KADMOS: Wait. His mind is surely distracted,
His thoughts sheer delirium. Son, remember
That dreadful death your cousin Actaeon died
When those man-eating hounds reared
By his own hands savaged him, tore him
Limb from limb for boasting that his prowess
In the hunt surpassed the skill of Artemis.
Do not let his fate be yours.

PENTHEUS [*grimly.*]: It won't. But I thank you for suggesting a most
Befitting fate for that sorcerer when we find him.

KADMOS: Not sorcerer. God. And even if your mind
Will not accept his person—I know appearances
Do more than prejudice even men of reason—
Since you must know within yourself, secretly
In the silence of your heart, this force *exists*
Take him simply as high priest of the rites, and
Semele is at least mother of a seer
Conferring great distinction on your family.
[*Misjudging the thoughtful mood of Pentheus, he thinks he has at
least mollified his stand. He removes the wreath from his own head.*]

KADMOS: Here, take mine. Let me wreathe
Your head with leaves of ivy. Come with us,
Glorify the god!

PENTHEUS [*knocks it off.*]: Take your hands off me! Get out!
Go and play Bacchae, but don't wipe
Your drooling idiocy off on me. Don't you dare
Touch my person again. As for you Tiresias,
Your punishment need not wait
One moment longer. I'll make you pay
Dearly for this folly of yours.
[*turns to his attendants.*]
                              Go, this instant!
Find the place where this prophet sits
Faking revelations out of birdsong. Go.
Pry it up with crowbars, heave it over
Upside down. Demolish everything you see.
Throw his fillets out to wind and weather.
That will teach you! The rest of you,

Go scour the city, bring me this foreigner
This thing of doubtful gender who infects
Our women with his strange disease and pollutes
Our marriage beds. Find him. Clap him in chains.
Drag him here. He'll suffer stoning to death
The nearest fate I can devise to Actaeon's
Piecemeal death at the jaws of his hunting hounds.
He'll find Thebes a harder bed than he had
Bargained for with his Bacchic jigs.
[*The attendants hesitate. They move as far as the exit, stop.*]

TIRESIAS: You are mad. Do you realize what you're saying?
You made little enough sense before but now—
You are raving! Lead me out of here Kadmos.
It's almost an impiety to stay beside such folly.
We must no longer think of him, only of us,
Pray that for the sake of Thebes, this folly
Is overlooked. We must harness this great force
For our common good.
[*as they exit.*]
Kadmos, in Greek the name Pentheus signifies
Sorrow. Does that mean anything? Let's hope not.

PENTHEUS [*turns round, attracted by whispering. He is surprised to see his attendants still there.*]:
Are you still here?
[*An Old Man comes forward.*]

OLD SLAVE: We wondered . . . about the hut of the holy man . . .
you would not . . . really want it destroyed?
[*For reply Pentheus fetches him a slap which knocks him flat.*]

PENTHEUS: Slave! Is that language simple enough even for a slave?
Something is wrong with the old men of this city. It affects
freemen and slaves alike.

LEADER: Back! Keep back!

VARIOUS:—Keep away!
—   This is filth, stain
—   Smear, decay.
—   Abomination

LEADER: Back! Leave him there
Let him lie there and accuse him!

VARIOUS:—With the scorn that dripped

Scathing, corroding from his mouth
Fouling Dionysos, child of his own city.
—   I am a stranger, but I think
Now I know Dionysos.

PENTHEUS [*his hand on his sword.*]:
Do you slaves defy me?

VARIOUS: We are strangers but we know the meaning of madness
—   To hit an old servant
With frost on his head
Such a one as has stood
At the gateway of Mysteries.

LEADER: You know it. This
Was the body of the Old Year Dying
The choice of the priests of Eleusis
Till good Tiresias stepped in his place.

SLAVE: And now you'll pull down the Old Seer's hut.

LEADER: You said to the Master of Revels
Take him—perhaps he'll live, or the gods
Will claim him—he's old enough.
Is such a one to be violated by you?

VARIOUS: Oh the scorn on his lips. Such
Inhuman indifference. Corrosive
As his hate for Dionysos.
—   Age is holy
To hit an old man
Or demolish the roof of a sage?
—   Yet we are the barbarians
And Greece the boast of civilization.
We are slaves and have no souls.

LEADER: No one will touch him where he lies
The world must see it.
Dionysos shall avenge this profanity.
I live to share
The feast of the vengeance of joy. O-oh
I have heard earth turn at the tramp
Of dancing Bacchantes, and my heart
Has leapt. At the sound of flutes, whole
Galaxies have fallen in my cupped hands
I have drunk the stars . . .

[*He bows his head suddenly and intones, the others repeating each
line after him, as if this is a practised liturgy. Pentheus's face
registers horror and disbelief as he recognizes the implications of this.*]
And yielded to the power of life, the god in me
To the seminal flood that courses earth and me
The alliance of blood to wine, the bond
Of ether and flesh, earth, and the breath in me.
And this is what this day we celebrate
Our feet at the dance are the feet of men
Grape-pressing, grain-winnowing, our joy
Is the great joy of union with mother earth
And the end of separation between man and man.

LEADER [*alone.*]:
Said Bromius,
I am the gentle comb of breezes on the slope of vines
The autumn flush on clustered joy of grapes
I am the autumn sacrament, the bond, word, pledge
The blood rejuvenated from a dying world
I am the life that's trodden by the dance of joy
My flesh, my death, my re-birth is the song
That rises from men's lips, they know not how.
But also,
The wild blood of the predator that's held in leash
The fearful flames that prowl the thicket of the night
I melt as wax the wilful barriers of the human mind
Gently even in this, except to the tyrant mind
That thinks to dam the flood-tide from the hills.
I am Dionysos.
[*A pause of an instant, then, powerfully.*]
                    Lead us Bromius!

SLAVES: Lead us—!

PENTHEUS [*He has snatched out his sword.*]: Shut up! [*dead silence.*]
I'll cut out the tongue of the next man that utters that name
Bromius. Or Dionysos!
[*Enter Dionysos, captive, surrounded by soldiers. Three or four
Bacchae are with him, their hands similarly tied.*]

DIONYSOS: Who calls on Dionysos? You, Pentheus?
[*Freeze. Hold for between thirty and forty-five seconds, sixty if
possible.*]

[*Pentheus moves first, approaches the prisoner and inspects him in silence. The officer begins his report, Pentheus continues his inspection.*]

OFFICER: We found him Pentheus. The hunt is over.
Here is the animal you sent us after.
And not so dangerous after all, quite docile
To tell the truth. We had no trouble over him.
Handed himself over without a murmur
Held out his arms for the chains, no attempt
To run or hide, or escape our dragnet.
To confess the truth, that bothered me.
I was—well—quite embarrassed. It seemed
Not quite playing the game. For a professional—
Code of conflict and all that—well—I felt
Quite ashamed. I said to him, Stranger,
I am not here by choice. I take orders and
My orders were to bring you live to Pentheus.
He seemed to understand. Oh, another thing—
The women you locked up in gaol are free.
They've shed their chains, they're up and away
In the forests and mountains, running like deer,
Calling on their god Bromius. He seems to be
Their master, governs them completely.
Naturally, I probed the matter. I am
Compelled to report the truth. It was
No human hands that snapped those chains, no
Human cunning picked the locks on those
Iron gates. The thing is beyond me. Thebes
Is suddenly full of miracles—I say no more.
The rest is your affair.

PENTHEUS: Untie his hands. He is fast within our net
And cannot escape.
[*They untie him. Dionysos and Pentheus stand face to face.*]
So. You are not at all bad-looking
Quite attractive I am sure, to women.
Perhaps it was this that brought you to Thebes—
Our women have a reputation for being easy game . . .
Long hair, all nicely curled. Hold out your hands.
[*Dionysos obeys.*]
I thought so. You have never wrestled

Or done a day's work in the fields. The arts
Of war must be just as strange to you. Your skin
Is smooth. You cultivate the shadows, the dark
For the larks of Aphrodite. Ah yes,
And what they call a handsome profile, quite
An asset in your style of life. Now answer straight:
Who are you? Where do you come from?

DIONYSOS: I am . . .
Nothing of note, nothing to boast of.
As for where—have you heard of a river
Called Tmolus. It runs
Through fields of flowers.

PENTHEUS: Yes, I know that river.
It circles the city of Sardis.

DIONYSOS: I come from there.
My country is Lydia.

PENTHEUS: Hm, that fits with my reports.
And who is this new god whose worship
You have brought to us in Hellas?

DIONYSOS: Dionysos, the son of Zeus. The god himself
Initiated me.

PENTHEUS: You have some local Zeus there
Who spawns new gods?

DIONYSOS: He is the same as yours.
The Zeus who sowed his seed
In earth.

PENTHEUS: And he initiated you. Was it
In truth-defining day, or was it by night
This 'inspiration' came to you.

DIONYSOS: Will you reduce it all to a court
Of inquiry? A fact-finding commission such as
One might set up to decide the cause
Of a revolt in your salt-mines, or a slave uprising?
These matters are beyond the routine machinery of state.

PENTHEUS: Answer me!

DIONYSOS: How does the earth take seed? By night
Or day? When heaven opens forth and,
Swarms and probes earth's thirsty womb, do you ask
Did her 'inspiration' come by night or day?

And when the grape begins to swell, its purple juice
Pounding on the tender skin or, at the sight
Of the bursting udder of a cow
Do you wait to date and time
Her 'inspiration' or simply fetch the milk-pail?
Do you demand of earth the secret of the vine or
Tread the grapes and say a prayer of thanks to heaven?

PENTHEUS: So it is all, and must remain a secret?

DIONYSOS: To those in whom Dionysos is not born.
To others there are no secrets for
Their minds are open.

PENTHEUS: You are clever, but not clever enough.
If there were no shameful acts in this
New worship, you would hardly wait to speak.

DIONYSOS: Mysteries are only for the initiates.
And in this worship all, even you Pentheus
May enter into the Mysteries.

PENTHEUS: Very clever. Your answers are designed
To make me curious. Tell me this at least
What benefits do the initiates derive,
The followers of this god?

DIONYSOS: Again I am forbidden to say. But they are
Well worth knowing.

PENTHEUS: I see your game, it is so transparent.
You think to play on my curiosity.

DIONYSOS: Our Mysteries abhor an unbelieving man.

PENTHEUS: You say you saw the god? What form
Did he assume?

DIONYSOS: The form of all men, all beasts
And all nature. He chose at will.

PENTHEUS: You evade my question.

DIONYSOS: Talk truth to a deaf man and he
Begs your pardon.

PENTHEUS: You grow bold stranger. In a moment
You shall learn how unwise that is.
Now, are we the first to suffer your visitation
Or have you spread your dirt in other cities?

DIONYSOS: The world everywhere now dances for Dionysos.

PENTHEUS: We have more sense than barbarians.

Greece has a culture.

DIONYSOS: Just how much have you travelled Pentheus?
I have seen even among your so-called
Barbarian slaves, natives of lands whose cultures
Beggar yours.

PENTHEUS: Don't try to wander off the subject.
These sacred practices of your god, this worship
The rites of great devotion, do they
Hold at night, or in the day?

DIONYSOS [*kindly, very gently and without scorn or attack.*]:
Poor Pentheus, how you must suffer, tying
So rigidly the hour of day and night with sin or virtue.
We hold our rites mostly at night, but only
Because it is cooler. And the lamps
Lend atmosphere and feeling to the heart in worship.
The lighting of a lamp is in itself
A votive act. Oil is an offering. A woman
Bears a lamp and the ring of light that falls
Around her frame is magic, holy,
A secretive and tender kind of grace. Think of a dark mountain
Pierced by myriads of tiny flames, then see
The human mind as that dark mountain whose caves
Are filled with self-inflicted fears. Dionysos
Is the flame that puts such fears to flight, a flame
That must be gently lit or else consume you.

PENTHEUS [*violently.*]: And I say night hours are dangerous
Lascivious hours, lechery . . .

DIONYSOS: You'll find debauchery in daylight too.

PENTHEUS: You wrestle well—with words. You will regret
Your ill-timed cleverness.

DIONYSOS [*wearily.*]: And you, your stupid blasphemies.

PENTHEUS: Enough! You, bring me the shears!

DIONYSOS: Shears? What terrible fate am I to undergo?

PENTHEUS: First, we shall rid you of your girlish curls.

DIONYSOS: My hair is holy. My curls belong to god.
[*Pentheus shears off his hair.*]

PENTHEUS: Next, you will surrender the wand.

DIONYSOS: You will have to take it. It belongs to Dionysos.

PENTHEUS [*snatching it.*]: You think I fear a common

Conjurer's wand? And now we will place you
Under guard and confine you to the palace.

DIONYSOS: Dionysos will set me free whenever I request it.

PENTHEUS: Yes, when you get your followers round you
And 'summon his presence'!

DIONYSOS: He sees. He is here. This minute he knows
What is being done to me.

PENTHEUS: Where is he then? Is he always invisible?
Why doesn't he show himself?

DIONYSOS: He does. But you being crass and insensitive
You can see nothing.

PENTHEUS: You insult me? You must be raving!
[to the Guards.]
He insults your king. He insults Thebes.
Load him with chains! The man is insane.

DIONYSOS: I am sane, but you are not. I warn you,
Set me free.

PENTHEUS: Chain him I say! Weight him down with chains.
I'll show you who has the power here.

DIONYSOS: You do not know what life is. You do not know
What you do. You do not know the limits
Of your power. You will not be forgiven.

PENTHEUS: What are you all waiting for. Chain him I said.
[The Guards with obvious reluctance approach him with chains.]

DIONYSOS: I give you sober warning Pentheus.
Place no chains on me.
[The Guards chain him quickly, move away as if from a distasteful
job.]

PENTHEUS: I am Pentheus, son of Ichion.
You are—nothing.

DIONYSOS: Pentheus. The name befits a doomed man.

PENTHEUS: Oh take him away. Get him out of my sight.
He talks and talks. Lock him up somewhere near—
In the stables—yes, leave him in the stables
Let him thrash in the hay and light up his darkness
With the flame of Dionysos. Dance in there.
And the creatures you brought with you, your
Accomplices in subversion, I shall have them
Sold to slavery. They'll work at the looms or carry

Water for the troops, day and night—that
Will silence their drums. [*Exit Pentheus.*]
[*As Dionysos is chained, his Bacchantes begin a noise, a kind of
ululating which is found among some African and Oriental peoples
and signifies great distress, warning, or agitation. Sometimes all
combined. It increases in volume. As Dionysos is led away it
spreads towards the Chorus of Slaves, swelling into deafening
proportions.*]

DIONYSOS: I leave you now. I go, not to suffer
For that cannot be. But Dionysos whose
Godhead you deny will call you to account.
When you set chains on me, you manacle the god.
[*From within the shrieking intensity of sound protesting the
sacrilege, a Bacchante's voice rises.*]

BACCHANTE: He rages. He is full of the mad wind
Of rage. Pentheus, son of Ichion and Agave
I know now you are mad. You have chained
The messenger of god.

SLAVE: Why am I rejected? Why am I a second time
Rejected O blessed Nile. First, banished
From your banks into this city, a slave. And now to see
The promise broken, the messenger of Bromius in chains
Heavier than mine! Rejected? Pentheus!
By the clustered grapes on the hills I swear
You shall come to know the name of Bromius!

BACCHANTE: He, a second time rejected, sweet Dirce
Life-stream to these fields! Again
Rejected from your sweet breast, from
Banks that were a cradle for the new-born child.

BACCHANTE: I heard the voice of Zeus in thunder
Saying, Welcome my son,
Welcome to the world, spirit of all
That lives and moves. . . .

SLAVE: Free spirit, soul of liberty, seed of the new order.

BACCHANTE: Yet this river spurns the god a second time!
Come not near. No ivy crowns on my banks
No gatherings, no dances, no flutes
To ruffle flowers on my beds.

BACCHANTE: Oh some day you'll thirst, ache

Parched, long for this immortal
Communion.
Yes, some day, you'll crave
Dionysos.

SLAVE: Such fury from his eyes, yet not he
Violated, outraged. But the fury!
With spite with hate he rages. No, not a man.
A beast run wild. A crop of dragon's teeth
That earth has never tamed with nursing.
A freak, a monster
Gorged and rank with pestilence . . .

BACCHANTE: A fiend, murderous to the bone. And this
This thing means to shut me up, to
Plunge me in the darkness of his mind!
I am not his. I belong
To Dionysos!

BACCHANTE: In a dungeon, in a sightless pit
He buries our leader.

OLD SLAVE: He is nothing. A trickster. Windbag. A commonplace
Illusionist. Beyond that, nothing.
Briefly I dreamt I saw salvation. Now
The breeder of false cravings lies
Bound in the net of his own spinning,
Crushed.

1ST BACCHANTE: CRUSHED?

SEVERAL: NO! NO! NO!

1ST BACCHANTE: Chained, but like a tower of gold.

BACCHANTE: A column of the sun that touches
Earth from Olympus.

ALL: Come Dionysos!

BACCHANTE: With a tree in his hand, the rockhills
Of his brow are drawn, they frown . . .

BACCHANTE: Down on the palace walls of Pentheus—
Come Dionysos!

LEADER: Pentheus! Retribution lowers
From the brow of a prisoner.

SLAVES: Come Dionysos!

LEADER: Prestidigitator god.

1ST BACCHANTE: Apocalyptic utterance.

LEADER: Bromius, come, COME! Be manifest!
VARIOUS: —Come from the mountain forests
—   Glide from the wild beast's lair
—   Spring from a cruel peak
—   Leap from a whirlwind dance
—   Burst from a thousand oaks
—   Rise from the silent valley
       A tree-leafed menace
       Like the end of Orpheus' spell
       On the hounds of death
—   Breaking the forest netting
       On limbs of mahogany
—   From out of mountain torrents
       Heralded on drumming feet
—   Surge over waves towards us
       Over green plains, a raging stallion
SLAVE: Break interminable shackles
       Break bonds of oppressors
       Break the beast of blood
       Break bars that sprout
       In travesty of growth
1ST BACCHANTE: Wounding the farmlands
       Bruising the grapes
       Lashing the late buds
       Ploughing the hills
       Watering the fields
       In torrents of wine
       Spirit of motion
       Quickener of life
       Oh let your sweet grape burst in me
       Come Dionysos!
ALL: [*ecstatically*.]: Bromius! Bromius! BROMIUS!
       [*a loud rumble, as of thunder. A hush falls on the scene.*]
1ST BACCHANTE: It is happening. Do you hear it?
       I know it is happening.
CHORUS [*a whisper*.]: Bromius?
1ST BACCHANTE: It is happening. I hear him
       In footsteps of the earthquake.
CHORUS: Bromius?

IST BACCHANTE: In the chords that Orpheus fingered
  In the hunger of women
CHORUS: Bromius?
IST BACCHANTE: In the terror of children
  And the anger of slaves.
CHORUS: Now. Now is the time. Bromius
  Be manifest! Come, the new order!
BACCHANTE: Shatter the floor of the world!
SLAVE LEADER: It's happening. The palace of Pentheus
  Totters, bulges, quivers. Rot gapes
  In the angry light of lightning. Roots
  Long trapped in evil crevices have burgeoned
  Their strength empowers me, the strength
  Of a Master. . . . Join him! Power his will!
CHORUS: Come BROMIUS!
  [*Again, another rending as of deep thunder rolling off into a distance.
  Like heavy breathing—In–Out:*]
IST BACCHANTE: Earth—
CHORUS: —Shake!
IST BACCHANTE: Earth—
CHORUS: —Retch!
IST BACCHANTE: Earth—
CHORUS: —Melt!
IST BACCHANTE: Earth—
CHORUS: —Swarm!
IST BACCHANTE: Earth—
CHORUS: —Take!
IST BACCHANTE: Earth—
CHORUS: —Swell!
IST BACCHANTE: Earth—
CHORUS: —Grow!
IST BACCHANTE: Earth—
CHORUS: —Move!
IST BACCHANTE: Earth—
CHORUS: —Strain!
IST BACCHANTE: Earth—
CHORUS: —Groan!
IST BACCHANTE: Earth—
CHORUS: —Clutch!

1ST BACCHANTE: Earth—

CHORUS: —Thrust!

1ST BACCHANTE: Earth—

CHORUS: —Burst!

1ST BACCHANTE: Earth—

CHORUS: —TAKE!

1ST BACCHANTE: Earth—

CHORUS: —Breathe! Live! Blow upon the walls of
                         darkness.
                         Melt marble, pillars, take! Take! TAKE!

1ST BACCHANTE: Adore him!

CHORUS: We adore him.

[*Darkness, thunder, flames. Roar of collapsing masonry. From
among it all, the music of Dionysos.*]

1ST BACCHANTE: Flames! The fevered flames around the grave
Of Semele, charred earth that no one walks upon
Except . . .

DIONYSOS: Dionysos.

[*He is revealed as first seen standing on the charred ruin of the grave
of Semele. The flames are higher round his feet. The Bacchantes
and the Chorus are down on their faces.*]

BACCHANTE: We do not move, or look, or breathe.

DIONYSOS: Afraid, my companions from distant lands?
Look at you, hugging the earth, terror struck.
You saw the house of darkness split and sundered—
For Dionysos was there. You willed him,
Summoned him, your needs
Invoked his presence. Why do you tremble?
Look up. Look up at me. The mortal ribs of Pentheus
Crumble, sundered by the presence
Of the eternal. Look up. All is well.

BACCHANTE: The dawn we know, our life-light departed
When you left in chains.

DIONYSOS: Did you think I would be buried in those
Death cells of Pentheus' darkness, and so
Settle down to despair?

OLD SLAVE: You are free?

DIONYSOS: You willed my freedom. I could not resist.

SLAVE: How did you do it? How did you escape?

DIONYSOS: With ease. No effort was required.
SLAVE: With manacles on your wrists? That man
    Had blood-lust in his eyes.
DIONYSOS: Oh, but there I fooled him. It was my turn
    To humiliate the godless fool, serve him
    Outrage for outrage. I made the sick desires
    Of his mind his goal, and he pursued them.
    He fed on vapours of his own malignant
    Hate, pursued and roped mirages in the stable—
    Manacled hooves and horns of a docile bull,
    Stumbled on pails, wrestled beams, lost his way
    In collapsing hay, slipped on manure
    Then sat in a lather of sweat, chewing his lips
    Cursing the stranger from Phrygia.
    I sat nearby, quietly watching. Untouched.
    That moment came Dionysos.
    He shook the roof of the palace of Pentheus
    Touched the living grave and cradle of his being
    And up leapt ribbons of fire. Pentheus looked up
    He saw—only his palace, possessions, his high estate
    Menaced by passionate flames. From end to end
    Of his palace he rushed, screaming at servants
    To pour water, more water on water till every slave
    Was working—over nothing. The fire existed
    Only in his unquiet mind. He left it suddenly—
    A fear had crept upon him that I might escape—
    Snatched up a long steel sword and hurled himself
    Back into the stables. His prisoner was gone,
    But there was bright, gleaming air where Dionysos
    Had been. At this emanation in the stable gloom
    Pentheus charged, stabbing and lunging, thinking
    To slake his vengeance in my blood. More folly.
    And it brought more havoc in its wake. For now Dionysos
    Razed the palace to the ground, reduced it
    To utter ruins. At that bitter sight
    Pentheus, spent and limp, threw away his sword
    Broken by the struggle. Well, he is only a man
    He exceeded himself, tried to fight a god.
    Quietly I left the house, came back to you.

He never touched me.

                    Listen. I hear footsteps
That would be him. He'll come out and rave and swear ...
But what can he say now? Let him bluster.
I'll manage him easily. The secret of life is
Balance, tolerance ... perhaps he's learnt that now.
[Enter Pentheus.]

PENTHEUS: I had him trussed up. He could not move.
Still, he got away. I have been tricked.
[He sees Dionysos.]

                                        What! You?
How did you escape? Answer me!

DIONYSOS: Tread lightly. Let your anger drain off ...
Slowly ... slowly ...

PENTHEUS [even more peremptorily.]: How did you escape?

DIONYSOS: Have you forgotten? Someone, I said
Would set me free.

PENTHEUS: Who? Spell out his name.

DIONYSOS: He who tends the grape for mankind.

PENTHEUS: He who sows drunkenness and disorder.

DIONYSOS: Poor Pentheus. He has learnt nothing.

PENTHEUS [to the Guards.]:
Surround the palace. Close every gate in the city.
Seal up every nook and cranny. I want the city
Bolted tight.

DIONYSOS: You are truly incurable. These powers
That you dispute move on a higher plane
Than towers and city walls.

PENTHEUS: Very clever talk, as usual. This time
It will not help you.

DIONYSOS: No. I use it thinking to help you. As usual
It is futile. You are a doomed man Pentheus.
Look, here comes someone with a message.
Listen to him first. Carefully. Don't hurry anything.
We are in no hurry. We'll wait for you.
Hear what he has to say; he comes from the mountains.

HERDSMAN: Pentheus, I am one of your subjects here
In Thebes. I am just from Kithairon. The snow
Is there still and white hills dazzle you. ....

PENTHEUS: Get to the point man! What is your news?

HERDSMAN: Sire, I have seen
    Miracles. The very stuff of ballads. You cannot . . .
    No, wait. If I must report faithfully . . .
    You see, it has to do with the Maenads, these
    Women who run barefoot from city to city . . .
    I have witnessed weird, fantastic things, but . . .
    Can I speak freely, and in my own way?
    Master, you have a cruel temper. We, your subjects
    Know it to our cost. And all too often.

PENTHEUS: You may speak freely. Do your duty and nothing
    Will happen to you. You have my promise.
    Tell me the worst things they've done, the worse
    It shall be for the man who began it.
    But you are safe—speak.

HERDSMAN: Well then—and may the god of oaths protect me—
    Our herds of cattle had just climbed a hill
    Grazing as they went—the dew was wet upon the grass,
    The sun being hardly warmed up that early hour—
    Well, by chance I stumble on this meadow, and in it
    Find a scene just like a painting on a vase—motionless—
    Three rings of women—fast asleep. One brief look
    Is enough. I say to myself—it's *them*. ·
    One is grouped round Autonoe—that would be your
    Auntie I think. The second I was more sure of—Agave
    Your mother. The third had to be Ino. Each ring
    Is formed around the leader, in a kind of
    Magic circle to my thinking. They were *still*,
    So peaceful it seemed a shame they had to wake.
    Some you'd find propped against the pine-tree trunks
    Others, curled up on a pile of oak leaves
    A few were simply pillowed on earth. I found there
    None of that drunkenness we'd heard so much about,
    None of the obscene abandon, or the wild music.
    No topping among the bushes. If I may describe it—
    A kind of radiant peace, like the sacred grove of a deity.
    Well, our cattle soon put an end to that. Their lowing
    Wakes up your mother, she leaps up, cries out
    And wakes the rest of the women. Her voice was clear

And strangely tuneful in those echoing hills, I heard her
Warn the others men and cattle were close by.
They shook off sleep from their eyes, yet even awake
That air of peace still controlled their actions . . .
And such beauties! We do have some treasures in Thebes.
Young supple limbs, maidens who have yet to know man—
Such jet and gold flew through the air when they let fall
Their hair. They brushed their clothes, then
Fastened them at the waist with . . . well, tell me I'm lying—
Snakes! *Live* snakes! I see their tongues still flickering
Clearly as I see you now! But that was nothing.
There was still more live wonder to come.
Have you ever seen a woman nurse a fawn
Exactly like a child? Or a wild wolf cub? I mean
To the point where she gives it suck? From—her—own—breast!
Heavy of breast those were, newly delivered,
Left their own babes at home—you know, the breast
Can get painful with milk—but to suckle a wild cub!
Again, that is nothing, for now rushed one miracle
After another. From weaving strands of ivy,
Oak-leaves, and flowering bryony to dress their hair,
One turned to twining leaves around a branch,
Like the most natural act you could conceive. She
Tapped a rock and—tell me I'm lying—out of that rock
Spouts—water! Clear, spring water, fresh as dew.
Another drove her fennel in the ground, and, where
The earth was wounded—another spring! But this time—
Wine! A wine-spring! Two women on their knees
Scrape the soil with fingers and out flows
Milk, creamier than the morning yield from a champion cow.
From all their ivy-covered branches, sweet honey
Dripped in golden cascades . . . Oh sire, if you had been there
If you had witnessed but a part you would be
On bended knees, giving thanks, praying the heavens
For help and guidance.

We met, shepherds and cowherds
Gathered in small groups to argue, comparing rumours
With this real event, for these were fantastic
Deeds! We could hardly believe our eyes. Now,

Up gets a city fellow, a great one for speeches,
Seizes his chance and addresses our group:
'Friends from the meadows of these mountains'—
Majestic meadows he said—I'll give him his due—
'Allow me to suggest a judicious and expedient hunt
One not without great expectations. Let us pursue
Agave the Queen-mother, rescue and bear her from these
Unmajestic orgiastics. Indubitably I declare
Pentheus will most royally reward us.' That did it.
Who would turn his back on such a profit? Straightway we
Devised an ambush for the women. We hid
Among the undergrowth, covered in leaves. We waited.
The hour for their ritual soon approached
Their ivy-covered staves were beating earth in rhythm—
It gets in your blood, that rhythm, it really does—
The chanting began—'Iacchos' 'Dionysos'
'Bromius!' 'Son of Zeus!'
                              Everything—
The very mountain seemed to sway to that one beat.
A beat like the hearts of a thousand men in unison.
The beasts moved with them, they seemed
Touched by a savage divinity.
                              It quickened.
The Maenads were swift upon their feet, rapt, unseeing,
Blind to all except the vision of their god.
Agave raced towards me, she flew close
Her arms were flashing like blades but I leapt,
My hands hot on the quarry. That scream!
I never will forget that screaming summons from her lips
To her swift hounds—for so she termed them—
Exhorting them to follow and turn hunter.
And they obeyed her. We changed roles and became the hunted,
Fleeing for sweet life. Another moment and
We would have been shredded like chaff.
Balked of their prey, the Maenads turned upon our herd.
Unarmed, they swooped down on our heifers grazing
In the meadows, nothing in their hands, nothing.
Their bare arms sufficed. They rent young, stocky
Heifers in two—you should have heard their death bellows,

Seen these frail-built creatures wrench
Full-grown cattle limb from limb, ribs, hooves
Spiral in the air, fall in torrents of blood,
Seen our dismembered livestock hang from branches
Blood spattering the leaves, seen wild bulls
With surging horns, unapproachable till now
Tripped, sprawled full-length on the ground
Bellow in unaccustomed terror as girlish limbs
Tore them apart, flayed them living.
There was a force within them; it drove them
Uphill, their feet hardly touching the ground.
Like invaders they swooped into Hysiae
Sacked Erythrae in the foothills of Kithairon.
Nothing withstood them, they pillaged and raided
Snatched children from homes, razed walls to the ground.
And all this plunder they piled on their backs,
Nothing held it, nothing. Yet neither bronze nor iron
Fell to the ground. Flames flickered in their curls but
Their hair remained unsinged.

Until at last,
Mad at these monstrosities, some villagers
Foolishly took to arms and made to attack them.
It was a terrible sight my masters. The men's
Spears and swords are lethal and sharp but,
They draw no blood, while the wands of the women . . .!
The men ran, yes, *ran*! Routed by women!
Master, it is not for me to say, but
Some god was surely with them. I watched them
Transformed in an instant, troop peacefully back
To where they had started, by those springs magically
Bestowed by their god, wash stains from their bodies
And the snakes licking the drops of blood
That clung to their hair.

Whoever this god may be
Sire, welcome him to Thebes. He is great
In other ways I hear. Didn't he make us
Mortal men the gift of wine? If that is true
You have much to thank him for—wine makes
Our labours bearable. Take wine away

And the world is without joy, tolerance or love.
[*Pentheus remains as he is for some moments.*]

PENTHEUS: It spreads. The craze, the violence,
Like a blazing fire. It comes close, close,
It comes too close. It contaminates even by report.
As a people we are disgraced, humiliated.
It's firmness now, no more hesitation.
[*To the Officer.*]
Go to the gates of Electra, order out
All the heavy-armoured infantry.
Call out the fastest troops of the cavalry
The mobile squadrons and the archers.
Issue a general call-up—all able-bodied men
Who can hold shield and spear. Set in motion
The standard drill for a state of emergency—
I have reasons for that—these restive dogs
Might see their chance to stage a slave uprising,
I have seen signs, so see to it!
I want the troops massed here directly.
We attack the Bacchae at once.

DIONYSOS: Pentheus . . .

PENTHEUS: Shut up! [*turns to a Guard.*] You. Give me the map of
Thebes.

DIONYSOS: Pentheus, you've done me wrong, Still
I warn you yet again, do not take arms
Against a god.
[*Pentheus begins to plot the attack.*]

PENTHEUS: You escaped from prison, let that suffice you.
Or else I'll take you first, before your women.

DIONYSOS: Stay quiet. Safe. Bromius will not let you
Drive his women from the hills.

PENTHEUS: If you had ever borne responsibility for
Law and order anywhere you might be worth
Attention. Since you have not
Be less glib with your advice.

DIONYSOS: And yet I offer only sane advice.
Sacrifice to this god. It is futile
To rage and kick against such power.
You are a man.

PENTHEUS: All the sacrifice your god will have already
    Lies in the glades of Kithairon. His women
    Have been lavish. The state has nothing more to offer.

DIONYSOS: And for this you raise the army of Thebes—
    Against women?

PENTHEUS: Those are not women. They are alien monsters
    Who have invaded Thebes. I have a duty to preserve
    The territorial integrity of Thebes.

DIONYSOS: You will actually *attack* them Pentheus?
    Draw sword, bow, cast spears, drive
    Your armoured chariots into—women?

PENTHEUS: They will have a chance to surrender
    Peacefully. If not—think who began the violence.
    Thebes must take measures for her own safety.

DIONYSOS: Thebes' well-being lies in acceptance
    Of this god. Your way leads to defeat,
    An ignominious rout. Bronze shields are no match
    For women's hands.

PENTHEUS: Will no man rid me of this pestilential tongue?
    All it does is wag. Whatever I do or say
    It's all the same. Yakkity-yak-yak-yak!

DIONYSOS: But there is a better way than yours. I ask
    Only for a chance to prove it.
    [*Pentheus ignores him, concentrates on plotting his campaign.*]
    I will bring the women here.
    Without use of force.

PENTHEUS: Brilliant. This is the great
    Master plan. The grand deception.

DIONYSOS: You are too distrustful. I wish you well.
    I want you, and Thebes, to keep whole.
    [*Pentheus has finished. He looks satisfied, prepared. Turns to the Guards.*]

PENTHEUS: Bring out my armour. And you—[*to Dionysos.*]
    Be quiet. I am not a simpleton.

DIONYSOS [*stops the Guards.*]:
    Wait! [*He moves close to Pentheus.*] You could see them.
    I mean, there, up in the hills.

PENTHEUS: Your mind is always busy, but I thought you
    Cleverer. Any fool can see through that trap.

DIONYSOS: Why do you fear me Pentheus?

PENTHEUS: Fear? I, son of Ichion?

DIONYSOS: Yes, you are afraid of me.

PENTHEUS: Because I will not follow you into a trap?

DIONYSOS: No. It goes deeper. I saw it from our first encounter.

PENTHEUS: If you refer to your cheap conjurer tricks
Don't let that swell your head. I have seen
Greater spectacles in market-places, greater feats
Of illusion. But now my mind is clear. I know you
For a charlatan. Perhaps a spy, an agent
Of subversion for some foreign power. Certainly
A degenerate, quite contemptible. Fear you?
Rid your mind of such conceit.

DIONYSOS: But you do fear me. You fear my presence here
May set you free.

PENTHEUS: Me? Who is the prisoner—You or I?

DIONYSOS: You Pentheus, because you are a man of chains. You
love chains. Have you uttered one phrase today that was not
hyphenated by chains? You breathe chains, talk chains, eat
chains, dream chains, think chains. Your world is bound in
manacles. Even in repose you are a cow chewing the cud,
but for you it is molten iron issuing from the furnace of your
so-called kingly will. It has replaced your umbilical cord and
issues from this point . . .
[He touches him on the navel, commences to turn Pentheus round
and round, gently. In spite of himself Pentheus is quite
submissive.]

                              . . . and winds about you all the way
back into your throat where it issues forth again in one
unending cycle.
[He holds out his hand before Pentheus's eyes, like a mirror.]

                              Look well in the mirror
Pentheus. What beast is it? Do you recognize it? Have you ever
seen the like? In all your wanderings have your eyes been
affronted by a creature so gross, so unnatural, so obscene?
[With a superhuman effort Pentheus shakes off his hypnotic state,
tries to snatch the 'mirror' but clutches at nothing. He backs off, his
face livid.]

PENTHEUS: Try that trick again! Touch our person once more and
it won't be mere chains for you. How dare you!

DIONYSOS: Again chains. You are so scared I shall cut through that chain and set you at liberty.

PENTHEUS [to the Guard.]: Has no one brought my armour?
[to Dionysos.] Better keep your hacksaw for yourself. You shall need it before long.

DIONYSOS: Hacksaw. Your thoughts are so metallic. Dionysos loosens chains by gentler means.

PENTHEUS: I know what those are.

DIONYSOS: Tell me Pentheus, wouldn't you give a lot to know the future—not yours, you have none—but the future of this god Dionysos. It's a short cut, but ... would you? Would you like to see something of his fate, the past and future legends of Dionysos—don't talk—look!

[In the direction in which he points, a scene lights up. Wedding scene. Music. The bridal procession enters, masked. The mask is the half-mask. The bridal retinue registers variations of hauteur, their clothes and attitude denote sixty-carat nobility, probably trade. The bride is veiled.

An altar to Aphrodite is set at the entrance. The bride's father pauses by it, is handed a jug by a servant and pours libation at its base. He hands the jug to the bride who also pours libation, makes a silent prayer. They proceed on to an elevated throne. A servant-girl brings wine, is waved away by the aristocratic front-liners. She finds takers in the very rear.

By the time she gets there the bridegroom arrives. His retinue is one, a sort of bestman. The bridegroom is clumsy, awkwardly dressed for the occasion in what must be his Sunday best. Bestman makes last-minute adjustments to groom's attire, pulls him back in time to the altar, where the jug has been left. In his nervousness he takes a swig, then hastily pours a libation.

In the hall the bridegroom is waved unceremoniously to a seat almost at the feet of the bridal group. He sweats, his collar (or whatever) is too tight. This is a creature who is not comfortable in clothes. The masks from on high turn on him and inspect him coldly. We can almost hear the sigh of resignation as they turn away.

Guests arrive, perfunctorily spilling a little libation. The wedding feast begins. Dancers perform. The bridegroom grows more and more uncomfortable. The serving-girl carries on a quiet flirtation with him, doesn't wait for his cup to empty before refilling it. The bridegroom *visibly responds to both charm and blandishments.*

A sudden clash of cymbals. All movements stop. Ceremonially the father rises, unveils the bride. From all the guests, hands and faces are lifted in unmistakable gestures of rapture. Except the bridegroom. On his face and on the face of his bestman are expressions of horror. The bride (also masked) is a picture of horrendous, irredeemable ugliness.

A movement (of light?) turns our attention to the bust of Aphrodite. The face is coming off. Underneath, the mocking face of Dionysos. He beams on the scene.

The wine-girl is almost never away from the bridegroom. The performing dancers resume their jigs. The bridegroom drinks. The bride transfers to and fro between devastating glares at the wine-girl and loving smirks at her groom. Her groom drinks more and more. Suddenly he leaps up, brushing aside the restraining arm of his bestman. He strides among the dancers, stops the musicians and gives them instructions. He begins to dance. Already, a transformation has commenced. The music quickens. He stops, flings off his mask and garments. Underneath, the Dionysian fawn-skin. The bridal group registers predictable shock at the scantiness. He begins to dance. He DANCES!

The dance ends with a leap on to the bridal table, upside down, his back to the shocked 'high table'. The bride screams, the father rises in fury. His lips move and over an amplified system, the historic exchange:]

FATHER-IN-LAW: Hippoclides, you have danced your wife away.

BRIDEGROOM [*a melon-sized grin on his face.*]: Hippoclides—
     does-not-care! οὐ φροντὶς Ἱπποκλείδη

     [*A snap black-out, except on the altar of Aphronysos.*]

DIONYSOS [*voice.*]: Look Pentheus!

     [*A new scene to another side. Again a wedding scene, but a huge contrast. All the noise—music, revellers, snatches of drunken singing comes from Off. What we see is the traditional Christ-figure, seated. But his halo is an ambiguous thorn-ivy-crown of Dionysos. At his feet a woman kneels, anointing them. Behind him, embroidering is a slightly more elderly woman. Her mask is beautiful, radiates an internal peace.*

     A woman enters, irate, with a pitcher under her arm. She frowns on this scene and points angrily to the kneeling woman. Turns the pitcher upside down to indicate the problem. Her angry gestures include the feminine logic (pace Fem. Lib.) that the wine shortage is related to the idle foot-anointer. The Christ-figure makes peace, indicates that the pitcher should be filled with the contents of a pot in a corner. Water is poured into the pitcher. He raises his hand, blesses it. Takes a cup and invites her to fill it from the pitcher. Tastes, nods, passes the cup to the irate woman. Her expression changes to rapture. She passes the cup to the kneeling woman, embraces the man. All taste, all are full of wonder, love and forgiveness. General embraces. She hurries out. Noise from Off indicates the success of this wine. The figure looks up, smiles beatifically in the direction of the sound.

The scene fades slowly, as lights come up on Dionysos and Pentheus. Dionysos is holding out a cup (the same as last seen) to Pentheus.]

PENTHEUS [*taking it.*]: Was that . . . he? Your god?

DIONYSOS: Does it matter? Drink!

PENTHEUS: Can I see some more? [*Slowly, dreamily, Pentheus raises the cup to his lips.*]

DIONYSOS: You are a king. You have to administer.
Don't take shadows too seriously. Reality
Is your only safety. Continue to reject illusion.

PENTHEUS: I do.

DIONYSOS: You found me out. I have the gift
Of magic, conjuring. But reality
Awaits you on the mountains.
Are you still afraid?

PENTHEUS: No. What do you suggest?

DIONYSOS: Come with me to the mountains. See for yourself.
Watch the Maenads, unseen. There are risks
A king must take for his own people.

PENTHEUS: Yes, yes, that is true.

DIONYSOS: You are king. Your blood provides its own
Immunity. Just the same, if I may suggest it—
It is foolhardiness to take avoidable risks. . . .

PENTHEUS: Go on. I am interested in your scheme. I find
Somehow, you are trustworthy. Your ways
Are strange, but . . . go on.

DIONYSOS: You must not be recognized. Cunning proves

Always more successful than a show of force. You must
Wear a disguise.

PENTHEUS: Yes, yes, I could dress as a common soldier,
Or a peasant, a herdsman . . . where is that cowherd?
I'll borrow his clothes.

DIONYSOS: You forget. He and his sycophantic companions
Fomented this trouble. The sight of a herdsman now . . .

PENTHEUS: True, true. How shall I go then? I long
To see them at their revels.

DIONYSOS: Do you? Then trust me. I shall lead you there
Safely.

PENTHEUS: And stay to bring me back? I may get lost.
I know so little of Thebes beyond the city.
Almost nothing of the country, come to think of it.

DIONYSOS: Your mother will bring you back, in triumph,
Leading a great procession. You will make your peace
With Dionysos.

PENTHEUS: Oh, oh, not so fast. But I'll come with you.
I shall do as you say—short of surrender
To your priest of sly subversion.

DIONYSOS: Then come disguised as one of those we go
To spy upon.

PENTHEUS: What! Dress myself as a Maenad? A woman?
Make the throne a laughing-stock in Thebes?

DIONYSOS: Suppose the madness has not left them?

PENTHEUS: Don't mention it again. It is too undignified.

DIONYSOS: Even more undignified it is to be severed
Limb from limb.

PENTHEUS: Forget it, I will not bring myself
Down to such a mockery of the throne.
I shall go as I am, or not at all.

DIONYSOS: As you wish. But wear your armour at least.
It may deflect a stone or two. Why seek bruises
From foolhardiness.
[Turns to the Old Slave, speaking with emphasis.]
Bring the king his armour. Bring out
His only protection against the Bacchae.

PENTHEUS: Yes, I shall go up the mountains as a king.
Alone. Except for you as guide.

DIONYSOS: In your royal armour.

PENTHEUS: Yes, I shall go with you in the battledress
Of a worthy king of Thebes.

DIONYSOS: It is by far the best plan. And if the Maenads
Spy you out, your royal presence will recall
Your mother and her sisters back to their
True heritage.

[*The slave returns—with a female Bacchic costume.*]
Here. I'll help you dress.

[*Dionysos begins to dress him. Pentheus strikes the customary stance
for when he is being armed by a retainer. The contrast is pathetic.*]

PENTHEUS [*as the first piece is slipped on.*]:
Strange, it feels so soft today. Hardly
Like bronze and steel.

DIONYSOS: It is the wine. It does create that effect.

PENTHEUS: And lighter. It has hardly any weight.

DIONYSOS: Wine lightens all burdens. You will discover
How lightly you walk, how your steps quicken
And turn to dance.

PENTHEUS: I feel it already. Hurry. You must restrain me
As we go. I feel I shall hardly conduct myself
As becomes a soldier and a king.

DIONYSOS: Trust me. I shall be your guide. There is a force
That blinds all men to diadems, swords and sceptres.
You feel the beginnings of it.

PENTHEUS [*as Dionysos fastens a jewelled brooch.*]:
You are a dark horse, full of hidden talents
To look at you, one would hardly think you knew those
Intricacies of an armour's chains and buckles
Yet you handle them like a practised armourer.
Is there anything you don't know?

DIONYSOS: Dionysos taught me all I know.

PENTHEUS [*chuckles, in very good humour.*]:
It is instructive to meet a fanatic. I could use
Such loyalty. Whatever I say is turned
And exploited by you to glorify Dionysos.
[*He tilts the cup.*]
Is there more of this nectar? I feel
A great thirst within me.

DIONYSOS [*stretching his hand.*]: Your cup is full.

PENTHEUS [*looks.*]: Ah. [*Takes a prolonged draught.*]

1ST BACCHANTE: Look! He stands at the gate of the trap
    He'll find the Bacchae and with his life
    He'll answer. He thrashes in the net
    Of Dionysos, his wits are distracted.
    Though he fought with the will of a Titan
    Yet, for all that, he's a man.

DIONYSOS: Some hair still shows beneath your head-piece
    Not very soldierly—I'll tuck it in.
    [*Places a wig on his head and ties it with a ribbon.*]

OLD SLAVE: He stands at the gate of retribution,
    The tyrant. Shall I pity him? I do not know.
    His thoughts are dislodged, his reason slithers.
    What sane mind struts in woman's clothing
    And thinks it an armour of bronze.

BACCHANTE: He'll raise a howl of derision all through Thebes
    Mincing like a camp-follower.

DIONYSOS: Dionysos will admit he's met his match
    To see such a figure of Ares walking the earth.

BACCHANTE: Once he mouthed fearsome threats. Now,
    He is dressed, a docile lamb, for a descent
    Into Hades. A rough caress by his mother
    Will ease him there.

SLAVE: A jealous joy, a ferocious, gentle joy
    Is my Dionysos.

BACCHANTE: Consummate god, most terrible, most gentle
    To mankind.

PENTHEUS: Mind you, I shall not forgive Tiresias,
    Or my grandfather. They should have set
    A good example and saved me all this bother.

DIONYSOS: You will meet them on your way. Your grandfather
    Shall be cruelly punished. And Agave . . .

PENTHEUS: She most especially. My own mother,
    What a disgrace! I hope we don't find her
    Doing something really disgusting at those revels
    I would be forced to kill her—for the honour
    Of the house of Kadmos—you understand?

DIONYSOS: Of course. Keep still while I fix this stubborn—

There, it's in ... About Agave, set your mind
At rest. I shall bring reconciliation to
Mother and son. You shall return, Pentheus
Cradled in your mother's arms.
[*A gradual commencement of light changes.*]

1ST BACCHANTE: Night—will it ever come
When what we know is done?
I seek release to a calm
Of green hills, white thighs
Flashing in the grass
The dew-soaked air kissing my throat.

LEADER: Night, night set me free
Sky of a million roe, highway of eyes
Dust on mothwing, let me ride
On ovary silences, freely
Drawn on the reins of dreams.

BACCHANTE: ... the dance of night
Where darkness is deepest.

SLAVE LEADER: Come, dawn, in the dance of the sun.
Come, dawn, herald of the new order.

1ST BACCHANTE: But gently, as the dance of the young deer, swathed
In emerald meadow, when the terror of the hunt is past,
The leap over knotted nets, the hunter's shrieks
Forgotten. Let the new order bring peace,
Repose, plenitude. ...

BACCHANTE: ... the lull
Of a sweet mothering copse, a timeless shade
Where no danger lurks ...

DIONYSOS [*still tucking in and tricking out Pentheus, his mouth is
full of pins and clips.*]:
Is your wish still white-hot for a peep
At the forbidden? I would hate to take this trouble
Over nothing. Is your resolve as strong as ever?

PENTHEUS [*with just a touch of tipsiness.*]:
Yes, but listen. I seem to see two suns
Blazing in the heavens. And now two Thebes
Two cities, each with seven gates. And you—
Are you a bull? There are horns newly
Sprouted from your head. Have you always been

A bull? Were you . . .

[*He searches foggily in his brain.*]

                   . . . yes, that bull, in there?

Was it you?

DIONYSOS: Now you see what you ought to see. Dionysos
Has been good to you with his gift of wine.

PENTHEUS: Funny. Inside, I went this way with my head
Then, that way—back, forward—back. It was
Almost a kind of trance. I dreamed I stabbed
A bull. A minotaur. Was that you?

DIONYSOS: I am whole. There—all that agitation has made
Your cuirass come loose. And the knee-guard.
Keep still till they are strapped in position.

[*He adjusts his sash, dolls out the pleats of his dress.*]

PENTHEUS: I shall make you my armourer, after this
campaign.

OLD SLAVE: What does it mean life? Dare one
Hope for better than merely warring, seeking
Change, seeking the better life? Can we
Control what threatens before the eruption?
Defeat what oppresses by anticipation? Can we?
Dare we surrender to what comes after, embrace
The ambiguous face of the future? It is enough
To concede awareness of the inexplicable, to wait
And watch the unfolding. . . .

SLAVE: For there are forces not ruled by us
And we obey them
Trust them. Though they travel inch by inch
They arrive.

OLD SLAVE: Dionysos? or—Nothing.
Not even a word for these forces.
They lack a name. We will call them
Spirits.
Gods.

SLAVE: Principles,
Elements,

SLAVE: Currents.
Laws, Eternal Causes.

SLAVE: But they are born in the blood

Unarguable, observed and preserved before time . . .

LEADER: As freedom. No teaching implants it
No divine revelation at the altar.
It is knotted in the blood, a covenant from birth.

DIONYSOS [*hands Pentheus a thyrsus.*]: Your sword. [*Pentheus sticks
it through the sash.*] Perfect. If your mind matches your appearance,
Then the enemies of Thebes have surprises to come.

PENTHEUS [*straighter than ever, conscious militaristic preening.*]:
I feel superhuman. I could hoist the whole of Kithairon
On one shoulder—with valleys full of women
Despite their dancing and madness . . . yes?

DIONYSOS: I do not doubt it. We'll find a hiding place
That suits you best.

PENTHEUS: Take me right through Thebes
Right through the centre. I am the only man here
With dare and courage.

DIONYSOS: Yes, you alone
Make sacrifices for your people, you alone.
The role belongs to a king. Like those gods, who yearly
Must be rent to spring anew, that also
Is the fate of heroes.

PENTHEUS: We'll march through Thebes. I lately imported
A famed drill-master for the troops. An expert.
He hails, I think, from . . . Phrygia! Hey, that's you.
Do you know him? Is he your countryman?

DIONYSOS: It is possible.

PENTHEUS: He's taught a new march to the household cavalry
A masterpiece of precision. We'll prance through
Thebes like those splendid horsemen. Wait,
I'll teach you the movements. It's simple—
Watch my feet!
[*He draws his 'sword', performs a brief salute forwards and sideways,
then strikes a dance pose.*]
                    Here we go—
One-Two-Back, One-Two-Back, One-Two-Back . . .
[*exactly like Tiresias. The music of Dionysos accompanies him,
welling in volume as Pentheus throws himself passionately into the
dance, exhorting Dionysos's efforts.*]
That's it. Very good. A little higher at the knees.

You're light on your feet I must say, quite
An accomplished dancer. Well, shall we advance?

DIONYSOS: Forward Pentheus!

PENTHEUS [lets off a loud yodel.]: Death to the Bacchae!
One-Two-Back! One-Two-Back! One-Two-Back!
[His voice dies off in the distance, punctuated to the last by fierce
yodels. Dionysos stands and speaks with more than a suspicion of
weariness from this now concluding conflict. It is not entirely a noble
victory.]

DIONYSOS: At last he comes, my Bacchantes
Prepare, you sisters, daughters of Kadmos
Agave, open your mothering arms—
Take him. Mother him. Smother him with joy.
[Exit Dionysos. As his speech ends, part of the Chorus of Slaves set
up a dog-howl, a wail of death. Instantly a section separate themselves,
move throughout the next speeches until they are joined with the
Bacchantes. They form, for this last part, a solid fanatic front with
the followers of Dionysos. The progress across should not be a dance,
but a terse series of dramatic motions which takes its motif from the
following invocation, the decisive gesture of throwing their lot with
the Bacchae, the casting off of the long vassalage in the House of
Pentheus.]

LEADER: A self-swollen and calloused soul
Tumoured and hard.
All your malignant growths of thought
Level now, pare, and crop
They move in the dark with a fading glimmer
The ruler is overruled
You countered and strove at your peril
Seeking Dionysos. Death follows your finding.

BACCHANTE: Go, track to the mountains
Swift hounds of madness
Run, dogs run,
Find the daughters of Kadmos

SLAVE: [separating.]:
Snap at their dancing heels
Sink your fangs into their brains
Then turn them loose
Turn them loose on the foolhardy

Ruler, who spies in flapping skirts.

ANOTHER: He's mad for the secret
He spies on the faithful possessed
His mother shall see him first
She'll cry to the Maenads:

BACCHANTE: LOOK! See what creeps across the hillside
[*begins a stylized mime of the hunt. It ends just before the 'coup de grace' at the entry of the Officer. Only three or four of the Bacchae take part.*]
What creature is this?
What monstrous obscenity!
It surely was born of no woman
It took life from a rotting foetus
That heaved from a dying gorgon.

SLAVE: Watch him sniffing up our mountains
Watch him drag like the spawn of a reptile.

ANOTHER: Now we shall see the balance restored
O Justice! O Spirit of Equity, Restitution
Be manifest! A sharp clear sword
With blood on its edge—drive
To the gullet of Pentheus.

BACCHANTE: Intent with sick passion
His mind is a sewer rat
Rooting and sniffing to the living heart
Madly assailing, profaning
The rites of the mother of god.
[*A steady beat of the chant 'Bromius Bromius' by the Bacchantes commences as counterpoint to the dog-howl of the remnant Slave Chorus, gradually gaining ascendancy until the arrival of the Messenger.*]

LEADER: Come, god
Of seven paths: oil, wine, blood, spring, rain
Sap and sperm, O dirge of shadows, dark-shod feet
Seven-ply crossroads, hands of camwood
Breath of indigo, O god of the seven roads
Farm, hill, forge, breath, field of battle
Death and the recreative flint . . .

SLAVE: He runs, against the unassailable.
Runs with violence against his, my

Forever-free spirit, unchainable,
He runs, with chains in his hand
With manacles for the encounter—
Death will counter his inventions
Death will end him!

OLD SLAVE [*he remains with the Slave Chorus.*]:
Headlong he runs to his death
The gods do humble us with death
Lest we forget
We are not such as gods are made of.
I say accept, accept.
Humility is wise, is blessed
There are great things unfathomable
The mind cannot grasp them.

SLAVE: Where do we seek him? Where find him?
Where conflict rages, where sweat
Is torrents of rain, where flesh springs
Of blood fill him with longing as the rush
Of wine. There seek the hunter god.

LEADER: Justice! Restitution! O Spirit of Equity
Be manifest! Bright clear sword, a gleam
Of blood on its edge—drive!
Destroy the earth-spurning evil spawn of Ichion.

1ST BACCHANTE: Reveal yourself Dionysos! Be manifest!
O Bacchus come! Come with your killing smile!
Come, a dragon with swarming heads, vomiting flames!
Come hunter, cast your noose.
Bring him down. Trample him
Underfoot with the herd of justice, your Maenads!
Bromius come! Master! Lover! Bull with horns
Of fire. Serpent with fangs of love. Lion
At my breasts, Eternal Ember in my hearth
Hunt this game to ground, Come Bromius!
[*Enter the Officer just as the arm of the miming Bacchante is raised
to strike the 'quarry'.*]

OFFICER: What is this? Has this god not done enough
That you still call here on Bromius?
[*Gradual silence. They turn to him.*]
In this house lived people who were once

The envy of all Greece—once—a family begun
In dragon's teeth, that summer harvest reaped
By Kadmos. It is winter now for this great race
I see no future spring.

CHORUS: What is it?
Have you news? Were you in the hills

OFFICER: I am only a soldier, nothing more, yet
I mourn the fortunes of this fallen house.
King Pentheus, son of Ichion, is dead.

BACCHANTE: All power to Bromius: Victory on this first day
Of his homecoming. Quickly, how did he die?

OFFICER: What is this? You dare rejoice
At the disasters of this house? My master
Is—DEAD!

SLAVE: Your master not mine.
I have another home, another life.
Nor will the fear of dungeons stop me
Manifesting my joy.

OFFICER: Your feelings can be forgiven. But this,
This exultation over terrible misfortune—
It's ugly.

BACCHANTE: Was it truly terrible? Tell us. Were you
there?

OFFICER: There were three of us in all: Pentheus, I
Attending the king, and that stranger who offered
His services as guide. We soon left behind us
The last outlying farms of Thebes, forded
The Aesopus, then struck into the barren scrubland
Of Kithairon.

                    There, we halted in a grassy glen
Unmoving, wordless, taking all precaution
Not to be discovered. It was there we saw them,
In a sudden meadow carved in rockface of the cliffs
Water ran freely there, and the pines grew dense
With shade—there the Maenads rested, their hands
Busy with their normal tasks, singing. They were
Weird, disturbing tunes.

                    But our king, Pentheus
Unhappy man, found his view obscured by springy

Undergrowth. 'Stranger,' he said, 'from here I can see
Little of these counterfeiting worshippers.
What if I climbed that towering fir that overhangs
The banks, do you think I might see them better at
Their shameless orgies?
                              And now the stranger worked a miracle!
He reached up to the highest branch of a great fir
Bent it down, down to the dark earth
Till it was curved, a drawn bow in giant hands
A wooden rim bent to encase a wheel for the chariot
Of the sun. I was awed. No mortal could have done this.
He seated Pentheus on the highest tip and,
With great control he eased aloft the trunk
Slowly, gently, most careful not to throw our king
From his new throne among the leaves.
And that fir rose, towering back to heaven
With my master proudly seated at the top.
You know that saying?—A man the whole world seeks to roast
Rubs himself in oil, crouches beside an open fire
Moaning, I have a chill: the rest is soon told.
The stranger had vanished. Only his voice, a bull's roar
Filled the mountains, stayed to set his doom in train.
'Maenads, look up!' it bellowed. They obeyed. The women
Saw King Pentheus stark against the sky
Clearer than he could see them. Hell broke loose.
Like startled doves, through grove and torrent
Over jagged rocks they flew, their feet excited
By the breath of god.
                              His mother took the lead
I heard the voice of Agave calling on her Maenads
To make a circle, shouting, 'This climbing beast
Must not escape lest he reveal the secrets
Of our god.' They made a ring. A hundred hands
A hundred supple arms heaved and strained. King Pentheus
Clutched at futile anchors on his naked nest
Hoping to keep death at bay. I heard the wrench of roots
From their long bed of earth and rocks. The fir was
Lifted out, it rose from earth, tilted, and down
From his high perch fell Pentheus, tumbling

Down to earth, sobbing and screaming as he fell.
He knew the end was near. His mother
First at the sacrifice of her own son
Fell upon him, angry priestess at the rites of death.
Pentheus, still miraculously alive, tore off wig
And snood, touched her face and hoped for recognition.
He mouthed a last despairing plea in silence, his voice
Broken from the fall.

                  She foamed at the mouth, her eyes
Rolled with frenzy. Agave was mad, stark mad
Possessed by Bacchus, blind to all plea for pity.
She seized the waving arm by the wrist, then
Planted her foot upon his chest and pulled,
Tore the arm clean off the shoulder. The tongue
Of Pentheus stretched out in agony, his mouth ran blood
But no sound came. Ino, on the other side of him
Began to peel his flesh. Then Autonoe, the swarming
Horde of Maenads homed on him, his other arm
Was torn, a foot flew up in air, still encased
Within its sandal. The last I saw, his rib-case
Dragged, clawed clean of flesh. They played
With lumps of flesh, tossed from hand to blood-stained
Hand until the hills and valleys of Kithairon
Were strewn with fragments of his body.

                      The pitiful remains lie scattered
One piece among sharp rocks, others
Lost among the leaves in forest depths.
His mother seized the head, impaled it on a wand
And seems to think it is a mountain lion's head
She bears in triumph through the thickness of
Kithairon. She calls on Bromius: he is her 'fellow-huntsman'
'Comrade of the chase'; she is 'crowned with victory'.
All the victory you will find on her is that grisly prize
And her own loss.

                I must go. Best to flee
This place before the caryatid of grief returns and,
Proves flesh and blood in the hour of truth.
Let who can console the house of Kadmos.

                              [*Exit.*]

OLD SLAVE: The ways of god are hard to understand
We know full well that some must die, chosen
To bear the burden of decay, lest we all die—
The farms, the wheatfields, cattle, even the
Vineyards up on the hills. And yet, this knowledge
Cannot blunt the edge of pain, the cruel
Nature of this death. Oh this is a heartless
Deity, bitter, unnatural in his revenge.
To make a mother rip her son like bread
Across a banqueting board! I pity her.

LEADER: Who pities us? When the mine-prop falls and pulps
Our bones with mud, who pities us? When harvest
Fails, who goes without? And you, if you had
Died at the feast of Eleusis, would Thebes
Have remembered you with pity?

OLD SLAVE: I pity her. But I fear she'll prove
Beyond mortal consolation.

IST BACCHANTE: Look! Here she comes, the priestess
Of hunting rites. Take her, enfold the new triumphant
Bride of Bromius.
[*Agave runs in with her trophy stuck on a thyrsus but invisible
under gold ribbons. She raises the stave and the ribbons flow
around her as she runs once round the stage.*]

AGAVE: Women of the hills ... Bacchae!

CHORUS: Speak Agave! Welcome!

AGAVE: Do you see this bough, this fresh-cut
Spray from the mountains? Observe
How it streams. Can you see it?

CHORUS: We see it Agave.

IST BACCHANTE: We know it Agave and for this
We sing your praise. Tell us of the hunt.
We've heard of the snarling beast whose towering
Pride was humbled by the might of Bromius.

AGAVE: Have you known a mountain lion
Wild-fanged, red-eyed indomitable whelp.
Have you known such savagery ever
Trapped without net or noose? Without
Weapons, without beaters or other
Time-consuming subterfuge. Answer me.

CHORUS: It is unheard-of.

AGAVE: Then look on this? Look at the prize.
  Is it noble?

OLD SLAVE: It is royal, Agave. Where did you find it?

AGAVE: On the mountains of Kithairon. Happy,
  Happy was the hunting!

OLD SLAVE: Who killed him?

AGAVE: I, Agave. I struck first, tore off
  A limb that launched its unsheathed claws
  Against my face. Thus—my foot was planted
  Crushing its rib-case! I heard sweet sounds of sinews
  Yielding at the socket as I tugged. The beast's snarl
  Turned to agony. I swung its lifeless limb
  Up in the air, the first taste of the hunt
  To Dionysos. The Maenads call me
  Agave the Blest.

BACCHANTE: Blessed Agave, thrice blessed daughter of
  Kadmos!

OLD SLAVE: Tell the rest Agave.

AGAVE: All the daughters of Kadmos are blest.
  Ino, Autonoe came after. But mine was the first
  Hand on the quarry. I struck the death-blow.
  Later, we rested. My sisters wove a worthy
  Garland for the noble prize. See how it flows.
  A god-like mane for a royal beast. It flows bountifully
  Like my golden joy.

OLD SLAVE: Joy indeed. Joyful Kadmos. Joyful Thebes.

AGAVE: All must share in my glory. I summon you all
  To a feast of celebration.

OLD SLAVE: A feast . . . ? Oh Agave.

SLAVE LEADER: To eat of this—lion, Agave?

AGAVE: This bull, lion, this swift mountain-goat
  This flash of the wind in grassland,
  This dew-skinned deer . . .

                              Oh, our god is generous
  Cunningly, cleverly, Bacchus the hunter
  Launched the Maenads on his prey.

OLD SLAVE: Yes, he is a great hunter. He knows
  The way to a death-hunt of the self.

AGAVE: Ah, you praise him now.

CHORUS: We praise Dionysos.

AGAVE: And the blessed Agave?

CHORUS: We praise the blessed Mother.

OLD SLAVE: And your son?

AGAVE: Will praise the Mother who caught
    And offered the sacrifice.

                        Oh he'll wear his pride
As palpably as mine, his joy will mount
In full flood-tide higher than mine.
I feel a strength in me like the purity
Of Dionysos. And here is the proof—
This boon of our chase, this golden gift
Of Dionysos.

OLD SLAVE: Then poor woman, unshroud this great prize
    Show the citizens of Thebes, this trophy
    Of the god of joy.

AGAVE: Why? Can't they see it?
    [*She looks up at the thyrsus.*]

                      Ah! The shroud of gold
Obscures him. Maenads! Catch this billowing mane.
[*She takes the thyrsus in both hands and whirls it. The Maenads
chase and catch the ribbons as they unfurl and float outwards. With
Agave in the centre, a Maypole dance evolves naturally from their
positions. It is a soft graceful dance.*]
Men and women of Thebes, the city of high
Towers, impregnable, behold the trophy of your—
Women, captured in the hunt. Behold our offering
To this year of Dionysos. We tracked him down
Not with nets nor spears forged in workshops
Of Thessaly, but with the untried, delicate hands
That give birth. What are they worth, those clumsy
Tools you fabricate, your armour and swords?
We caught this beast, we brought him to the altar,
Our fair mothers' hands our only weapons. Tell me
Do you know of any greater than the power
Of our creative wombs?

                      But ... where is father?
He should be here. And my son, Pentheus?

Fetch them someone. And bring a ladder too.
I want it set against the wall. This masthead must
Fly high upon our palace walls.
[*Exit the Slave Leader. A Bacchante relieves Agave at the Maypole
and she takes her place. Instantly the dance grows frenzied and works
up to a high pitch. The Slave Leader re-enters with a ladder, stands
watching for some moments. He sets the ladder in position and
shouts above the music.*]

SLAVE LEADER [*a mock-bow.*]:
The Ladder, Queen Mother Agave!
[*She looks up, rushes back and snatches the thyrsus and 'flies' up
the ladder with it. Enter Kadmos supported by Tiresias followed by
attendants who carry a covered bier, the remnants of Pentheus.*]

KADMOS: This way ... follow me. Is the burden heavy?
My grief is heavier. Set him down, there
Before the palace.
Pentheus has come home.
It was a long, weary search, there was so much
Of my dismembered son, and set so wide apart
Through the forest. No two pieces in a single place.
Tiresias and I, we had paid our tribute to Dionysos
And were back in the city. The news found us here
Of this unseasonable harvest reaped upon the mountains.
Oh the mountains of Kithairon boast a gory crop!
Unlucky house ... I saw them at the mountainside
Aristaus' wife, mother of Actaeon, Autonoe and Ino
All still stung with madness. Agave I hear
Is still possessed ... what was in their minds?
What moved them to do this thing? Why couldn't ...
[*violently.*] She should have known him!
[*Raising his head, he sees her.*]
                                        No ... no ...
I don't want to see!

TIRESIAS: What is it Kadmos?

AGAVE [*turning from her task.*]:
Did I hear ... ? Ah, you at last. No! Don't look.
Turn around. Wait until this silken mane is
Fully displayed in all its splendour. Then you can tell me
How it looks from there? No royal wall

Ever boasted ornament to equal this.
Have rumours reached you yet? If not
I have such news for you. You are the proud
Father of brave daughters. I tell you, nowhere
Can such prowess be excelled. We have left our
Shuttle in the loom, raised our sights
To higher things. We hunt. We kill. Now, look!
A royal masthead! Look Father. Turn around!
Glory in my kill, my new-found prowess, invite
All Thebes to a great celebration. You are blessed father
By this great deed of mine.

KADMOS: Oh gods, can I measure grief like this?
I cannot look. This is awful murder, child.
This, this is the noble victim you have slaughtered
To the gods? To share this *glory* you invite
All Thebes and me.

                    Oh gods!
How terribly I pity you and then myself.
The things you've done, the horror, the abomination,
Oh fling your thanksgiving before what deity you please
Not ask my grief to come and celebrate!
Celebrate . . .
[*He breaks down.*]
Dioynsos is just. But he is not fair!
Though he had right on his side, he lacks
Compassion, the deeper justice. And he was born
Here. This . . . is his home . . . this soil gave him breath.
[*Agave comes down slowly, right up to him.*]

AGAVE: Oh look at him, old sourpuss. Monopoly
Of the sacrificial knife passes
Into women's hands
And turns him crabbed and sour.
I hope Pentheus takes after me, and wins as I
The laurels of the hunt when he goes hunting
With the younger men of Thebes. Alas, all he does
Is quarrel with god. You should talk to him.
You're the one to do it. Yes, someone call him out
Let him witness his mother's triumph.

KADMOS [*anguished.*]:

You'll know. You must! You'll see the horror
In your deed, then pain will wring blood from your eyes
Though, if I could grant ... a boon ... I would
You never woke up from your present state until
You die. It won't be happiness, but ...
You'll feel no pain.

AGAVE: Why do you reproach me? Is something wrong?

KADMOS: Look up at the sky.

[*Agave obeys.*]

AGAVE: So? What do you expect me to see.

KADMOS: Does it look the same to you? Or has it changed?

AGAVE: It seems ... somehow ... clearer, brighter than before.
There is red glow of sunset, a colour of blood.

KADMOS: And inside you, do you still
Feel the same sense of floating?

AGAVE: Floating? No. And it's quieter ... restful.
I feel ... a sense of changing. The world
No longer heaves as if within my womb.
There was a wind too but ... I think ... it's ... dropped.

KADMOS: Can you still hear me? Do you know what I'm saying?
Do you remember what you said before?

AGAVE: I ... no. What were we talking about?

KADMOS: Who was your husband?

AGAVE: Ichion, born they say of the dragon seed.

KADMOS: And the name of the child you bore him?

AGAVE: Pentheus?

KADMOS: Is he living?

AGAVE: Assuredly.

KADMOS: Now look up at the face you've set
Upon that wall. Whose head is it?

AGAVE: Whose ... ? [*violently.*] It's a lion!
It's ... I ... think ...

KADMOS: Look at it. Look directly at it.

AGAVE: No. What is it? First tell me what it is.

KADMOS: You must look. Look closely and carefully.

[*She brings herself to obey him.*]

AGAVE: Oh. Another slave? But why did I nail it
Right over the entrance?

KADMOS: Closer. Move closer. Go right up to it.

[*She moves closer until she is standing almost directly under it, looking up. She stiffens suddenly, her body shudders and she whirls round screaming.*]

AGAVE: Bring him down! Bring him down! Bring him ...

[*Kadmos has moved closer, and she collapses into his shoulders sobbing.*]

KADMOS [*to the Slaves.*]: Bring down the head.

[*But they all retreat and look down, as if they dare not touch him. After a while Kadmos realizes that no one has moved to obey him.*]

Did no one hear me? Take down my son!

AGAVE [*suddenly calmer.*]:

Let no hand but mine be laid on him.
I am his mother. I brought him out to life
I shall prepare him for his grave.

[*She turns towards the ladder, stops.*]

How did he die!

KADMOS: He mocked the god Dionysos, spied on his Mysteries.

[*Goes towards the bier and lifts a corner of the cover.*]

Here is his body. A long weary search.
I gathered him together, piece by piece
On the mountains of Kithairon.

AGAVE: Kithairon ... but ...

KADMOS: Where Actaeon was torn to pieces.

AGAVE: And Pentheus?

KADMOS: The whole city was possessed by Dionysos.

He drove you mad. You rushed to the mountains ...

AGAVE: Of Kithairon? Yes ... was I not there?

KADMOS: You killed him.

AGAVE: I?

KADMOS: You and your sisters. You were possessed.

AGAVE [*a soft sigh.*]: A-ah.

[*She stands stock-still. Then turns towards the ladder.*]

It is time to bring him down. [*Begins to climb, slowly.*]

KADMOS: Console her Tiresias. I no longer understand
The ways of god. I may blaspheme.

TIRESIAS: Understanding of these things is far beyond us.
Perhaps ... perhaps our life-sustaining earth
Demands ... a little more ... sometimes, a more
Than token offering for her own needful renewal.

And who, more than we should know it? For all too many
The soil of Thebes has proved a most unfeeling
Host, harsh, unyielding, as if the dragon's teeth
That gave it birth still farms its subsoil.
They feel this, same as I, even through calloused soles.
O Kadmos, it was a cause beyond madness, this
Scattering of his flesh to the seven winds, the rain
Of blood that streamed out endlessly to soak
Our land. Remember when I said, Kadmos, we seem to be upon
Sheer rockface, yet moisture oozes up at every
Step? Blood you replied, blood. His blood
Is everywhere. The leaves of Kithairon have turned red with it.

KADMOS [*The cry is wrung from him.*]: Why us?

AGAVE [*Her hands are on Pentheus's head, about to lift it. Quietly.*]:
Why not?
[*The theme music of Dionysos begins, welling up and filling the
stage with the god's presence.*
*A powerful red glow shines suddenly as if from within the head of
Pentheus, rendering it near-luminous. The stage is bathed in it and,
instantly, from every orifice of the impaled head spring red jets,
spurting in every direction. Reactions of horror and panic. Agave
screams and flattens herself below the head, hugging the ladder.*]

TIRESIAS: What is it Kadmos? What is it?

KADMOS: Again blood Tiresias. Nothing but blood.

TIRESIAS [*He feels his way nearer the fount. A spray hits him and he
holds out a hand, catches some of the fluid and sniffs. Tastes it.*]:
No. It's wine.
[*Slowly, dream-like, they all move towards the fountain, cup their
hands and drink. Agave raises herself at last to observe them, then
tilts her head backwards to let a jet flush full in her face and flush her
mouth. The light contracts to a final glow around the heads of
Pentheus and Agave.*]

THE END

OXFORD

MORE OXFORD PAPERBACKS

This book is just one of nearly 1000 Oxford Paper-
backs currently in print. If you would like details of
other Oxford Paperbacks, including titles in the
World's Classics, Oxford Reference, Oxford
Books, OPUS, Past Masters, Oxford Authors, and
Oxford Shakespeare series, please write to:

UK and Europe: Oxford Paperbacks Publicity Man-
ager, Arts and Reference Publicity Department,
Oxford University Press, Walton Street, Oxford
OX2 6DP.

Customers in UK and Europe will find Oxford
Paperbacks available in all good bookshops. But in
case of difficulty please send orders to the Cash-
with-Order Department, Oxford University Press
Distribution Services, Saxon Way West, Corby,
Northants NN18 9ES. Tel: 01536 741519; Fax:
01536 746337. Please send a cheque for the total cost
of the books, plus £1.75 postage and packing for
orders under £20; £2.75 for orders over £20. Customers outside the UK should add 10% of the cost
of the books for postage and packing.

USA: Oxford Paperbacks Marketing Manager,
Oxford University Press, Inc., 200 Madison Av-
enue, New York, N.Y. 10016.

Canada: Trade Department, Oxford University
Press, 70 Wynford Drive, Don Mills, Ontario M3C
1J9.

Australia: Trade Marketing Manager, Oxford University Press, G.P.O. Box 2784Y, Melbourne 3001,
Victoria.

South Africa: Oxford University Press, P.O. Box
1141, Cape Town 8000.

Oxford Paperback Reference

THE CONCISE OXFORD COMPANION TO ENGLISH LITERATURE

Edited by Margaret Drabble and Jenny Stringer

Derived from the acclaimed *Oxford Companion to English Literature*, the concise maintains the wide coverage of its parent volume. It is an indispensable, compact guide to all aspects of English literature. For this revised edition, existing entries have been fully updated and revised with 60 new entries added on contemporary writers.

* **Over 5,000 entries on the lives and works of authors, poets and playwrights**

* **The most comprehensive and authoritative paperback guide to English literature**

* **New entries include Peter Ackroyd, Martin Amis, Toni Morrison, and Jeanette Winterson**

* **New appendices list major literary prize-winners**

From the reviews of its parent volume:

'It earns its place at the head of the best sellers: every home should have one'
Sunday Times

OPUS

General Editors: Walter Bodmer,
Christopher Butler, Robert Evans,
John Skorupski

CLASSICAL THOUGHT

Terence Irwin

Spanning over a thousand years from Homer to Saint Augustine, *Classical Thought* encompasses a vast range of material, in succinct style, while remaining clear and lucid even to those with no philosophical or Classical background.

The major philosophers and philosophical schools are examined—the Presocratics, Socrates, Plato, Aristotle, Stoicism, Epicureanism, Neoplatonism; but other important thinkers, such as Greek tragedians, historians, medical writers, and early Christian writers, are also discussed. The emphasis is naturally on questions of philosophical interest (although the literary and historical background to Classical philosophy is not ignored), and again the scope is broad—ethics, the theory of knowledge, philosophy of mind, philosophical theology. All this is presented in a fully integrated, highly readable text which covers many of the most important areas of ancient thought and in which stress is laid on the variety and continuity of philosophical thinking after Aristotle.

ILLUSTRATED HISTORIES IN
OXFORD PAPERBACKS

THE OXFORD ILLUSTRATED HISTORY
OF ENGLISH LITERATURE

Edited by Pat Rogers

Britain possesses a literary heritage which is almost
unrivalled in the Western world. In this volume, the
richness, diversity, and continuity of that tradition
are explored by a group of Britain's foremost literary scholars.

Chapter by chapter the authors trace the history
of English literature, from its first stirrings in Anglo-
Saxon poetry to the present day. At its heart towers
the figure of Shakespeare, who is accorded a special
chapter to himself. Other major figures such as
Chaucer, Milton, Donne, Wordsworth, Dickens,
Eliot, and Auden are treated in depth, and the story
is brought up to date with discussion of living
authors such as Seamus Heaney and Edward Bond.

'[a] lovely volume . . . put in your thumb and pull
out plums' Michael Foot

'scholarly and enthusiastic people have written in-
spiring essays that induce an eagerness in their read-
ers to return to the writers they admire' *Economist*